FOUNDING FATHERS, SECRET SOCIETIES

"Robert Hieronimus's historical analysis could not come at a more crucial time. The United States has reached a critical point in its history, one that will not only affect its destiny but that of the rest of the world. Hieronimus has made an in-depth analysis of the founders of the United States, starting with the League of Iroquois and the European esoteric societies, proceeding to the impact of Masonic symbolism and the creation of the Great Seal, especially the images on its reverse side. He delivers an inspiring message of hope for a culture that is badly torn, a culture critically in need of the renewed vision described in this remarkable book."

STANLEY KRIPPNER, PH.D.,
PROFESSOR OF PSYCHOLOGY, SAYBROOK GRADUATE SCHOOL,
COEDITOR OF *VARIETIES OF ANOMALOUS EXPERIENCE*

"A vision that can unite, guide, and inspire us is increasingly possible when we know more of the rich history that helped launch our nation. Too much of this history has been unknown; too many facts have been hard to come by. It is a special delight to learn more of our history with Robert Hieronimus who is so careful to not exaggerate sources or certainty."

DAVID A. BURNET,
GRAND COUNCILOR EMERITUS AND
FORMER TREASURER OF THE ENGLISH GRAND LODGE,
ROSICRUCIAN ORDER, AMORC

"Anyone turning the pages of *Founding Fathers, Secret Societies* opens a secret door to the lost history of our country. By exposing the hidden roots of the United States, Robert Hieronimus has restored a sense of American destiny."

Frank Joseph,
author of *The Lost Treasure of King Juba*

". . . makes an intriguing case that combines a number of historical threads to provide a new interpretation of the United States' founding. Most importantly, Robert Hieronimus starts at the beginning, with our truly American founding, notably with the Great Law of the Haudenosaunee (Iroquois) Confederacy. This work should put to rest any remaining notions that the founding was a result of spontaneous intellectual combustion in a Philadelphia meeting room."

Bruce E. Johansen,
author of *Forgotten Founders:
How the Iroquois Helped Shape Democracy*

FOUNDING FATHERS, SECRET SOCIETIES

FREEMASONS, ILLUMINATI, ROSICRUCIANS, AND THE DECODING OF THE GREAT SEAL

Robert Hieronimus, Ph.D.

with Laura Cortner

Destiny Books
Rochester, Vermont

Destiny Books
One Park Street
Rochester, Vermont 05767
www.InnerTraditions.com

Destiny Books is a division of Inner Traditions International

Library of Congress Cataloging-in-Publication Data
Hieronimus, Robert.
  Founding fathers, secret societies, Freemasons, Illuminati, Rosicrucians, and the decoding of the Great Seal / Robert Hieronimus, with Laura Cortner.
       p. cm.
  Originally published: America's secret destiny. 1989.
  Summary: "An exploration of the influence of secret societies on the formative documents and symbols of the United States"—Provided by publisher.
  Includes bibliographical references and index.
  ISBN 1-59477-087-5 (pbk.)
  1. United States—Seal. 2. Secret societies—United States—History—Miscellanea.
3. Occultism—United States—History—Miscellanea. 4. United States—History—Miscellanea. I. Cortner, Laura. II. Title.
  CD5610.H545 2006
  929.90973—dc22
                                                                            2005028215

Printed and bound in the United States by Lake Book Manufacturing, Inc.

10 9 8 7 6 5 4 3 2 1

Text design and layout by Jonathan Desautels
This book was typeset in Sabon with Bernhard Modern used as a display typeface

In my darkest hour entered a soul of light who turned tragedy into self-fulfillment. Without Zohara Meyerhoff Hieronimus this book would have remained forever a work in progress. This work is dedicated to her—the flower of the universe in the garden of my heart.

CONTENTS

Acknowledgments

Many have made this book possible. First among them is my wife, Zohara Meyerhoff Hieronimus, to whom this work is dedicated. A glance at the afterword will tell you why.

Laura Cortner provided invaluable assistance editing, researching, and rewriting for both the first and second editions. Her extreme dedication to the project made it possible to meet the deadline for the revised edition, and I am very grateful for her contributions. Other transcribers were Rebekah Grossman, Janet Kinne, Lisa Burke, and Nate Thompson, the senior producer for Hieronimus & Co. productions. Thanks also to Leyan Darlington and Dr. Peter Hinderberger for keeping my body healthy while I worked under stressful conditions.

My alma mater, Saybrook Institute; my doctoral committee adviser, Stanley Krippner, Ph.D.; and outside reader, Willis Harman, Ph.D., were instrumental in guiding my doctoral studies upon which much of this book is based. This publication would not have taken its present form without their direction. My friendship with David Ovason and his encouragement and advice and extraordinary publications (see bibliography) were paramount in keeping me centered during difficult and trying times. My dear friends and coworkers Margie Herskowitz and Paul Trattner provided timely help with the astrological charts of the Founding Fathers. Thank you also to Jamaica Burns, our editor at Destiny Books, for many excellent suggestions and refinements.

My son, Plato, and daughters, Maré and Anna, have patiently listened to their father's enthusiasm for this work, which always gives me great pleasure. Inspiration was also provided by the spirits of my patron, Mari H. Milholland; my late mother-in-law, Mrs. Lyn P. Meyerhoff; and my distant uncle, Thomas Galen Hieronymus.

Many thanks also to White Eagle.

INTRODUCTION

I began my research into the Great Seal of the United States in 1966, just after graduating from college, when I discovered the pyramid on the back of one of my few remaining dollar bills. I was familiar with the Great Seal's obverse or eagle side, but that day the symbols on the seal's reverse captured my attention and filled me with wonder. I wrote the State Department asking about its history and meaning, and their reply was a full-color folder on the seal's obverse that made no mention of the seal's other side. Thinking this an oversight, I inquired again. They responded with a black-and-white photograph of the seal's reverse, but still no explanation. I took that to mean I had to look elsewhere.

The Great Seal's reverse entered my life at a critical point. I saw America at that time as a disintegrating culture. To me, the imagery on the seal's less well known side suggested a nation with a greater destiny than wars and hypocrisy. I was perplexed by and disappointed with our government's apparent disinterest in this important symbol of our national purpose.

On my own, I soon found several works that fed my curiosity about the reverse's meaning and the mysterious origins of its symbols. Some authors asserted that the seal's design had originated from secret societies: Freemasons, Rosicrucians, and Illuminati. For these writers the seal was emblematic of a nation in transformation. I felt that I had discovered a potent image that stood for America's greatness.

All nations and humans have a special destiny, which, if fulfilled, leads to their enlightenment. How does one discover national or world destiny? There are many ways, but often the destiny of a nation is embedded in its national coat of arms or Great Seal—especially if the nation's founders are conscious of the importance of symbols—and America's founders were especially adroit at choosing symbols that expressed the philosophy of the new republic.

It is one thing to express something, however, and another to have it heard, understood, and acted on. The Founding Fathers' intention to have a two-sided seal was signed into law on June 20, 1782. Since that time, the State Department and Congress have kept half of the Great Seal in the dark, and at times intentionally. The more familiar obverse of America's Great Seal is dominated by the eagle. The reverse of the seal bears an eye in a triangle over a pyramid and two Latin mottoes. Most people have seen this symbol only on the back of the one dollar bill, and before 1935, when it was placed on currency, very few Americans had ever seen it at all.

It was not until 1891 that the State Department allowed access to its department files on the Great Seal and, because of this, early seal historians and subsequent generations of historians who depended on sources predating 1891 were often misinformed.

In 1976 the State Department published the definitive history of America's Great Seal, *The Eagle and the Shield*. This book is a godsend to those who wish to know the seal's history. Like earlier State Department publications, however, it rejects the idea of cutting a die, making a metal impress, of the seal's reverse for use on official documents.

What the State Department has not considered are the consequences of not recognizing the importance of the founders' vision of America. Will our neglect impair the fulfillment of our national destiny? It seems to me that, by ignoring the vision of our Founding Fathers, we have altered our capacity to fulfill the goals established by those distinguished men. In effect, as interest grows in our national symbol, especially its reverse, the whole country is experiencing a greater capacity to comprehend the spiritual vision of those who brought America into being.

By the mid-1990s many other authors and researchers had begun focusing on the Founding Fathers and the Great Seal, and until now it had not seemed necessary to update this book with so many others writing on the subject. To my surprise, however, none of the other books that deal with the Founding Fathers and the Great Seal have made the connection to the influence of the League of Iroquois that I discuss in chapter 1. This is a connection that has only strengthened in evidence since the first edition of this book, and chapter 1 is one of the main sections that has been updated for this edition.

Other new sections are the discussions of the Freemasonic links to both the Knights Templar and the Native American Indians; John Dee and Francis Bacon and the New World; the Order of Skull and Bones; background on the three Great Seal committees; the archetype of the Unknown Man and the seal; the rise of feminine consciousness; the synchronicity of the return of the reverse of the Great Seal with information on morphic resonance and conscious acts of creation; a mathematical decoding of the dollar bill; and a numerological analysis of the mottoes on the seal and dollar. I have also rearranged the chapters that deal with the symbolic and mythological analyses of the seal in the hopes that they will read more easily, and added information on talismans, archetypes, and personal mythology. There are also two new appendices to update readers on the extraordinary leaps in research into the monuments at the Giza plateau in the past decade and to offer more information on the nature of talismans.

Judging by the blockbuster success of *The Da Vinci Code* (nineteen million and counting) and Touchstone Pictures' film *National Treasure,* interest in codes, ciphers, and symbols left behind by the Founding Fathers is at an all-time high—with the mysterious pyramid and eye in the triangle getting particular attention. Granted, the poetic license taken by the writers of these thrillers may create more misconceptions, pseudohistory, and antagonism from fundamentalists and establishment historians, but they are meant to be entertainment. I am just cheered by seeing them use much of the good research drawn from credible new sources that are usually ignored and ridiculed by the gatekeepers of what we know as "history." Perhaps future blockbusters will feature in equally stunning ways the contributions of the Native Americans to the foundation of this American nation. If any budding filmmakers or studio executives are reading this, you will find an irresistible hero by the name of Canassatego discussed in chapter 1, who, in my opinion, should receive credit as one of our nation's Founding Fathers.

America has a noble purpose and meaning and the vision of our

Founding Fathers is far more profound than we have ever suspected. By looking to the reverse of the Great Seal, those of us who are depressed about the future of this country can find hope and encouragement. The reverse of the Great Seal is reminding us that the true destiny of America is to spread the transformation of human consciousness beyond our individual country and to the planet. The reverse seal is a diagram of who we are as individuals, a country, and a planet, for when "thine eye be single, thy whole body shall be full of light" (Matthew 6:22).

Our nation (and the world) faces a very bleak period ahead, perhaps as dark as the times at Valley Forge. But unlike General Washington, we have been provided a lamp of wisdom to show the way. That lamp is America's Great Seal, and the illumination it is providing is currently only at half strength. We can adjust the power of our torch by increasing knowledge about its use and knowing where to shine it. This book provides such knowledge. Our willful use of this knowledge may determine America's success in achieving its goals and fulfilling its spiritual destiny.

1

THE LEAGUE OF THE IROQUOIS AND THE GREAT LAW OF PEACE

I love these two sayings: "History is the lie commonly agreed on," and "History is something that never happened, written by people who were not there." I think the first one was said by Voltaire and the second by Francis Bacon, but I was not there, so I can't be sure. It was America's own Henry Ford who was once credited with saying, "History is bunk!" and though he later said he was quoted out of context, he still agreed with the sentiment expressed. In the 1739 edition of *Poor Richard's Almanac,* Ben Franklin said it another way: "Historians relate, not so much what is done, as what they would have believed." Mark Twain's own twist on it goes like this: "The very ink with which history is written is merely fluid prejudice." And George Orwell summed it up this way: "History is written by the winners."

Bacon, Voltaire, and Franklin were painfully conscious that historical accounts, if they were to survive, must not offend those in charge. For these writers, history was at best a compromise, full of codes and ciphers to protect not only the authors but also their messages.

Contemporary examinations of America's Founding Fathers must consider just such deliberately disguised truths. It is very difficult to understand the founders if we depend only on what historians say about them. Our founders espoused too many controversial views that they recognized must be carefully phrased. We cannot expect to read the inner truths of history if we look only at the surface of written accounts.

Although there may be more information available today on America's democratic origins, the average person is usually not conscious of our country's unfolding. When I say that our view of the historical origins and founding of American democratic institutions is distorted and incomplete, I do not say it merely to generate controversy. Consider the discovery and colonization of America. What confidence could we have in a professor who clung to the pronouncement that Columbus discovered America? Not much, especially if we already knew that Leif Ericson, the Vikings, and perhaps even the Phoenicians, Africans, and Jews visited America fifteen hundred years before Columbus arrived.

During my undergraduate days I learned that American democracy came from Europe and that this republic was the child of the Age of Reason, out of which grew the democratic ideal. While Europe dreamed of a utopian type of representative government, America manifested it. The distance from Europe afforded us by the Atlantic Ocean played a key role in our successful development of representative government, and the political philosophies of Kant, Montesquieu, Locke, and others influenced the thoughts of the men who established the republic. But that's just part of the story. Until recently, one of the most important influences on our Founding Fathers has been unrecognized, in part because it is alien to the way we have come to view the "noble savages" who called America their home long before the white man came.

Within the past few decades another view of the Native Americans has developed. It has long been acknowledged that a group of six Indian tribes in the Northeast joined together as the League of the Iroquois to promote peace and human rights. What has emerged more recently is a detailed examination of the very major influence that this league had on Ben Franklin, Thomas Jefferson, George Washington, and Thomas Paine. Franklin and Jefferson borrowed consciously and freely from the democratic methods by which these people had governed themselves for four centuries. Without the league's guidance and advice, Franklin and Jefferson would not have achieved their goals so well.

We are born at the right time and place to rediscover how the Native Americans influenced our fledgling democracy because Donald A. Grinde Jr. and Bruce E. Johansen have reignited the controversy with their groundbreaking work. Much of the material in this chapter can be attributed to their individual and coauthored works; their thesis has strengthened even further since the first edition of this book in 1989. From Grinde's *The Iroquois and the Founding of the American Nation* (1977) to Johansen's *Forgotten Founders* (1982) (which Dee Brown, author of *Bury My Heart at Wounded Knee,* highly praised), to their coauthored 1991 book, *Exemplar of Liberty,* and their more recently published papers (1996, 1999, 2003)—by acknowledging the American Indian contribution to the U.S. Constitution, Grinde and Johansen impart justice that is long overdue.

The League of the Iroquois

The Indians of the northeast corridor of North America (figure 1.1) were not always a peaceful race. In fact, they were perennially at war with one another until, as the Iroquois tradition states, Deganawidah, a Huron from what is now eastern Ontario, proposed the creation of a league of five Indian nations. He found a spokesperson, Hiawatha, to undertake the

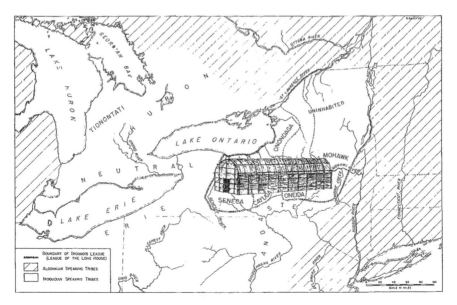

Figure 1.1. Map of the Iroquois league, showing the location of the northern Iroquoian tribes, circa 1600 C.E. (Printed with permission of the New York State Museum, Albany.)

arduous task of negotiating with the warring Indian nations. Hiawatha succeeded in accomplishing Deganawidah's dream, and the Senecas, Onondagas, Oneidas, Mohawks, and Cayugas ceased their struggle and formed a federal union. A sixth nation, the Tuscaroras, moved northward from the Carolinas, joining the league around 1714.

There is some disagreement about when the league began. There is a good scholarly case to substantiate the traditional oral accounts suggesting the 1100s C.E. as the founding of the Haudenosaunee confederacy (the Iroquois called themselves Haudenosaunee, meaning "people of the longhouse"). Barbara Alice Mann and Jerry Fields have more or less established the date 1142 C.E. for the Senecas' approval of the Great Law.[1] Arthur C. Parker placed the date at 1390 C.E. and others, such as Paul A. W. Wallace, at 1450 C.E.[2] Probably by *at least* 1450—forty-two years before Columbus's voyage from the decadent Old World—the so-called savages of the New World had formed a federation that would be the envy of Franklin, Jefferson, and Washington.

Cadwallader Colden, a contemporary of Benjamin Franklin's, wrote that the Iroquois had "outdone the Romans." As Bruce Johansen puts it:

> Colden was writing of a social and political system so old that the immigrant Europeans knew nothing of its origins—a federal union of five (and later six) Indian nations that had put into practice concepts of popular participation and natural rights that the European savants had thus far only theorized. The Iroquoian system, expressed through its constitution, "The Great Law of Peace," rested on assumptions foreign to monarchies of Europe: it regarded leaders as servants of the people, rather than their masters, and made provisions for the leaders' impeachment for errant behavior. The Iroquois' law and custom upheld freedom of expression in political and religious matters, and it forbade the unauthorized entry of homes. It provided for political participation by women and the relatively equitable distribution of wealth. . . . [3]

Nineteenth- and twentieth-century historians supported Cadwallader Colden's conclusions. Lewis Henry Morgan, for example, observed in

1851, after a decade of close association with the Iroquois, that their civil policy prevented the concentration of power in the hands of any single individual and inclined rather to the division of power among many equals. The Iroquois prized individual independence, and their government was set up so as to preserve that independence. The Iroquois confederation contained the "germ of modern parliament, congress and legislature."[4]

The symbol of the Iroquois league's Great Law of Peace was the Great Tree of Peace. Paul A. W. Wallace, in *The White Roots of Peace*, related that "the Iroquois fed their minds and guided their actions by means of symbols. When Deganawidah stood before the first council of the United Nations at Onondaga and planted the Tree of the Great Peace, he planted in the hearts of his people a symbol that was to give power and permanence to their union."[5]

The Iroquois excelled at the management of human relationships. To them, peace was the law. Peace was righteousness in action and the great good. They used the white pine tree as their symbol for peace (see figure 1.2) and likened its roots stretching to all corners of the earth to the extension of peace and law to all humankind. The branches symbolized shelter, security, and protection provided by the law of peace. If the law of peace was the constitution of the union of the tribes, then the tree was the living symbol of their constitution.

The eagle atop the tree symbolized watchfulness and a need to be ever vigilant and farseeing, and to stand guard to defend liberty, the peace, the union, and the constitution. The war club beneath the tree symbolized the burial of weapons of war because hostilities between the five nations ended in their union. Starting in October 1775, the flag flown from the American fleet to intercept British supplies coming to Boston had a design that may have been inspired by the Iroquois league's Great Tree of Peace. It shows a white ground with a green pine tree and the motto "An Appeal to Heaven." The standard explanation for this design relates the tree to the important income-producing lumber trade, but I wonder what Deganawidah would have thought of that?

In Arthur C. Parker's account of the Iroquois Great Law of Peace he notes, "Here, then, we find the right of popular nomination, the right of recall and woman suffrage flourishing in the old America of the Red Man." This was all in place "centuries before it became the clamor of

Figure 1.2. The Great Tree of Peace, the primary Iroquois symbol for the confederacy. (Illustration by John Kahionhes Fadden.)

John Kahionhes Fadden, who drew many of the illustrations in this chapter, is a Mohawk artist and director of the Six Nations Indian Museum in the northeastern Adirondack Mountains. The museum has been family-owned since its opening in 1954 by Ray, Christine, and John Fadden, who are of Mohawk Akwesasne descent. The museum contains precontact and postcontact artifacts, contemporary arts and crafts, diagrammatic charts, posters, and other items of Haudenosaunee culture as well as of other Native American cultures. The Six Nations Indian Museum is open in July and August and by appointment to groups in June and September. It is located at 1462 County Route 60, Onchiota, NY 12989 and may be reached by telephone at (518) 891–2299 or by e-mail at redmaple@northnet.org.

the New America of the white invader. . . ."[6] J. N. B. Hewitt observed that the Iroquois league significantly departed from tradition in separating military and civil affairs and in tolerating all forms of religion.[7] Arthur Pound noted that the unwritten Iroquois constitution—perhaps the world's oldest—also contained almost "all the safeguards" ever instituted "in historic parliaments to protect home affairs from centralized authority."[8] This rich Native American democratic tradition was the real source for the new Americans' distinctive political ideals. Indeed, centuries before Columbus arrived in the New World, democracy was alive and well, just waiting for the Founding Fathers to discover it.

Is it surprising that the American Indians established a democratic government of their own before the time of the white man? The colonists also borrowed from their diet (corn, potatoes, turkey, squash, avocados, tomatoes, apples), some of their medicine, language, and clothing. Early settlers—and later Americans—owed their very existence to the Indians. As Felix Cohen asserted, "The real epic of America is the yet unfinished story of the Americanization of the white man."[9]

The Anglo-Iroquois Alliance and the Albany Plan

Benjamin Franklin became aware of the accomplishments of the Iroquois league and spread the word through his work as a printer. Besides his newspaper, the *Pennsylvania Gazette,* which could be found in Philadelphia's most prominent homes, he published booklets detailing the proceedings of Indian treaty councils as early as 1736. One such council was held in 1744 in Lancaster, Pennsylvania, where representatives from Maryland, Virginia, and Pennsylvania met with the chiefs of the Iroquois league and agreed to an Anglo-Iroquois alliance. Both sides needed this alliance to halt France's determination to dominate the New World. The colonies agreed to control the recurrent problem of Scotch-Irish frontiersmen who were squatting on Indian land without permission, and in return the Indians would side with the English against France.

In the course of this meeting on July 4, 1744, the Indian spokesperson, Canassatego, much revered by both Indians and colonists, advised that the colonies unite, just as the Indians had done centuries before (see figure 1.3). Johansen provides this intriguing sketch of what could truly be called one of America's native Founding Fathers:

> Canassatego was praised for his dignity and forcefulness of speech and his uncanny understanding of the whites. At the 1744 treaty council, Canassatego reportedly carried off "all honors in oratory, logical argument, and adroit negotiation," according to Witham Marshe, who observed the treaty council. Marshe wrote afterward that "ye Indians seem superior to ye commissioners in point of sense and argument." His words were meant for Canassatego. An unusually tall man in the days when the average height was only slightly over five feet, Canassatego was well muscled, especially in the legs and chest, and athletic well past his fiftieth year. His size and booming voice, aided by a commanding presence gave him what later writers would call charisma—conversation stopped when he walked into a room. Outgoing to the point of radiance, Canassatego, by his own admission, drank too much of the white man's rum, and when inebriated was known for being unflatteringly direct in front of people he disliked. Because of his oratory, which was noted for both dignity and power, Canassatego was the elected speaker of the Grand Council at Onondaga during these crucial years.[10]

In 1747, Cadwallader Colden published the second edition of his *History of the Five Indian Nations Depending on the Province of New York in America,* and Franklin read it. Franklin began his campaign for federal union soon after. In 1751, Archibald Kennedy published a brochure entitled *The Importance of Gaining and Preserving the Friendship of the Indians to the British Interest Considered.* As Johansen notes, Franklin wrote to Kennedy's publisher in 1751:

> "I am of the opinion . . . that securing the friendship of the Indians is of the greatest consequence for these colonies . . . [T]he surest means of doing it are to regulate Indian trade, so as to convince them [the Indians] that they may have the best and cheapest goods, and the fairest dealings with the English." Franklin also thought . . . that the colonists should accept the Iroquois' advice to form a union in common

defense under a common, federal government. . . . "It would be a very strange thing if Six Nations of Ignorant Savages should be capable of forming a Scheme for such an Union and be able to execute it in such a manner, as that it has subsisted Ages, and appears indissoluble, and yet a like union should be impracticable for ten or a dozen English colonies."[11]

Franklin served as one of the colony's commissioners at a meeting in 1753 with the six nations in Carlisle, Pennsylvania. The Carlisle Treaty, which supported national defense against the French, began Franklin's diplomatic career. A year later the Albany Congress convened to cement the alliance with the Iroquois and to formulate and

Figure 1.3. Canassatego speaking to the treaty council in 1744, Lancaster, Pennsylvania. "Our wise forefathers established Union and Amity between the Five Nations. This has made us formidable; this has given us great Weight and Authority with our neighboring Nations. We are a powerful Confederacy; and by your observing the same methods, our wise forefathers have taken, you will acquire such Strength and power. Therefore, whatever befalls you, never fall out with one another."[12] (Illustration by John Kahionhes Fadden.)

ratify a plan of uniting the colonies, as Canassatego had proposed ten years earlier.

The similarities are obvious between the Albany plan of union created by Franklin and the League of the Iroquois Nations. Franklin proposed that a president-general appointed by the crown preside over the colonies. Each state would retain its internal sovereignty and constitution so that distrust among states due to wide diversity of opinions and geographical separation could be somewhat neutralized. The Iroquois resolved this difficulty by requiring that all "states" agree on a particular action before putting it into effect. Another similarity was that Franklin's proposed Grand Council and the Iroquois Great Council were both unicameral, unlike the British bicameral system.

Each colony was to have a quantity of representatives based on population and the number of enlisted military personnel, just as the Iroquois allowed for varying numbers for each of its five nations. Even the numbers of delegates allowed by the Iroquois and Franklin were nearly identical: Franklin suggested forty-eight; the Iroquois allowed fifty.

On the issue of military conscription Franklin took the middle road. While the crown made it involuntary and the Iroquois voluntary, he suggested that the federal government should not be allowed "to impress men in any colonies without the consent of its legislature."[13] The Albany Plan also regulated Indian trade and prevented colonial settlers from seizing land the Iroquois wanted.

Franklin's leadership in proposing the Albany Plan made him the progenitor of the colonial union and a federalist system of government. He was too far ahead of his time, though, and the Albany Plan died in the state legislatures, which pleased the British. It was to resurface two decades later, after the Stamp Act united the colonies, and eventually would result in the Articles of Confederation.

In 1775, on the eve of the Revolution, a delegation from the colonies met in hopes of negotiating an alliance against the British with chiefs of the Six Nations at Philadelphia. The commissioners repeated almost word for word the speech of Canassatego, which had been published by Franklin in his account of the Lancaster treaty in 1744:

Brothers, our forefathers rejoiced to hear Canassatego speak. . . . [His words] sunk deep into our hearts. The advice was good. It was kind. They said to one another: "The Six Nations are a wise people, let us hearken to them, and take their counsel; and teach our children to follow it." Our old men have done so. They have frequently taken a single arrow and said, Children, see how easily it is broken. Then they have taken and tied twelve arrows together with a strong string or cord and our strongest men could not break them. See, said they, this is what the Six Nations mean. Divided, a single man may destroy you; United, you are a match for the whole world. We thank the great God that we are all united; that we have a strong confederacy, composed of twelve provinces. . . . These provinces have lighted a great council fire at Philadelphia and sent sixty-five counselors to speak and act in the name of the whole, and to consult for the common good of the people. . . .[14]

Figure 1.4. On June 11, 1776, an Onondaga sachem gave John Hancock the Iroquois name Karanduawn, or The Great Tree, at Independence Hall. (Illustration by John Kahionhes Fadden.)

Without the example of the Native Americans' democratic union and their assistance, our own republic would likely have taken on a different form. Franklin borrowed heavily from the organization and ideals of the Iroquois league in his early proposals for the structure of the new government. All of the founders drew encouragement from the fact that the Iroquois league had been strong for some four centuries—twice as long as the current union on North American soil. Unfortunately, the United States that the American Indians helped to bring into being ultimately used its strength to obliterate these natives.

More Evidence to Show the Critics

In the 1990s there was a lot of noisy criticism from conservative pundits protesting against the concept that Native Americans had influenced any of the Founding Fathers in their conception of our new government. In effect, these pundits are the would-be gatekeepers of what passes for history, as they control and prevent discussion of theories that counter their mandate by discrediting those whose views expose their own shortcomings and challenge their cherished beliefs.

All of the criticism appears to be emotionally based, using labels such as "fiction" (George Will), "idiocy" (Pat Buchanan), an "elaborate hoax" (Elisabeth Tooker), spread by the "Visigoths in tweed" (Dinesh D'Souza). Phyllis Schlafly and Rush Limbaugh said that acknowledging the Iroquoian influence was no more than appeasement of the multiculturalists. Robert H. Bork, who as a legal scholar should have known better, said in his 1996 book, *Slouching towards Gomorrah: Modern Liberalism and American Decline*, "The official promulgation of this idea was not due to any research that disclosed its truth," but to the fact that "the Iroquois had an intensive lobbying campaign."[15]

Mr. Bork obviously did not look very hard, because in fact there is a great deal of research that discloses this truth. All one needs to do is examine the original writings of Benjamin Franklin, Thomas Jefferson, John Adams, and Thomas Paine, and there is no question they were all deeply impressed and influenced by the Iroquois league. Rather than being a political correctness horror story like the biased bigots would have us believe, the influence of the Iroquois league is so well documented that as of 2003 Johansen and Grinde report that only a few brushfires of academic criticism remain. This knowledge has moved into the mainstream. Some authors, such as Vine Deloria Jr., believe that if the case for the Native American influence on American democracy were submitted to a court hearing any fair jury would demand that the Six Nations be paid reparations by the anthropologists who have successfully hidden the truth for so long.[16]

Here is a collection of thoughts on the subject directly from the pens of the founders themselves.

Thomas Paine:

> To understand what the state of society ought to be, it is necessary to have some idea of the natural and primitive state of man; such as it is at this day among the Indians of North America. There is not, in that state, any of those spectacles of human misery which poverty and want present to our eyes in all the towns and streets of Europe.[17]

Thomas Jefferson:

> [Native American societies] enjoy, in their general mass an infinitely greater degree of happiness than those who live under European government.
>
> JEFFERSON TO EDWARD CARRINGTON, JAN. 16, 1787[18]

> As for France and England, the one is a den of robbers, and the other of pirates. . . . I would rather wish our country to be ignorant, honest and estimable as our neighboring savages are.
>
> JEFFERSON TO ADAMS, JAN. 21, 1812[19]

Jefferson did not, however, believe that Native American ways could successfully be applied to white civilization due to their sheer number. The Iroquois also acknowledged that once a population surpassed a certain number, their system of government would not work as efficiently.

Societies . . . without government as among our Indians [may be] . . . best. But I believe [them] . . . inconsistent with any great degree of population.

JEFFERSON TO MADISON, JAN. 30, 1787[20]

Benjamin Franklin:

Having frequent Occasions to hold public Councils, they have acquired great Order and Decency in conducting them. The old Men sit in the foremost ranks, the Warriors in the next, and the Women and Children in the hindmost. The business of the Women is to take exact notice of what passes, imprint it in their memories, for they have no Writing, and communicate it to their children. They are the Records of the Council, and they preserve the Stipulations in Treaties a hundred Years back, which when we compare with our Writings we always find exact. He that would speak rises. The rest observe a profound Silence. When he has finished and sits down, they leave him for five or six Minutes to recollect, that if he has omitted anything . . . he may rise again and deliver it. . . . How different this is from the Conduct of a polite British House of Commons, where scarce a Day passes without some Confusion that makes the Speaker hoarse in calling to order.[21]

John Adams, in the preface to his *Defence of the Constitution*:

Great philosophers and politicians of the age are attempting to set up governments of . . . modern Indians.[22]

Grinde and Johansen go on to say that Adams's *Defence of the Constitution*

was a critical survey of world government, which included a description of the Iroquois and other Native American government in its analysis. In the preface, Adams mentioned the Inca, Manco Capac, and the political structure "of the Peruvians." He also noted that tribes in "North America have certain families from which their leaders are always chosen." He believed that American Indian governments collected their authority in one center (a simple or unicameral model), and he also observed that, in matters of government, "the people" believed that "all depended on them."[23]

The proximity of the two cultures is a factor to consider when judging the impact of the native peoples on the colonials. When one considers that just a few decades before the American Revolution the colonies were literally surrounded by native people, the colonists could not help but be shaped by their example. Franklin and Jefferson in particular were fascinated by the Indian societies and spent much time observing their social and political systems firsthand.

Figure 1.5. John Adams discussed the Iroquois political system in his *Defence of the Constitution*. James Madison believed that Adams's book "would be praised and become a powerful engine in forming the public Opinion."[24] (Illustration by John Kahionhes Fadden.)

One of the most common mistakes made by critics of the Iroquois influence theory is in overstating its tenets, an emotional tactic used by those who have not studied the literature. There is no question that the Iroquois instructed the American revolutionary leaders on the virtues of unity, and there is ample evidence that they also served as examples of democracy to them. Acknowledging the role of the Iroquois does not in any way depreciate the roles of the classical Greek or English influences on the fledgling American government. The question is not *whether* they had influence but *how much* influence they had.

As Grinde and Johansen assert:

> In essence, American democracy is a synthesis of Native American and European political theories; there is an abundance of inferential and direct evidence to support the thesis that American government was influenced by Native American political concepts. The founders did not copy the British Constitution, the Magna Carta, the ancients, or the Iroquois Confederacy, but they did examine and use European and American Indian ideas in the creation of our American government. This was a time when the character of Native American societies was a subject of inquiry not only by the founders of the United States but also by important European philosophers, whose concepts of "natural man" and "natural law" were, in turn, exported to America. Our political traditions are not the product of any single heritage, but of a unique amalgam that is incomplete without an awareness of our American Indian roots.[25]

We, the Iroquois

Based on the number of articles and books that have been written about this subject in the past few decades, the influence of the League of the Iroquois is a highly debated topic. As of July 2005, Grinde and Johansen had tallied 1,362 annotations: 355 books, including 12 textbooks, 5 conference proceedings, 2 reports of the Canadian Royal Commission, 34 encyclopedias or dictionaries, and 1 public-information booklet from the Interior Department; 186 scholarly journal articles, monographs, commentaries, Ph.D. dissertations, letters to the editor, book and film reviews, or bibliographies; 99 specialty journal articles or book reviews; 73 trade or news magazine articles or book reviews; 377 newspaper or news service articles, columns, letters, or book reviews; 190 Internet Web sites; and 82 other venues (documentary films, speeches, college course outlines, and school curricula).[26] Despite the racial biases of its detractors, the idea does seem to have caught on.

Even staunch antimulticulturalists like President George H. W. Bush have endorsed the Iroquois influence idea (as did President Clinton). In August 1990 the first President Bush declared November to be National American Indian Heritage Month, saying that "activities planned will focus on Native American contributions to this nation for the past five centuries, such as the foundation of the U.S. Constitution that was based upon the government of the Iroquois Confederacy of Nations."[27]

In 1990 Hugh Downs talked about "We, the Iroquois," in his ten-minute *Perspectives* aired on the ABC Radio Network.[28] Larry King, Janet Reno, and Joe Clark, Canadian minister of Constitutional Affairs, have all focused on the Iroquois influence, as have an increasing number of educational institutions and political science curricula throughout the United States. In 2002 the Public Broadcasting Service (PBS) aired a two-part documentary discussing the Native American Iroquois cultural, political, and religious systems, among others. Even the Fourteenth Dalai Lama of Tibet saw the importance of giving credit to the Six Nations:

> The inspiration for the American founding forefathers, Thomas Paine and Benjamin Franklin, by their comprehensive studies of the Iroquois Confederacy and the thousand-year-old "Great Law of Peace" given by the Peacemaker [and] Hiawatha, provided them with the foundation stone for our United States Constitution and the Declaration of Independence! The early drafts of the American Constitution included some of the Iroquois language, for the English words were too limiting![29]

Earlier references to the influence of the Iroquois have also surfaced. Of particular note is a 1781 book on customs around the world by

Jacques Grasset de Saint-Sauveur who wrote about the Native Americans: "The form of their government has a simplicity and at the same time a wisdom that our profound legislators have not yet been able to achieve in their sophisticated codes. . . . Is it necessary then to go to the Iroquois to find a model of legislation?"[30]

I believe that we are at a point in time when we are witnessing a change in the historical record, a change in the discipline of historical writing that, as Vine Deloria Jr. put it, moves away from the "centuries-long simplistic doctrinal interpretation of history as a good white man/bad Indian scenario."[31] Despite the continued but dwindling efforts of the gatekeepers to ignore the importance of the Native Americans in the formulation of the American government, the hard evidence supports the fact that their representative form of democracy predated the U.S. Constitution and helped shape it and other fundamental expressions of the American character.

Another hidden aspect of the Founding Fathers' activities lies in the roles that secret societies played. In the next chapter we will examine not only the unifying influence of the Freemasons and Rosicrucians upon the colonials, but also other esoteric interpretations of the leaders, including their visions, their daily self-assessments of personal morality, and the astrological and graphological profiles of Washington, Franklin, and Jefferson.

2

SECRET SOCIETIES
AND THE FOUNDING
OF A NATION

Although contemporary historians characterize the seventeenth and eighteenth centuries as the Age of Reason and the Enlightenment, respectively, not all of the mental energy of this period was spent in trying to prove that everything in the world operated under predictable laws. In fact, other underestimated influences on the founders' ideas (besides the Iroquois league) were various forms of mysticism, occultism, and Illuminism, which used the tools of astrology, alchemy, and the Kabbalah.

In the colonies, watered-down versions of esoteric teachings could be found in publications known as almanacs. Although not of American origin, the almanacs became more popular here than in the Old World. Tens of thousands of these almanacs, published by Nathaniel Ames and Benjamin Franklin, found their way into almost every home, where they were consulted perhaps as frequently as the Bible. In fact, Franklin made his fortune through the extremely popular *Poor Richard's Almanac*. Besides newspapers and the Bible, the almanacs were by and large the colonies' only generally disseminated reading material. They contained scientific and quasi-scientific medicine and Newtonian science for the common people, as well as a great deal of astrology, which was of widespread public interest. Almanacs carried yearly predictions of eclipses of the sun and moon as well as the phases of the moon and weather forecasts, essential for the planting of crops.

While the general public had almanacs, those of the upper classes who wanted to gain more direct access to esoteric knowledge sought out the secret societies that protected it. According to two major authorities in the esoteric tradition, Dane Rudhyar and Manly Palmer Hall, many of the Founding Fathers were active members of these organizations.

While some esoteric historians, including Hall,[1] assert that fifty of the signers of the Declaration of Independence were Freemasons, others, such as Ronald Heaton,[2] who uses much stricter protocols to verify membership, place the number as low as nine. The wide discrepancy in these figures is due to records missing or destroyed during the Revolutionary War and to the uneven quality of the remaining evidence of Masonic membership. The date and lodge of initiation constitute the best and clearest evidence—which in the case of the signers yields a total of nine members. While some historians use dates of lodge attendance and attendance at Masonic functions as proof of membership, such evidence cannot be considered conclusive. Unfortunately, many contemporary authors unquestioningly quote the more sensational count of fifty, ignoring the fact that only nine of those can be firmly proved.

Four of the nation's founders discussed in this book are alleged to have been Rosicrucians (Washington, Jefferson, Franklin, and Charles Thomson), and three (Franklin, Jefferson, and Adams) were suspected to be initiates in the Illuminati order.[3] All claims of the Founding Fathers' involvement with the Rosicrucians and Illuminati originated from the organizations themselves or other unverifiable sources.*

Secret Societies: A Definition

The secret society tradition is an ancient one. Esoteric historian Charles Heckethorn believes that the great secret societies of antiquity were justified in their exclusive practices because the knowledge they guarded was so profound and important that it could not be made available to everyone.[4] Their procedures were to lead the initiate in stages to an understanding of the

---

*A lengthy treatment of Freemasons, Rosicrucians, and Illuminati and their reputed influence on George Washington, Benjamin Franklin, and Thomas Jefferson can be found in my 1975 article, "Were Our Founding Fathers Occultists?" My 1976 booklet, *The Two Great Seals of America*, contains a summary of the topic.

universal mysteries of life. Contemporary secret societies do not hide their existence; their general activities, with some care and discrimination, can be investigated. Their inner sanctum, however, is still largely unknown.

The inner teachings of most secret societies deal with self-transformation, that is, knowledge and mastery of humanity's physical, emotional, mental, and spiritual powers. Noted Theosophical and Masonic authority Charles Leadbeater revealed how the process of self-transformation is woven into the fabric of Freemasonry's three degrees:

> In each of the previous Degrees I have referred to certain currents of etheric force which flow through and around the spine of every human being. . . .
>
> It is part of the plan of Freemasonry to stimulate the activity of these forces in the human body in order that evolution may be quickened. . . . The first Degree . . . affects the "Ida" or feminine aspect of the force, thus making it easier for the candidate to control passion and emotion; in the Second Degree it is the "Pingala" or masculine aspect which is strengthened in order to facilitate the control of the mind; but in this Third Degree it is the central energy itself, the "Sushumna" which is aroused, thereby opening the way for the influence of the pure spirit on high. It is by passing up through this channel . . . that a yogi leaves his physical body at will in such a manner that he can retain full consciousness on higher planes, and bring back . . . a clear memory of his experiences.[5]

Just as there is a light and dark side to humanity, so it is with secret societies. To some, personal self-transformation extended itself beyond the spiritual planes and locked into transformation of their physical and emotional world, at the expense of any wisdom that might be gained. Often this led to the expansion of one's physical and personal power. The Knights Templar and other secret societies, rebelling against the corruption and misrule of the Church, would become as corrupt and powerful as those they sought to change. It has been shown that some secret orders were organizers of piracy, smuggling, drug trafficking, and the slave trade.[6]

At least two important references contemporaneous with the Founding Fathers sought to discredit the Masons and Illuminati. *Mémoires pour servir a L'histoire du jacobinisme* by Abbé Augustin de Barruel was published in 1797, and John Robison's *Proofs of a Conspiracy Against All the Religions and Governments of Europe Carried on in the Secret Meetings of Freemasons, Illuminati, and Reading Societies* was published in 1798.

Barruel claimed to have been initiated as a Master Mason but, not having made a vow of secrecy, felt he should warn the public about the dangers he perceived in the order. It is important to note, however, that Barruel was educated by the Jesuits, who allegedly pledge to infiltrate other religious groups and cultures in order to better defend Catholicism.

John Robison was a professor of natural philosophy at the University of Edinburgh and had indeed been initiated as a Mason in the early 1770s, but discontinued his membership soon after. He was one of the first to allege there was a Masonic/Illuminati conspiracy behind the American Revolution.

Freemasons

Albert Mackey, a Masonic author and historian whose views many contemporary Masonic lodges share, states that the term *freemason* was used to distinguish the Mason from operative (working) masons or stonemasons, who were considered an inferior class of workmen.[7] Freemasons were free in the sense that they were able to travel across national borders and work on any great building. Their secret passwords and rituals allowed a Mason to identify himself to his fellows and find employment.

William Brown acknowledges as many as twelve sources of Freemasonry, including ageless wisdom teachings, the Crusaders, the Knights Templar, the Roman College of Artificers, the operative masons or traveling masons of the Middle Ages, the Rosicrucians, the British throne, Oliver Cromwell, James the Pretender, and Christopher Wren.[8] More conservative Masonic historians, such as Mackey,[9] think that Masonry was reborn through the efforts of John Desaguliers and James Anderson, compilers of the celebrated *Book of Constitutions*.[10]

Although twentieth-century Freemasonry expresses itself through philanthropy and charity, some suggest that its real purpose is the eternal search for truth, "the truth about God, and the immortality of the soul! The various degrees represent the different levels through which the human mind passes while moving from ignorance toward knowledge."[11]

Others note that the role of the creative/intuitive mind in decision making was central to eighteenth- and nineteenth-century Freemasonry, which directed its members in the service of the Divine Architect.[12]

Masonic lodges met (and still meet) at regular intervals to carry out instruction and ceremonies. Many of the ceremonies resemble the rites of ancient religious orders and chivalric brotherhoods. In its early years in America, Masonry developed into two forms: the lodge, with a fixed meeting place, where esteemed members might participate in laying the cornerstones for imposing edifices; and the military lodge, which depended less on location and more on the strong bonds of brotherhood within the new armies. George Washington would draw great strength from the military lodges. Because Masonic members took great pride in such affiliation, numerous histories of individual lodges were eventually made public. Other reports of rituals and ceremonies came from disaffected members or from those who sought to form their own, more public, societies.

Native Americans and Freemasonry

There are many anecdotes about American Indians responding to the secret distress signals from colonial Masons, leading to the conjecture of a link between the two groups. The tales usually involve a Mason about to be put to death, only to be saved at the last minute by an Indian chief who recognized the hand gesture given by the Mason in desperation. How did the Native Americans come to learn these Masonic secrets? To date there has not been enough solid academic investigation of Native American rites and initiatory practices and their relationship to the West because most of this information comes in the form of oral tradition, which discourages modern scholars. Until a proper academic study is made, these anecdotal accounts should still be recorded.

One of the best-known accounts involves the Mohawk war chief Joseph Brant, an ally of the British who had become a Freemason during his first trip to England (see figure 2.1). As recounted in Sidney Morse's *Freemasonry in the American Revolution*:

At the commencement of the Revolution, Colonel John McKinstry, a member of Hudson Lodge, No. 13, of New York, who had seen service in the French War, joined the American army. He was at the battle of Bunker Hill and at many of the principal Northern battles. At the battle of the Cedars, on the St. Lawrence River, he was captured by the Indians under Brant, and came near losing his life to gratify savage revenge. He was bound to a stake and the fagots piled around him when, remembering that Brant was a Freemason, he communicated to him a Masonic sign which caused his immediate release and subsequent good treatment. From that time Brant and Colonel McKinstry were fast friends through life.[13]

Figure 2.1. The Mohawk Joseph Brant (Thayendanegea) is one of the best-known Indian Masons of the American Revolution era. The rituals and mystical aspects of the Iroquois Little Water Society and the Iroquois Eagle Dance were similar to the rites of Freemasonry. Portrait by George Romney, 1776. (Courtesy of National Gallery of Canada, Ottawa.)

Another similar tale is told in the Masonic magazine *The Builder* (May 1916), featuring Indians in Nevada in 1867 responding to a Masonic signal:

About 2 o'clock in the afternoon a band of Indians, finely mounted, appeared on a ridge above the valley, and he saw they were in hostile array, and said he hardly knew what to do, but thought if the G.H.S. [a secret Masonic gesture] would ever do any good, now was the time to try it; so he gave it, and the leader of the Indians at once dismounted, stuck a spear he carried in the ground, and left the band, came down, took Heath by the hand, led him behind the wagon, and, as he expressed it, gave him more grips and signs than he knew, and gave him to understand that his party must leave and return to Virginia City. The Indians then remained with them a day or two and escorted them out of the hostile country, and until they were safely on their journey and in sight of Virginia City, when the Chief parted with his white Brother, taking his men with him, and were soon out of sight.[14]

During encounters when Masons had the opportunity to question various tribes or war parties about where they received their "Masonic" words, grips, and symbols, the answer was generally that the medicine men had received this knowledge from the Great Spirit. It was unknown how long the natives had been initiated into these secrets, but they were never given to any member of the tribe below a subchief.[15] Some reports indicated that the Masons had been spared their lives because they were believed to be medicine men and had medicine secrets the Indians wished to obtain.

E. Cecil McGavin reports on an initiation ceremony of an Indian chief into Freemasonry during which the chief acted as though he was no stranger to the various aspects of the ritual. Afterward, the chief thanked him and said he wanted to make the grand master a medicine man according to the rules of his tribe, the highest honor they can confer on any person:

At the time set he went to the place with the chief and there met a number of medicine men, and they conferred upon him the mysteries of a medicine man in ample form, in *three degrees,* but whether all at the same meeting or not I cannot now recollect. In going through these ceremonies the brother Mason I speak of was as much surprised as the chief had been on going through the mysteries of the Masonic Lodge. Neither one was surprised by finding anything new, but in finding only that of which he had long been a *teacher*. My informant assured me that the work of those medicine men was well performed, and that it was in all its parts, except as to one word, substantially the same as the work of the three degrees of Masonry.[16]

Arthur C. Parker also noted the similarity of ceremonies and legends of the Freemasons and Indians.[17] One American Indian initiation ritual in particular contained many elements of the Hiramic legend. The candidate assumed the role of Red Hand, a beloved chief with mystic powers who had been struck down by a poisoned arrow. His assassin unsuccessfully demanded the secrets of his power and scalped him. Denslow's *Freemasonry and the American Indian* also publishes this account, which is remarkably similar to the Freemasonic Hiramic legend in which the beloved architect of Solomon's temple is assassinated as he refuses to reveal the password to the master's degree.[18]

The Hopi, Zuni, and in particular the Pueblo tribes not only have fraternities, they also have lodge rooms, altars, and secret rites. During colonial times Masonic emblems, including the royal arch and others hammered and cut from silver coins by Iroquois silversmiths, were procured from the Seneca Indians. One Masonic historian reported that the first settlers found Masonic symbols in the possession of American Indians in what was then called the Susquehanna country. In 1779, while the military was sent into the wilderness of Pennsylvania to squelch Indian raids under Major General Sullivan, one of his artillery officers, Colonel Proctor, obtained from the Grand Lodge of Pennsylvania a warrant to hold a movable lodge of Freemasons in the camp. At one encampment, as the soldiers were clearing away growth that appeared to have been there for centuries, much to their surprise, they located a very decayed iron square. Those of the soldiers who were also Masons put it to excellent use whenever the lodge was formed during the remainder of their expedition. They found it most remarkable that this item was found in a perfect wilderness where it was believed that "no white man had ever previously ventured thus far into the wild haunts of savage man, and still more savage beasts."[19]

Dennis Chornenky has connected the role of the medicine man or *psychopompos* (conductor of the soul) to that of the senior deacon in Freemasonry, both providing guidance to the initiates.[20]

Theories abound as to how the American Indians may have been introduced to rites and rituals similar to Freemasonry. Some say that Freemasonry ultimately originated in an Atlantean culture that spread both to the west and to the east at its destruction. Alternatively, the Native Americans may have inherited these secret rites from one of the many pre-Columbian settlers of America. As the field of archeology grows more sophisticated and open-minded, it becomes more evident that numerous Old World cultures visited and settled in the New World long before Columbus. The Welsh bardic tale of Prince Madoc tells of just one such instance. Prince Madoc was "lost at sea" in 1172, and some have supposed that the ocean currents carried him to North America. That is why in 1909, when two Welsh miners looking for gold in Arizona came across an Indian tribe rehearsing a Masonic ceremony in Welsh, they concluded that Madoc's descendents were responsible.[21]

While McGavin is open to the likelihood of an early emigration from Wales, he prefers the idea in James William S. Mitchell's *History of Freemasonry* that the knowledge of Freemasonry possessed by these Indians must have been derived from the Druids. "The Menominees and Iroquois may have learned their mysteries from the Welch Indians; or, on the supposition that they did not, their knowledge of the mysterious might be traced to a more ancient source—even the same from which the Druids themselves derived them."[22]

Another theory has the American Indians descending from the Lost Tribes of Israel, pointing to the similarities between both groups' ideas for a holy of holies sanctum; a succession of high priests; rituals of purification and anointing; and particular habiliments inherited from their fathers of remote antiquity. Dr. Cyrus Gordon reported a successful translation of a stone found in Bat Creek, Tennessee, inscribed in Canaanite and translated "for the Land of Judah."[23] Hebrew and Roman coins were also unearthed in three nearby Kentucky locations (Hopkinson, Louisville, and Clay City), indicating a date of 135 C.E. which corresponds with the refugees from Judea fleeing from the Romans during the first (66–70 C.E.) and second rebellions (132–135 C.E.). After studying inscriptions on numerous coins and artifacts, Dr. Barry Fell concluded that America's visitations started by at least 325–250 B.C.E. with the Carthaginians and Phoenicians.[24] They were followed by Libyan Greeks in 264–241 B.C.E. and Roman traders from 100 B.C.E. to 400 C.E. Jews settled in Kentucky and Tennessee by 69 C.E., with a second wave of refugees arriving in 132 C.E. Frank Joseph lays a compelling case for the settlement of Africans from Mauritania around the same time.[25] Robert Schoch shows how "primeval sailors traveled from the Eastern continents, primarily southeast Asia, and spread the idea of pyramids across the Earth, involving the human species in a far greater degree of contact and exchange than experts have previously thought possible."[26] Yet another theory suggests that the Native Americans obtained their Masonic knowledge from a renegade Mormon lodge in Idaho that lost its dispensation in 1842–43.

Any number of these early visitors could have influenced Native American ritualistic practices by passing along Masonic knowledge. Or perhaps the source for both is that Atlantean culture that spread in both directions at its destruction. Regardless of origins, it is clear that the roots of Masonic and Indian philosophies are in harmony. No wonder that those Founding Fathers who had "the eyes to see and the ears to hear" were able to work together with the League of the Iroquois in establishing a new representative form of government.

Freemasonic Links to the Knights Templar

Since the first edition of this book, many new books have appeared tracing the origins of Freemasonry back to the medieval order of warrior monks called the Knights Templar. While earlier historians, such as William Brown in 1968, cited the Knights Templar as one of twelve possible sources of Freemasonry, contemporary authors, such as Robinson, Baigent and Leigh, Knight and Lomas, and Sora, confirm this suspected link.

The Knights Templar started out as a band of just nine French knights mostly from the region of Champagne, all from the Merovingian line of descent, who traveled to the Holy Land to offer their services to the newly crowned Christian king there, Baldwin I. Their proposal to start a separate order of fighting monks was accepted, "and they took up residence in the royal palace of Jerusalem, which was believed to lie on the site of Solomon's Temple. As monks, they took vows of poverty, chastity and obedience in a ceremony on Christmas Day in the year 1119."[27]

Their stated mission was to protect pilgrims on their trek from Europe to the Holy Land, something that nine men alone could not possibly accomplish; it therefore seems reasonable to conclude that the Knights Templar had a hidden agenda. "Besides the fact that the task of protecting the highways was perilous, if not impossible, they did not actually spend time on the highways. Instead, they spent the first decade of their history excavating the site of Solomon's Temple, specifically under the stables. It is likely they had received some knowledge of either sacred treasure or religious artifacts, and finding them was their primary mission."[28]

Others, like Mark Amaru Pinkham, have revealed the influence on the Templars of their Sufi and Islamic neighbors, particularly the Druses and Assassins, tenth- and eleventh-century sects. Their influence was carried on through the Templars to the Western mystery traditions of the Freemasons and Rosicrucians.

> The Druses, who existed in mountainous compounds proximal to the Templar fortresses of Lebanon, observed a mystery religion that began as a synthesis of Judaism, Islam and Christianity. The structure and rites of the Druses, including the sect's foundational three degrees, reflected those of the Templars and betrayed a connection between the two organizations. . . . [Their rites are] nearly identical to the observances of European Freemasonry, a later organization founded by the Knights Templar that was based upon their ancient rites.[29]

For close to two hundred years the Knights Templar flourished in both the Holy Land and across Europe, their numbers soaring as they accumulated vast quantities of wealth and inspired enmity from the highest quarters. Their estates and banking empire continued to grow even after they were defeated and forced out of the Holy Land, in part because they were not subject to any taxes of the king, answering as they did only to the higher power of the pope. Philip IV, king of France, grew indebted to them and, in a grandiose attempt to bolster his financial situation, tried to seize their wealth by convincing the pope to accuse them of heresy. The end of the order began on Friday, October 13, 1307, when Philip's armies arrested Templars all over France, but as Steven Sora pointed out, "the greatest military organization in the world most likely had an equally powerful intelligence system."[30] Apparently the Templars had been effectively informed about the coming crackdown, and the massive treasure alleged to have been in Paris was nowhere to be found. According to testimony at a later Templar trial, the wealth of the world's largest bank was carried by wagon train to the Templar port city of La Rochelle, where it departed for points unknown, but most likely to Scotland in care of the St. Clair/Sinclair family.

The eradication of the Templars in France was brutal and violent, but Philip was powerless against the Templars in other countries. The best he could do was to convince the pope to pressure other kings for arrests, which he did.[31] Nowhere else were the Templars persecuted so mercilessly as in France, but the order itself was effectively broken. Their lands and wealth were mostly divided up between the ruling monarchs, the Church, and competing orders.

It now appears certain that as the surviving Templars went underground they were assisted by, or they evolved into, the society of Freemasons. A secret society of mutual protection blossomed in Britain where brothers were hidden, given money, and even provided with the "lodging" that gave Freemasonry the unique term for its chapters and meeting rooms.[32] John J. Robinson and other scholars contend that the fugitive Knights Templar, already exquisitely adept at secret operations, reorganized themselves so that their heritage lives on six hundred years later in the largest fraternal organization ever known, the Freemasons.

Rosicrucians

A second secret society claims that several of America's founders were members of its order—the Rosicrucians. The Rosicrucian order may have originated in Germany with the publications of *The Fama of the Fraternity of the Meritorious Order of the Rosy Cross Addressed to the Learned in General and the Governors of Europe* in 1614, and in 1615 the *Confessio Fraternatatis* (Confession of the Fraternity). These books were purportedly the work of an anonymous group of adepts who wanted to work toward the "moral renewal and perfection" of mankind. The group proposed "that all men of learning throughout the world should join forces for the establishment of a synthesis of science, through which would be discovered the perfect method of all the arts."[33] The probable author of both books was Johann Valentin Andreae, a German theologian and Rosicrucian.

Many historians—including Heckethorn, Regardie, Waite, and Wittemans—have speculated on the obscure roots of the Rosicrucian fraternity. The Rosicrucian order AMORC (Ancient and Mystical Order of the Rosy Cross) of San Jose, California, teaches that its founder was the "heretical" Egyptian pharaoh Akhenaton (1370–1353 B.C.E.), the founder of monotheism.[34] Other contemporary writers attribute the founding of Rosicrucianism to Christian Rosenkreutz, who is supposed to have lived in the sixteenth and seventeenth centuries and who is cited in the *Fama Fraternitatis* (1614) as having learned the "sublime science" of alchemy in the East.[35]

One of the preeminent nineteenth-century Freemasonic scholars of highest degree, Albert Pike, explained the purpose of the Rosicrucians:

The obligations of our Ancient Brethren of the Rose were to fulfill all the duties of friendship, cheerfulness, charity, peace, liberality, temperance and chastity: and scrupulously to avoid impurity, haughtiness, hatred, anger, and every other kind of vice. They took their philosophy from the old Theology of the Egyptians, as Moses and Solomon had done, and borrowed its hieroglyphics and cyphers of the Hebrews. Their principal rules were, to exercise the profession of medicine charitably and without fee, to advance the cause of virtue, enlarge the sciences, and induce men to live as in the primitive times of the world.[36]

The word *rosicrucian* is also of uncertain origin. It may have been derived from the name of its alleged founder, Christian Rosenkreutz. It may have been composed from the Latin words *ros* (dew) and *crux* (cross): *ros* representing the alchemical dew of the philosophers, the most powerful solvent of gold; and the cross symbolizing light.[37]

Only in the past few decades have contemporary scholars turned their attention to the origins and meaning of Rosicrucianism. According to Peter French, "The Rosicrucian mode of thinking . . . tended toward secrecy and science mixed with magic."[38] Frances Yates, fellow of the

British Academy and the Royal Society of Literature, sees Rosicrucianism in a historical context.[39] For her, it represents a phase in European culture intermediate between the Renaissance and the scientific revolution of the seventeenth century. "It is a phase in which the Renaissance Hermetic-Kabbalist tradition has received the influx of another Hermetic tradition, that of alchemy." Yates supports the thesis that the Rosicrucian movement arose from an alliance of Protestant sympathizers that was formed to counteract the Catholic League. European culture was in need of reform—in its society, education, and religion—and the Catholic League opposed and temporarily subdued such reforms until Renaissance science brought into being the scientific revolution. In contrast, the Rosicrucian enlightenment strove not only for the advancement of intellectual knowledge, but also for spiritual illumination.

Many authors have noted that Rosicrucians and Freemasons share many symbols and beliefs, but there is disagreement as to which order preceded the other.[40] Some writers suggest that the Masonic and Rosicrucian orders cooperated with one another in colonizing the New World. According to the esoteric tradition, Sir Francis Bacon (1561–1626) was a prime mover of both Rosicrucian and Freemasonic orders. He zealously lobbied Queen Elizabeth I to colonize the New World to prevent its domination by Spain, and hence by the Catholic League, which, as noted, opposed the social, economic, and religious reforms proposed by Freemasonry and Rosicrucianism.[41]

Fr. Wittemans describes the difference between the two organizations in this way:

> The Freemasons and the Rosicrucians have become disunited . . . in order to propagate, as to the former, philosophical ideas, philanthropy, religious liberty, cosmopolitanism; as for the latter, in order to continue Kabbalistic, alchemical and magical dreams of their predecessors. In order to keep to the probable, it is necessary to recognize in these illuminati several characteristics: That of guardians of the esoteric tradition; that of interpreters of the light of the Gospels; that of physicians of bodies, souls and societies; finally that of forerunners, or precursors of the Holy Spirit.[42]

Wittemans also suggested that Freemasonry is "exoteric Rosicrucian-ism," by which he meant that it was a worldly expression of the fundamental ideals of the Rosicrucians.

Sir Francis Bacon's publications *The Advancement of Learning* (1605) and *Novum Organum* (1620), and his unfinished *New Atlantis* (1627), led to the establishment of the Royal Society (1660), whose members were not only scientists, but alchemists, hermeticists, and Kabbalists. Bacon is also alleged to have been involved in establishing either or both Freemasonry and the Rosicrucian order. In *The Advancement of Learning* he demands "that there should be a fraternity or brotherhood in learning, through which learned men might exchange knowledge and help one another. The universities do not at present promote such exchange, for there is not sufficient mutual intelligence between the universities of Europe. The brotherhood of learning should transcend national boundaries."[43] Of significance is Bacon's choice of words comparing learning with illumination when he says, "so in learning there cannot but be a fraternity in learning and illumination, relating to that paternity which is attributed to God, who is called the father of illumination or lights."[44]

In *The Rosicrucian Enlightenment*, Frances Yates points out that, nine years later, the Rosicrucian *Fama* presented "the Brothers R.C. as a fraternity of illuminati, as a band of learned men joined together in brotherly love; it was to urge that learned magicians and Cabalists should communicate their knowledge to one another; and it was to proclaim that the time was at hand of a great advance in knowledge of nature."[45]

While Yates suggests that a closer examination of the parallels between Francis Bacon and the Rosicrucian movement would be revealing, even more emphasis of late has been put on Dr. John Dee (1527–1608) as a possible Rosicrucian. Peter French's 1972 biography, *John Dee: The World of an Elizabethan Magus*, described Dee as

one of the most celebrated and remarkable men of the Elizabethan age. Philosopher, mathematician, technologist, antiquarian, teacher and friend of powerful people, Dee was at the centre of some of the major developments of the English Renaissance; in fact, he inspired several of these developments through his writings and his teaching. But Dee was also a magician deeply immersed in the most extreme forms of occultism. . . . [His] worldview was thoroughly of the Renaissance, though it was one which is unfamiliar today . . . [where] philosophers lived in a world that was half magical, half scientific. . . . Dee can plausibly be identified with the Rosicrucian mode of thinking, which tended toward secrecy and science mixed with magic, but only if Rosicrucian is used as a generic term. It is improbable that he was a Rosicrucian in the sense of belonging to a secret fraternity with formal rules, secret ceremonies, and so forth. Actually, there is still question about whether or not the group even existed in Dee's lifetime.[46]

Frances Yates explains that Dee's life and work divide into two halves. First, there was his career in England as "the mathematical magician who inspired the Elizabethan technical advance, and the more esoteric and mystical side of whose thought inspired Sidney and his circle and the Elizabethan poetic movement which they led." And his second career began in 1583 when he traveled to central Europe and became the leader of an alchemical-kabbalistic religious movement of some kind. She concludes that the Rosicrucian movement in Germany followed from both of these sides of Dee's work. "It is in one sense an export of the Elizabethan period and of the inspirations behind it, scientific, mystical, and poetic."[47]

The Illuminati

A third secret society that is often tenuously linked to a few of the Founding Fathers is the Illuminati. The name Illuminati has been adopted by a number of sects but the best-known and most mentioned in connection with several of the Founding Fathers is the Bavarian Society of the Illuminati. Founded in May of 1776 by Adam Weishaupt, a professor of law at Ingolstadt University, the Bavarian Illuminati comprised an original five members sworn to remove all heads of church and state. At its height, the group achieved a membership of about two thousand—some of them the most distinguished men in Germany—but it was short lived as an organized force and disintegrated after 1784 when the elector of Bavaria issued an edict for the society's suppression.[48] Robison, Carr, Webster, and others believe the Illuminati continues to function to this day.[49]

Manly Hall believed that the Bavarian Illuminati represented but a fragment of a larger movement: "Weishaupt emerged as a faithful servant of a higher cause; behind him moved the intricate machinery of the secret schools. As usual, they did not trust their full weight to any perishable institution. The physical history of the Bavarian Illuminati extended over a period of only twelve years. It is difficult to understand therefore, the profound stir which this movement caused in the political life of Europe. We are forced to the realization that this Bavarian group was only a fragment of a large and composite design."[50]

Weishaupt's Illuminati Society was divided into three classes, the middle of which he named Masonry, inferring a link between the Illuminati and Masonic Orders.[51] As the legend of a secret society within a secret society grew, it produced more myths than facts. By the end of the eighteenth century, critics were already pointing to the Illuminati as manipulators of both the American and French Revolutions.[52] In the United States, Federalists encouraged people to believe that Thomas Jefferson and the Democratic–Republican party were controlled by the Illuminati in Europe.

It is important to remember that the word *illuminati* also referred to one who was enlightened by receiving knowledge from an exalted or higher source. The term was first used to describe baptized Christians but may have had its origin in the Mystery Schools of the East. The Rosicrucian Order, as well as other esoteric groups, use the term *illuminati* to refer to the higher grades of initiation. More conservative historians agree with Charles Heckethorn, who believes that the Illuminati "was instituted for the purpose of lessening the evils resulting from the want of information from tyranny, political and ecclesiastical."[53] Indeed, if we accept this definition, most of our Founding Fathers could have been called Illuminati, for they supported these same goals and founded America on freedom of information and against political and ecclesiastical tyranny.

The Order of Skull and Bones

Ostensibly founded in the 1830s, Yale University's most infamous secret society has no direct connection to our nation's founding, although some have noted its possible inspiration from the Illuminati. Since so many members of this powerful club have become presidents of the United States, however, it is worthy of mention here.

According to the legends, this society started out with Yale student William H. Russell, who went to study in Germany in the early 1830s. When he returned from his study abroad, he found that Phi Beta Kappa, the national honor society, had been stripped of its secrecy in an anti-Masonic fervor. He was so incensed that he installed Skull and Bones at Yale University as the American chapter of a German secret society he'd encountered while abroad, allegedly called the Brotherhood of Death or, more informally, the Order of Skull and Bones. This organization is said to have plotted an underground conspiracy to dominate the world.

People point to a suspicious number of Bonesmen who have gone on to positions of power and influence, including President George W. Bush, and his father, George H. W. Bush, our forty-first president, and his grandfather, Prescott Bush. In fact, the Bush family dynasty in Skull and Bones is only one of many prominent and recognizable family names on the register of the society, including Bundy, Buckley, Harriman, Rockefeller, Taft, and Whitney. The only way to become a member of Skull and Bones is to be an undergraduate at Yale who has distinguished himself on campus by the time of his junior year. Every president of this country so far who has been an undergraduate at Yale has also been a member of Skull and Bones.

According to Alexandra Robbins, Skull and Bones is the only society at Yale that exists only for its own good. "No community service, no donations to anybody. . . . It is the only society that has this very specific agenda, which is to get members into positions of power, and to have those members hire other Bonesmen to positions of prominence and prestige." Some of our most popular news outlets, like *Time* and *Newsweek,* for example, have Skull and Bones at their foundings, and many prominent journalists today are members of Skull and Bones.[54]

The Metaphysical Leanings of the Founders

Although it is generally recognized that many of the founders were affiliated with secret societies, this element of their lives is usually ignored or acknowledged only in derogatory remarks. Two examples of such discrediting illustrate this common practice. One of Washington's biographers captioned a painting of Washington presiding over a lodge: "Below: a lithograph by Duval and Hunter showing Washington in a Masonic Lodge. He was a member but not a very active one. Undoubtedly the illustration was used by the order to capitalize on what was only a nominal membership."[55] Franklin's involvement with Masonry was similarly downplayed by Alfred Owen Aldridge:

> A few years before the Kinnersley affair, Franklin became a Mason; and subsequently took an active part in both the Philadelphia Lodge and the Parisian Lodge of the Nine Sisters. Since Eighteenth century Masonic doctrine was almost inseparable from deism, there is little purpose in detailing this segment of Franklin's religious history. In his Masonic rites he referred to God as "the Supreme Architect" and to his fellow members as "brothers," but otherwise, Masonic ritual had but little to contribute to his spiritual life.[56]

The authors do not appear to be familiar with the true extent of either Washington's or Franklin's participation in Masonry, nor do they seem to have much knowledge of Masonic beliefs and practices.

George Washington

Mackey's *Revised Encyclopedia of Freemasonry* clearly shows that Washington's membership in the order was more than token (see figure 2.2).

> Washington was initiated, in 1752, in the Lodge at Fredericksburg, Virginia, and the records of that Lodge, still in existence, present the following entries on the subject. The first entry is thus: "Nov. 4th. 1752. This evening Mr. George Washington was initiated as an Entered Apprentice." . . . On March 3 in the following year, "Mr. George Washington" is recorded as having been passed a Fellow Craft; and on August 4, same year, 1753, the record of the transactions of the evening states that "Mr. George Washington" and others whose names are mentioned, have been raised to the Sublime Degree of Master Mason.[57]

Figure 2.2. George Washington as master of the Alexandria-Washington Lodge No. 22. Washington viewed the Masonic institution as one whose liberal principles were founded on the immutable laws of "Truth and Justice," and whose grand object was "to promote the happiness of the human race."[58] Portrait by Hattie Burdette. (Copyright the George Washington Masonic National Memorial Association, All Rights Reserved. Photography by Arthur W. Pierson, Pierson Photography.)

Marquis de Lafayette and General Washington shared not only a close friendship but membership in the Craft (a commonly used name for Freemasonry), and on two occasions it is alleged that Lafayette presented a Masonic apron to Washington. One of Washington's Masonic aprons bears the emblems of the Holy Royal Arch degree (figure 2.3). This has led to much speculation that Washington was raised to that degree, which may be of considerable importance, for the "Royal Arch degree is the

Figure 2.3. Sketch of George Washington's white satin Masonic apron embroidered with Masonic emblems. (Collections of the Grand Lodge of Pennsylvania on deposit with the Masonic Library and Museum of Pennsylvania.)

salient, spiritual degree of Freemasonry, not excepting the degree of Master Mason."[59]

While he was commander in chief of the American armies during the Revolutionary War, Washington frequently attended the meetings of military lodges. He presided over Masonic ceremonies initiating his officers and frequently attended the Communications of the Brethren (lodge meetings). Washington was nominated for grand mastership of the Independent Grand Lodge, an office he declined. In 1805, this lodge was renamed Alexandria Washington in his honor. To Masonic authorities, the evidence is clear that Washington was the master of a lodge. Testimony given by Timothy Bigelow in a eulogy before the Grand Lodge of Massachusetts two months after Washington's death indicates that Washington's Masonic experience was more than perfunctory.

> The information received from our Brethren who had the happiness to be members of the Lodge over which he presided for many years, and of which he died the Master, furnishes abundant proof of his persevering zeal for the prosperity of the Institution. Constant and punctual in his attendance, scrupulous in his observance of the regulations of the Lodge, and solicitous, at all times, to communicate light and instruction, he discharged the duties of the Chair with uncommon dignity and intelligence in all the mysteries of our art.[60]

In his letters and addresses to Masonic bodies, Washington repeated his profound esteem for their principles. In 1797, he addressed the Grand Lodge of Massachusetts: "My attachment to the Society of which we are all members will dispose me always to contribute my best endeavors to promote the honor and prosperity of the Craft."[61] Later in the same speech he said that the Masonic institution was one whose liberal principles were founded on the immutable laws of truth and justice and whose grand object was to promote the happiness of the human race. Only thirteen months before his death he declared to the Grand Lodge of Maryland, "So far as I am acquainted with the doctrines and principles of Freemasonry, I conceive them to be founded in benevolence, and to be exercised only for the good of mankind. I cannot, therefore, upon this ground, withdraw my approbation from it."[62]

Historians have offered many reasons for the fact that a ragtag American army, led by a general who had to go to the library to brush up on battle tactics, could defeat the strongest military power in the world. Many valid factors have been cited—the barrier of the Atlantic Ocean, the weakness of King George and his problems at home, the guerrilla tactics of the American army, and so on—but what has been overlooked is the influence of secret societies, especially Freemasonry, on America's leaders. As previously noted, some esoteric historians cite that of the fifty-six signers of the Declaration of Independence, at least fifty were Freemasons.[63] Whether this is a fact or not cannot be presently corroborated, but substantial information supports that many of the officers and enlisted men in the American military were Freemasons, and many practiced the Craft in the military lodges. According to Marquis de Lafayette (a General and Freemason himself), Washington "never willingly gave independent command to officers who were not Freemasons. Nearly all the members of his official family, as well as most other officers who shared his inmost confidence, were his brethren of the mystic tie."[64]

The lists in figure 2.4 (see page 46) have been compiled by Masonic historian Ronald Heaton. They show that nine confirmed Masons were signers of the Declaration of Independence, thirteen confirmed Masons signed the Constitution, and thirty-three confirmed Masons served as general officers in the Continental Army.

Freemasonry allowed Washington greater control of and influence on his army. Those who breached military and Masonic secrets faced the penalty of death. Manly Hall and Paul Foster Case report that the number of Washington's generals who were Freemasons accounted in part for their strong allegiance during America's darkest hours.[65]

The underlying philosophy of Freemasonry ("the brotherhood of man and the Fatherhood of God") was the foundation of political, religious, social, and educational reform, which was opposed by the monarchies of Europe and ecclesiastical authorities as well. Washington's leadership and involvement with the Craft gave him the confidence that America's military secrets were safe. His involvement in Freemasonry, as master of the lodge, provided him with more than confidence, because the function of the lodge rituals was to elevate the participants' consciousness.

Founding Fathers Identified as Masons

Signers of the Declaration of Independence (9)

William Ellery

Benjamin Franklin

John Hancock

Joseph Hewes

William Hooper

Robert Treat Paine

Richard Stockton

George Walton

William Whipple

Signers of the Constitution of the United States (13)

Gunning Bedford Jr.

John Blair

David Breatley

Jacob Broom

Daniel Carroll

Jonathan Dayton

John Dickinson

Benjamin Franklin

Nicholas Gilman

Rufus King

James McHenry

William Paterson

George Washington

General Officers in the Continental Army (33)

Benedict Arnold

James Clinton

Elias Dayton

Joseph Frye

Mordecai Gist

John Glover

John Greaton

Edward Hand

James Hogun

Henry Knox

Marquis de Lafayette

Benjamin Lincoln

William Maxwell

Hugh Mercer

Richard Montgomery

John Peter Gabriel Muhlenberg

John Nixon

Samuel Holden Parsons

John Paterson

Israel Putnam

Rufus Putnam

Arthur St. Clair

John Stark

Friedrich W. A. von Steuben

John Sullivan

Jethro Sumner

William Thompson

James Mitchell Varnum

George Washington

George Weedon

Otho Holland Williams

William Woodford

David Wooster

Figure 2.4. Signers of the Declaration and the Constitution and officers in the Continental Army who were Masons. (From Heaton, *Masonic Membership of the Founding Fathers.*)

For the Freemasons, experiencing the rituals and initiations as a group in an altered state of awareness provided them the internal strength and fortitude to grasp the importance of the American revolutionary experience, along with its meaning for humanity as a whole.

Thus, the Atlantic Ocean, guerrilla tactics, and King George's conflicts contributed to the defeat of the English army, and so did the Freemasonic experience. It provided Washington the will and capacity to vanquish the British when everyone expected America's defeat.

Washington's reputed involvement in the American Rosicrucian Supreme Council is documented in an account entitled "The Fulfillment of the Prophecy, The Consecration of Washington, The Deliverer, The Wissahickon." The Wissahickon, a creek in Philadelphia, has a special meaning for Rosicrucians as the location of the settlement of the German Pietists, believed to be the forerunners of the Rosicrucian Order AMORC.

> Wissahickon is much more than a word, or the name of a stream, however beautiful. To the true American it is synonymous with a pure Mystic religion, with the freedom of all religious sects, for it was here that the many sectarians established themselves; with the founding of the American Republic, because here was conceived the Constitution, and here was held the first American Rosicrucian Supreme Council, here was Washington, one of its Acolytes consecrated, and here formed the Grand Temple of the Rosy Cross. Wissahickon the beautiful and to many of us, sacred as the Ganges is to the Hindu.[66]

Our Story of Atlantis; or, The Three Steps describes the part the mystics of the Wissahickon played in founding America. There can be no doubt that Washington was familiar with and admired several of these mystics and occultists, including Peter Miller, who translated the Declaration of Independence into European languages, and Conrad Beissel. It was Miller who convinced General Washington not to hang one of America's first traitors but to release him to Miller's custody. Anyone familiar with Washington's policies toward traitors to the American cause can appreciate the magnitude of Washington's favor. It seems clear that

Washington respected Miller and the mystics of the Wissahickon, but the nature of the friendship between the two men remains a mystery.

Washington's views on the Illuminati, however, are very clear. He condemned them as "self-created societies" and dealt them a blow that led to their disappearance. When questioned about whether or not Illuminism had spread to Masonry in America, Washington answered that he "did not believe that the lodges of Freemasons in this country had as societies, endeavored to propagate the diabolical tenets of the . . . [Illuminati] or pernicious principles of [Jacobinism]."[67]

George Washington's metaphysical leanings are fairly well known; the depth of his spirituality is less so. During the Valley Forge episode his inner strength was perhaps the deciding factor in his ability to hold together what was left of his army (whom he sometimes referred to as his "Christian soldiers"). Washington spent a long time each day in prayer and meditation. This habit of his was often observed, and etchings of Washington on his knees beneath the trees of Valley Forge are common. He carried his daily practice of prayer into the lives of his soldiers, ordering prayers to be said in the army every morning, and on Sundays when no chaplain was available he read the Bible to his men and led the prayers himself.[68]

Washington's speeches and correspondence held many indications of his spiritual nature. Writing to Governor Trumbull of Connecticut, Washington confessed that he could "almost trace the finger of Divine Providence" through those dark and mysterious days which led the colonists to assemble in convention, thereby laying the foundation for prosperity, when he had "too much reason to fear that misery and confusion were coming too rapidly upon us."[69]

General Washington's Vision

Esoteric tradition recognizes at least two prophecies related to Washington. One is a possible vision he had at Valley Forge, during which an angel showed him America's future. Another account is an alleged Indian prophecy given to Washington by an old chief in 1770.

The following was originally published in 1880, around the centennial of the revolution, by Wesley Bradshaw in the *National Tribune*. It is Bradshaw's retelling of his friend Anthony Sherman's firsthand memories of serving under Washington. Although an unverifiable second- and third-hand source, this story of Washington's vision has remained popular as an expression of the belief held by the founders that they were being led by divine providence.

From the opening of the Revolution we experienced all phases of fortune, now good and now ill, one time victorious and another conquered. The darkest period we had, I think, was when Washington, after several reverses, retreated to Valley Forge, where he resolved to pass the winter of 1777. Ah! I have often seen the tears coursing down our dear commander's careworn cheeks, as he would be conversing with a confidential officer about the condition of his poor soldiers. You have doubtless heard the story of Washington's going to the thicket to pray. Well, it was not only true, but he used often to pray in secret for aid and comfort from God, the interposition of whose Divine Providence brought us safely through the darkest days of tribulation.

One day, I remember it well, the chilly winds whistled through the leafless trees, though the sky was cloudless and the sun shone brightly, he remained in his quarters nearly all the afternoon alone. When he came out I noticed that his face was a shade paler than usual, and there seemed to be something on his mind of more than ordinary importance. Returning just after dusk, he dispatched an orderly to the quarters of the officer I mention who was presently in attendance. After a preliminary conversation of about half an hour, Washington, gazing upon his companion with that strange look of dignity which he alone could command, said to the latter:

"I do not know whether it is owing to the anxiety of my mind, or what, but this afternoon, as I was sitting at this table engaged in preparing a dispatch, something seemed to disturb me. Looking up, I beheld standing opposite me a singularly beautiful female. So astonished was I, for I had given strict orders not to be disturbed, that it was some moments before I found language to inquire the cause of her presence. A second, a third, and even a fourth time did I repeat my question, but received no answer from my mysterious visitor except a slight raising of her eyes. By this time I felt strange sensations spreading through me. I would have risen but the riveted gaze of the being before me rendered volition impossible."

The account continues with Washington again trying unsuccessfully to address his visitor, and then experiencing strange sensations as the space all around them filled with light.

"Presently I heard a voice saying, 'Son of the Republic, look and learn,' while at the same time my visitor extended her arm eastwardly. I now beheld a heavy white vapor at some distance rising fold upon fold. This gradually dissipated, and I looked upon a strange scene. Before me lay spread out in one vast plain all the countries of the world—Europe, Asia, Africa and America. I saw rolling and tossing between Europe and America the billows of the Atlantic, and between Asia and America lay the Pacific. 'Son of the Republic,' said the same mysterious voice as before, 'look and learn.' At that moment I beheld a dark, shadowy being, like an angel, standing, or rather floating in mid-air, between Europe and America. Dipping water out of the ocean in the hollow of each hand, he sprinkled some upon America, with his right hand, while with his left hand he cast some on Europe. Immediately a cloud raised from these countries, and joined in mid-ocean. For a while it remained stationary, and then moved slowly westward, until it enveloped America in its murky folds. Sharp flashes of lightning gleamed through it at intervals, and I heard the smothered groans and cries of the American people. A second time the angel dipped water from the ocean, and sprinkled it out as before. The dark cloud was then drawn back to the ocean, in whose heaving billows it sank from view. A third time I heard the mysterious voice saying, 'Son of the Republic, look and learn.' I cast my eyes upon America and beheld villages and towns and cities springing up one after another until the whole land from the Atlantic to the Pacific was dotted with them. Again, I heard the mysterious voice say, 'Son of the Republic, the end of the century cometh, look and learn.'"

The angel proceeded to describe two more conflicts to be encountered by America, one undoubtedly meant to be the Civil War. At the end of the third conflict, Washington once more "beheld the villages, towns and cities springing up" and the bright angel planted the standard among them crying out, "While the stars remain, and the heavens send down dew upon the earth, so long shall the Union last."[70]

A second prophecy related to Washington was given to him in 1770 by an Indian sachem who believed Washington would become the chief of many nations of a people yet unborn. The following is taken from *George Washington Plays,* "The Indian's Prophecy," which was based on the "Recollections of Washington" written by his adopted grandson, George Washington Parke Custis in 1827. It relates a meeting between Washington and an Indian chief who sought him out fifteen years after the battle of the Monongahela during the French and Indian War in order to hail him as the founder of a mighty empire. During that battle, the twenty-three-year-old Colonel Washington had been specifically targeted by the Indians because he was an officer, and his life literally hung in the balance for more than two hours as he rode back and forth on the battlefield delivering orders to the troops. According to David Barton in *The Bulletproof George Washington,* of the eighty-six American and British officers, sixty-three became casualties, and Washington was the only officer on horseback not shot down.[71]

GRAND SACHEM: I am a chief and ruler over many tribes. The hunting grounds of my people extend from the thunder of the Onigara and the Great Lakes to the far blue mountains. I have traveled the long and weary path of the wilderness road that I might once again look upon the young warrior of the great battle. By the waters of the Monongahela, we met the soldiers of the King beyond the Seas, who came to drive from the land my French Brothers. They came into the forest with much beating of drums and many flags flying in the breeze. Like a blind wolf they walked into our trap, and the faces of these red-clad warriors turned pale at the sound of our war-whoop. It was a day when the white man's blood mixed with the streams of our forests, and 'twas then I first beheld this Chief. *[Points to WASHINGTON.]* I called my young men and said: "Mark you tall and daring warrior! He is not of the red-coat tribe, he is of the Long-knives. He has an Indian's wisdom. His warriors fight as we do—himself alone is exposed to our fire. Quick! Let your aim be certain and he dies. Our muskets were leveled—muskets that, for all but him, knew not how to miss. I, who can bring the leaping squirrel from the top of the highest tree with a single shot, fired at this warrior more times than I have fingers. Our bullets killed his horses, knocked the war bonnet from his head, pierced his clothes, but 'twas in vain; a Power mightier far than we shielded him from harm. He cannot be killed in battle. I am old and soon shall be gathered to the great council fire of the Land of the Shades, but ere I go, there is something bids me speak in the voice of prophecy. Listen! Give ear to my words ye who are gathered here. The Great Spirit protects that man and guides his footsteps through the trails of life. He will become the chief of many nations, and when the sun is setting on the remaining few of my people and the game has departed from our forests and streams, a people yet unborn will hail him as the founder of a mighty empire. I have spoken.

WASHINGTON: *[After a pregnant silence.]* Our destinies are shaped by a mighty Power, and we can but strive to be worthy of what the Great Spirit holds in store for us. If I must needs have such a lot in life as our Red Brother presages, then I pray that the Great Spirit give unto me those qualities of fortitude, courage, and wisdom possessed by our Red Brother. I, the friend of the Indian, have spoken.[72]

An Astrological and Graphological Analysis of Washington

The astrological chart of George Washington computed for February 22, 1732, 10:00 a.m. (figure 2.5), as prepared by Margie Herskowitz, CA-NCGR (Certified Astrologer, National Council for Geocosmic Research), shows that at Washington's birth the sun was in the sign of Pisces, which predisposes natives to an intuitive, mystical, religious orientation. The chart also supports Washington's spiritual inclinations and his having direct access to his subconscious and unconscious minds, making him prone to unexpected vision and expanded consciousness. These abilities were tempered and structured by his lunar placement in the sign of Capricorn, the sign of structured hierarchical form, which gave Washington organizational stability. The ability to take abstract ideas and structure them into a philosophical system of life is shown by the moon in the ninth house, the house of higher mind and philosophy. An additional grounding influence is present in Washington's rising sign of Taurus. With Taurus as an ascendant, the president's demeanor would have been slow, thorough, and patient. Yet another force drawing his mystical ideas into form is the moon trining the ascendant.

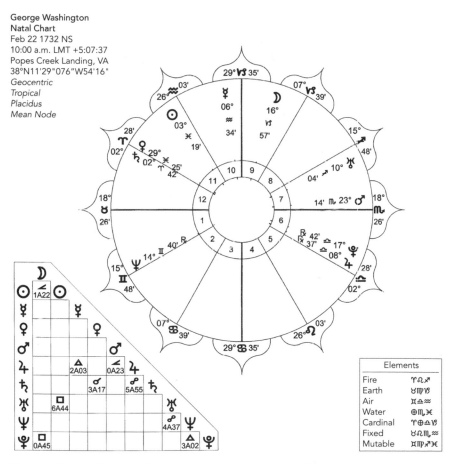

Figure 2.5. Astrological chart for George Washington, born on February 22, 1732, 10:00 a.m., in Popes Creek Landing, Virginia. (By Margie Herskowitz, CA-NCGR.)

Author Russell Arundel examines Washington's automatic writing, or doodling (figure 2.6), and makes the following comments: "From his early youth George Washington, like nearly all presidents, was a doodler. The [samples] were taken from original manuscripts. The central figure appeared in Washington's Copybook, now in the Library of Congress. It is obvious that Washington was neat to the point of fastidiousness. Analysis: meticulous, generous, studious, well-balanced mind."[73]

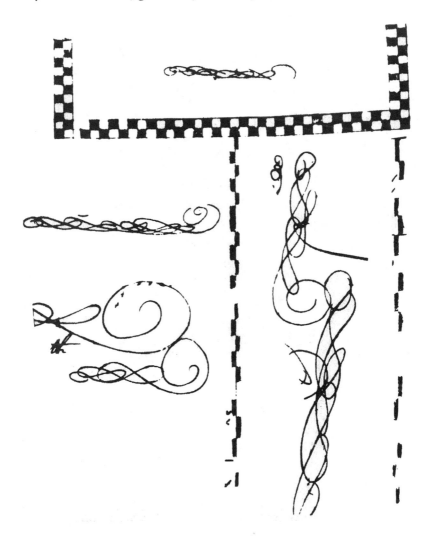

Figure 2.6. George Washington's doodles. A graphological analysis: "meticulous, generous, studious, well-balanced mind." (Illustration from Arundel, *Everybody's Pixillated: A Book of Doodles.*)

A mystic is one who has intuitions or intimations of the existence of inner and spiritual worlds, and who attempts to come into self-conscious communion with them. An occultist studies the hidden aspects of being, the science of life or universal nature. An occultist is one who studies the structure and operations as well as the origin and destiny of the cosmos. Mysticism is a product of the heart, while occultism is primarily a product of the mind.

The metaphysical leanings of George Washington were decidedly mystical rather than mental or occult; Washington was more heart-centered than mind-centered. Benjamin Franklin's metaphysical tendencies, in contrast, were more mental and practical.

Benjamin Franklin

Thomas Jefferson referred to Ben Franklin as the greatest ornament of the age and country in which he lived, while others, like William Pitt, have ranked Franklin with Isaac Newton as a scientist. Masonic historians consider this eighteenth-century genius the greatest American Mason of all time. This may surprise those who have read his autobiography, for he makes no mention of his affiliation even though he was involved with the Craft for sixty years of his life.[74] Little wonder that modern historians have rejected Freemasonry's influence on his spiritual life. Franklin may have chosen to omit his Masonic life from his autobiography because he took his vows of secrecy seriously. (Secrecy has always been of prime importance to Masonry, especially during the revolutionary period.) Because his autobiography was written piecemeal, no complete edition was available until 1868 (seventy-eight years after Franklin's death), which further complicates the issue of using it to verify his involvement with the Masons.

The subject of Masonry interested Ben Franklin years before he was qualified to apply for membership at age twenty-one. Since membership in the Craft was largely confined to the gentry, his entrance was delayed until he achieved greater status. His exclusion did not prevent him from publishing articles on Masonic events, however.

Franklin founded his own secret society called the Leather Apron Club after returning from his first trip to London in 1726 where he had perfected his skills as a printer and been exposed to the many streams of occultism currently in vogue. The name of the organization itself indicates a Masonic influence, since Masonic aprons were made of leather. The group evolved into the Junto Club in 1731 and eventually became the American Philosophical Society. James Logan, eminent Quaker scholar, denounced it as a political tool of Pennsylvania's Governor Keith. Corinne Heline, in *America's Invisible Guidance,* describes the Leather Apron Club as being small (twelve members) and devoted to preparing members for citizenship in a yet-to-be-born nation. Under the club's auspices, Franklin started the first circulating library and himself became its first librarian. "The Junto became the center for disseminating the highest idealism cultural and political, into the life of the growing state. In a deeply mystical ceremony, closely resembling the Masonic in form, the members of this club dedicated themselves "to build a universe of peace, devoid of fear and based on love."[75]

Meanwhile, Franklin had attained his heart's desire in being invited to join a Masonic group in Philadelphia in 1730 (figure 2.7). His subsequent Masonic career was highly distinguished, including service as grand master of Pennsylvania and provincial grand master.[76] In 1734, according to Masonic tradition, he and the brethren of Philadelphia's Saint John's Lodge laid the cornerstone of Independence Hall. Twenty years later, he helped to dedicate the first Masonic building in America, Philadelphia's Freemasons' Lodge.

Franklin's participation in lodge activities was serious and steady. Over a period of five years he missed only five lodge meetings, and he was never absent from a Grand Lodge meeting.[77] His involvement with Masonry reflected many of the public projects that Masonry was famous for, such as street lighting and street cleaning, and building hospitals and libraries.

Franklin is supposed to have founded yet another secret society, the Apollonian Society. Heline notes that, at Franklin's time, "Paris was now the center of Egyptian Masonry and occultism flourished everywhere. The [purpose of the] deeply esoteric Apollo Society . . . was yet again to further his lifelong dream of uniting science with religion. The society celebrated his eighty-third birthday by the erection of his statue crowned with myrtle and laurel."[78]

Benjamin Franklin had occultist tendencies. He was a student of the science of life and nature. Masonry provided some tools for Franklin to

Figure 2.7. Benjamin Franklin adorned in ceremonial Freemason apron. (Nineteenth-century Kurz and Allison print.)

plot his own course, as well as America's. He printed Masonic bylaws, manuals, and constitutions. Careful examination reveals that the structure and content of his daily life were in harmony with Freemasonic teachings. The methods by which he sought to improve his moral and ethical character, and his sincere desire to serve the public good through establishing services such as libraries, firehouses, street lighting, and hospitals, are supported by Freemasonry.

Around 1730 Franklin conceived of a plan to achieve moral perfection that consisted of a list of thirteen virtues to master, including frugality, temperance, sincerity, and order. Franklin examined himself mentally every day to determine whether or not he was nearing his desired goal. He then recorded the results in a little book and kept track of his progress. Franklin also held to a strict regimen of scheduling his daily business beginning at 5 a.m. with the question "What good shall I do this day?" and ending at 9 p.m. with the question "What good have I done today?"[79] (Figure 2.8.)

An examination of Franklin's ambitious program of scheduling business and moral perfection sheds light on his character. The virtues he prized are basic to the discipline of every true occultist. His scheduling and self-examination of his desire to do good comprise a basic practice of the mystics of the Wissahickon (Rosicrucians) and of occultists past and present. Taking the "resolution of the day" and the "examination of the day" can be found in the morning and evening exercises of many meditative groups.[80]

Soon after Franklin arrived in France to negotiate a treaty of alliance (December 4, 1776), he affiliated with the French Masonic lodges. He was present and assisted in the initiation of Voltaire in the Nine Sisters Lodge on April 7, 1778. The following year Franklin was elected worshipful master of the lodge of the Nine Sisters and served for two years, and was elected again in 1782. Franklin later affiliated with two other French lodges in 1785: Saint Jean de Jerusalem and Loge des Bons Amis.

Franklin used his French and American Masonic connections (especially the Marquis de Lafayette) to cement the Franco-American alliance that contributed immeasurably to America's military success. Diplomacy and secret negotiations are consistent with Masonic protocol, and Ben Franklin was a keen observer and a master practitioner.

Although no hard evidence exists to prove it, at least one Rosicrucian order has claimed Benjamin Franklin as a member. The former imperator of the Rosicrucian Order AMORC, Dr. H. Spencer Lewis, makes his case this way:

The truth of the matter is that Franklin did establish a secret group of Rosicrucians that met as a separate body in Philadelphia just as many members of the Rosicrucian Order today who are members of one lodge or another come together to establish a new Rosicrucian Lodge. In the case of Rosicrucianism, however, a single individual can be a founder, as well as a prime mover, in contradistinction to the customs in Freemasonry. After the first Rosicrucian foundation in Philadelphia beginning in 1694-5, the activities remained as a community nucleus for many, many years, and it was not until after 1720 that enough members had been attracted to the nucleus from various parts of the eastern seaboard and small lodges could be formed. The one started by Franklin was one of the earliest of the typical modern forms of lodges that were communities where the members lived together in a sort of secret community life.[81]

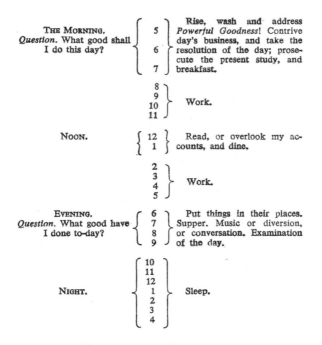

Figure 2.8. Benjamin Franklin's "Precept of Order," which required that every part of his business had its allotted time. Note his morning and evening questions dealing with what good he would do and what good he did do that day, a practice of Rosicrucians. (Illustration from Franklin, *The Autobiography of Benjamin Franklin*.)

Other sources also imply that Ben Franklin was a Rosicrucian. Heline mentions a group Franklin led that may have been the Rosicrucian lodge referred to above.

> A mystic brotherhood . . . was located in what is now the Germantown section of Philadelphia. . . . Upon the passing of its last leader its occult library was turned over to Benjamin Franklin. Naturally, this literature stimulated Franklin's interest in the Ancient Wisdom teachings still further and it was not long before he had gathered around him a group of brilliant youths who were also interested in metaphysical research. Their student occult practices led them far afield and into work more advanced than that pursued by the average twentieth century student of the subject.[82]

Historians for the Rosicrucian Order AMORC assert that Franklin's first connection with the Rosicrucians was through Conrad Beissel and Michael Wohlfarth of the Ephrata community, one of the groups of German Pietists in Pennsylvania. Joel Disher in the *Rosicrucian Digest* (November 1960) states that Beissel and Wohlfarth discussed publishing their religious material during their first meeting with Franklin.[83] Figures 2.9, 2.10, and 2.11, from Julius Sachse's *German Pietists of Provincial Pennsylvania,* document the extent of Rosicrucian teachings in their religious material. It is the friendship of Franklin, Jefferson, and other founders with these German Pietists that is used to show an interest in Rosicrucianism among the Founding Fathers.

It is impossible now to determine the facts of Franklin's Rosicrucian membership, but his involvement could also be reflected in his life and accomplishments. It was not until Franklin's return from London in 1726 that his life reflected any order or design, and one man may have been responsible for this change. Thomas Denham was a Quaker merchant who after a four-year relationship with Franklin had become, in Franklin's own words, a second father to him. Very little is known about Denham, but he is the one who paid for Franklin's voyage home from London and offered him a job as a clerk in his store.

The limited information available about Denham indicates that he was a quiet, successful, respected man of sound principles. Many of

Figure 2.9. In 1694 the German Pietists left the fatherland carrying several complete sets of Jacob Boehme's ten volumes of mystical works. These are some of their relics from the collection of Julius F. Sachse. This material shows that Franklin's Pietist friends of the Wissahickon were studying Rosicrucian texts. (Photograph from Sachse, *German Pietists of Provincial Pennsylvania*.)

Figure 2.10. The emblem of "Celestial Eve," which in Rosicrucian Theosophy typified "Theo-Sophia," divine wisdom or the spiritual aspect of nature as understood by the German Pietists. Note how the symbols of the sun over the triangle resemble the reverse of the Great Seal with its radiant eye over the pyramid. (Illustration from Sachse, *German Pietists of Provincial Pennsylvania*.)

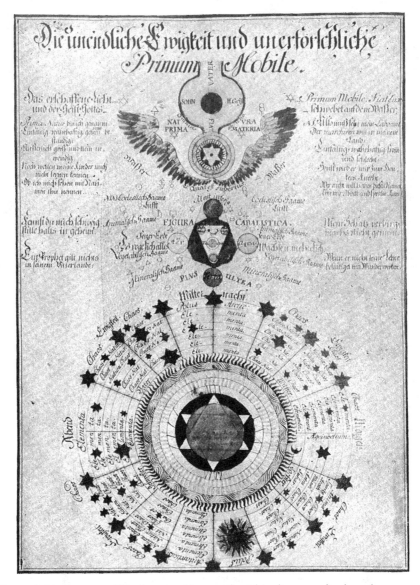

Figure 2.11. A page of Rosicrucian Theosophy. This diagram displays the Rosicrucian axiom of "As Above So Below." The six-pointed star with a dot in its center at the top represents the spiritual macrocosm. The same symbol is used below for the great universe, or the earth, but this time the dot is outside of the center. The physical universe (microcosm) is reflected in the spiritual universe (macrocosm). This is a dictum of Hermes Trismegistus and central to the teachings of the Rosicrucians and Ephrata community. (Illustration from Sachse, *German Pietists of Provincial Pennsylvania*.)

the conclusions Franklin set down as his own may have stemmed from the observations of the fatherlike figure he idolized. In my opinion, the unsentimental Franklin adopted Denham's ideas without crediting their source. The period following his four years with Denham gave birth to the Leather Apron Club, the Junto, and his entrance into Freemasonry.

Six months after returning to Philadelphia, and shortly after Franklin's twenty-first birthday, both Denham and Franklin became ill. Denham died and Franklin came close to death as well. After recovering, Franklin returned to the printing trade. Franklin's close call with death encouraged him to acquire from an unacknowledged source, or possibly to compose, his own epitaph. This piece of writing suggests that he believed in reincarnation: "The Body of B. Franklin Printer (like the cover of an old book, its contents torn out and stript of its lettering and gilding) lies here, food for worms, but the work shall not be lost; for it will (as he believed) appear once more, in a new and more elegant Edition Revised and corrected by the author."[84]

Prior to Franklin's relationship with Denham, he exhibited at least three characteristics that might be seen as Rosicrucian. The first is Franklin's youthful vegetarianism, a practice advised by many secret societies, and one that he believed gave him "greater clearness of head and quicker apprehension."[85] Second, he shared the Rosicrucian belief in the possibility of communication between the physical and spiritual worlds. He and his close friend, Charles Osborne, "made a serious agreement that the one who happen'd first to die should, if possible, make a friendly visit to the other, and acquaint him how he found things in that separate state. But he never fulfill'd his promise."[86] It was Osborne who died first but did not make contact with Franklin after his death. Third, Franklin showed a fascination for the metaphysical. He was alleged to have frequented a coffeehouse that served as a meeting place for "unconventional foreign travelers and soldiers of fortune. Here Franklin discovered a young medical student who was interested in esoteric subjects and so he acquired his intimate companionship. Together they practiced old alchemical formulas, rites and ceremonials."[87]

These three facets of his life do not prove Franklin's involvement in the Rosicrucian order, nor do they prove a predisposition to occultism, but they do show that his life could be interpreted in that light.

After Franklin's initiation into Masonry, he began to publish *Poor Richard's Almanac*. The origin of the almanac's title remains unsettled. Noted Franklin historian Carl Van Doren thinks that "the imaginary astrologer probably took his full name from an actual Englishman, Richard Saunders, compiler of the 'Apollo Angelicus,' though Denham's account book lists a Philadelphia Richard Saunders as one of the firm's customers."[88] Franklin, being Denham's clerk, was of course familiar with the name of Richard Saunders. Is this yet another way Denham influenced Franklin's life work?

Astrological Predictions of Death

Ben Franklin's first almanac appeared in 1733 and was a great success. What gained Franklin much notoriety, however, was the method with which he dealt with his "competition," rival almanac writer Titan Leeds, in the preface to this first edition:

> "He dies by my Calculation made at his Request, on Oct. 17, 1733, 3 ho., 29 m. P.M., at the very instant of the conjunction of Sun and Mercury. By his own Calculation he will survive till the 26th of the same Month. This small difference between us we have disputed whenever we have met these 9 Years past; but at length he is inclinable to agree with my Judgment. Which of us is most exact, a little Time will now determine."[89]

Even though Leeds failed to die at the appointed time, "Poor Richard" insisted year after year in each new edition that Mr. Leeds was dead, claiming that other men had assumed the publication of his almanac under his name. This continued until Leeds's actual death in 1738 and has caused much controversy over whether Franklin's interest in astrology was sincere or whimsical. Conservative historians insist Franklin's use of astrology was tongue-in-cheek, while the more liberal-minded see it as an indication that his interests were sincere.*

---

*For a complete discussion of the Franklin-Leeds astrology episode, see Hieronimus "Were Our Founding Fathers Occultists?" and "An Historical Analysis of the Reverse of America's Great Seal and Its Relationship to the Ideology of Humanistic Psychology."

An Astrological and Graphological Analysis of Franklin

Whether or not he was serious in his use of astrology, Franklin did use it in *Poor Richard's Almanac* to ensure subscribers. The almanac contained an ephemeris noting the planets' positions, phases of the moon, the changes in season, the length of days, and information on tides. Students of esoterica often refer to Franklin's astrological prowess, but there is little evidence to that effect.

Franklin's prediction of important technological advances does point to highly developed psychic and intuitive abilities. In writing to Joseph Priestley he noted:

The rapid progress true science now makes, occasions my regretting sometimes that I was born too soon. It is possible to imagine the height to which civilization may be carried in a thousand years, as man demonstrates his power over matter. We may, perhaps, learn to deprive larger masses of their gravity and give them absolute levity for the sake of easy transport [the airplane]. Agriculture may halve its labor and double its produce [scientific farming], all diseases may, by sure means, be prevented or cured—not excepting that of old age—and our lives lengthened at pleasure, even beyond the antediluvian standard [preventive medicine].[90]

Franklin's involvement with the esoteric sciences may be explained by his natal birth chart. According to the astrological chart Herskowitz erected for Franklin, his sun was in Capricorn in the eleventh house (see figure 2.12). This placement indicated an interest and drive in community efforts, events, or movements, where his creativity was highlighted. It also gave him an air of practicality and efficiency and an ability to work with power, in this case as a statesman. With his moon in Pisces in the twelfth house, he had a mystical and spiritual bent directed through universal concerns of mankind. His understanding was telepathic. His moon in Pisces ruling the fourth house describes a character trait of devotion to home and homeland, which was expressed inspirationally and creatively. Franklin also had an analytical mind of genius quality and a facility for communication associated with his strong Mercury. He was a writer and a master printer. He brought great zest as well as philosophical and religious interest to his work for occult and spiritual groups, for whom he printed Bibles. His Mars in Sagittarius in the ninth house of higher mind, abstract thought, religion, and foreign affairs predisposed him to such a combination of interests.

With Uranus in the fifth house, opposing Mercury in Aquarius, Franklin combined the qualities of the intuitive and rational mind. He also showed an interest in matters associated with Aquarian consciousness, such as astrology.

A graphological assessment of Franklin's character from his handwriting and doodling concludes: "By looking at the signatures of the

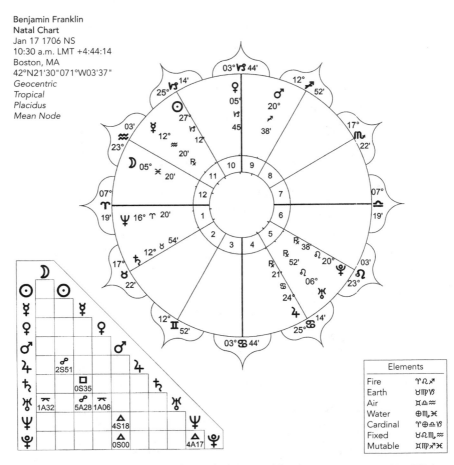

Figure 2.12. Astrological chart for Benjamin Franklin, born on January 17, 1706, 10:30 a.m., in Boston, Massachusetts. (By Margie Herskowitz, CA-NCGR.)

signers of the Declaration of Independence one finds a paragraph for the Graphologists. Franklin's handwriting shows gentleness, amenity, composure and refinement. Franklin's unusual terminal curls convince one of his inventiveness and ingenuity. The forward slope of his writing indicated he was of a loving and sympathetic nature."[91]

In *Everybody's Pixillated: A Book of Doodles,* Russell Arundel defines a doodle as something scribbled while the mind is consciously engaged in something unrelated, revealing thereby an "accurate picture of the subconscious mind."[92] The scarcity of writing materials in early America discouraged doodling, but many interesting specimens have survived. Benjamin Franklin's original manuscript for his *Autobiography* contains the doodles in figure 2.13 that reveal his restless nature.

Benjamin Franklin was more than familiar with the esoteric sciences. Whereas George Washington excelled in the areas usually referred to as mystical, Franklin's interests lay more with utilitarian occultism, or the practical occult sciences. This is not to say that Franklin was not visionary in some respects, for he was, but his emphasis was on practicality and mental pursuits rather than the emotional or purely spiritual. Returning from London, Franklin wrote: "The more deeply one studies the inner workings of life, the more wonderful and expansive they become. The more one studies the outer, the less it means and the more ignorant become those who engage in it solely."[93]

When the Constitutional Convention could not reach accord, Franklin made one of his best-known speeches, an appeal for spiritual help in creating the nation.

> God governs in the affairs of men. If a sparrow cannot fall to the ground without His notice, is it probable that an empire can rise without His aid? I . . . believe this and also that without His concurring aid, we shall succeed in this political building no better than the builders of Babel; . . . I therefore beg leave to move—that henceforth prayers imploring the assistance of Heaven and its Blessings on our deliberations be held in this Assembly every morning before we proceed to business. . . .[94]

Figure 2.13. Benjamin Franklin's doodles show rapid strokes that demonstrate he was "Very restless. Accurate. Self-confident." (Illustration from Arundel, *Everybody's Pixillated.*)

Franklin truly was a man ahead of his time, and some of his beliefs and visions were precursors of commonly held views today, such as this one on other intelligent life in the universe: "I believe that man is not the most perfect Being but One, rather that as there are many Degrees of Beings his inferiors so there are many Degrees of Beings superior to him."[95]

Thomas Jefferson

The third Founding Father considered here strikes a balance between George Washington's heart-centeredness and Benjamin Franklin's mind-centeredness. Jefferson's part in writing the Declaration of Independence, his desire for the end of slavery in America, and his statute on religious freedom in Virginia were essential to America's existence as a new, path-breaking nation. Without Jefferson's influence, Alexander Hamilton's views on monarchy might have succeeded, and America would have resembled Europe politically.

Jefferson might have been America's foremost scientist had not his political life interfered. He wrote to Harry Innes, "Science is my passion, politics, my duty." In California today there is a research center named after Jefferson based on Jefferson's behavioristic views and his unique approach to life. In his opinion the most pragmatic and useful sciences were botany, chemistry, zoology, anatomy, surgery, medicine, natural philosophy, agriculture, mathematics, astronomy, geography, politics, commerce, history, ethics, law, and the fine arts. His versatility in studying and writing in all these fields illustrates his special genius.

Because of his scientific attitude, one might be skeptical of his religious interests. In compiling a catalogue for the University of Virginia, which he founded, he refused to assign a special section to metaphysics and instead declared "Metaphysics have been incorporated with ethics, and little extension given to them. For while some attention may be usefully bestowed on the operations of thought, prolonged investigations of a faculty unamenable to the test of our senses is an expense of time, too unprofitable to be worthy of indulgence."[96] The eighteenth-century definition of metaphysics (literally, after or beyond physics) is not in harmony with today's idea that there are laws that are yet undiscovered, but supportive of physical laws and not in opposition to them. In the views of Dr. Willis Harman, former president of the Institute of Noetic Sciences, metaphysics (which concerns itself with the ultimate nature of existence) is moving away from a materialistic monism, in which matter gives rise to mind, and toward transcendental monism, in which mind gives rise to matter.

The metaphysical leanings of Jefferson may prove to be the most controversial of the three founders discussed here. Was Thomas Jefferson a member of any secret societies? Masonic sources say he was, but no one has turned up documentary evidence of his initiation. The Masonic Bible, however, has "unmistakable evidence that he was an active mason."[97] These include records of his name as a visitor in a cornerstone-laying ceremony and references in twenty-nine issues of Masonic journals to his status as a Mason. Jefferson's humanitarian beliefs were harmonious with eighteenth-century Masonry, and it has been suggested that Jefferson may have been initiated in France; if so, an American initiation record would not exist.

The Rosicrucians claim Washington and Franklin as members, but do not provide irrefutable evidence. In Jefferson's case, however, Dr. H. Spencer Lewis, former imperator of the Rosicrucian order, introduces a piece of substantial evidence. Lewis found among Jefferson's papers some "strange-looking characters" that previous researchers had assumed were a code Jefferson had invented (figure 2.14). "I recognized it as one of the old Rosicrucian codes used for many years before Thomas Jefferson became a Rosicrucian, and still to be found in many of the ancient Rosicrucian secret manuscripts."[98] An examination by Lewis of other ancient non-Rosicrucian ciphers failed to produce anything comparable to the one used by Jefferson.[99] I have submitted this code to several cryptographers and none has yet been successful in identifying it. Rex Daniels of Concord, Massachusetts, a former code-breaker with the Office of Strategic Services (OSS) and CIA, commented in a personal letter to me, "I have taken several tries at the code with no success for the standard ones. . . . You have hit upon something nobody else seems to know about."[100]

According to Lewis this code is another bit of evidence showing a Rosicrucian connection to Thomas Jefferson. In fact, one might also conclude that Jefferson had to have been one of the most important officers of the Rosicrucian colony in and around Philadelphia in order to have learned this secret code.

Jefferson's interest in codes and ciphers earned him the title of Father of American Cryptography. His wheel cipher (see figure 2.15), invented more than a century and a half ago, is still in active use today, according to David Kahn in *The Codebreakers.*

But then it was invented by a remarkable man, a well-known writer, agriculturist, bibliophile, architect, diplomat, gadgeteer, and statesman named Thomas Jefferson. . . . [I]t seems likely that he invented it either during 1790 to 1793 or during 1797 to 1800. During the first period he was America's first secretary of state, and the responsibilities of conducting foreign policy, the need to protect communications from England and France, the divided American cabinet, the spirit of invention that he found as administrator of the patent law, all spurred his own natural inventiveness; he was then also in contact with Dr. Robert Patterson, a mathematician of the Univer-

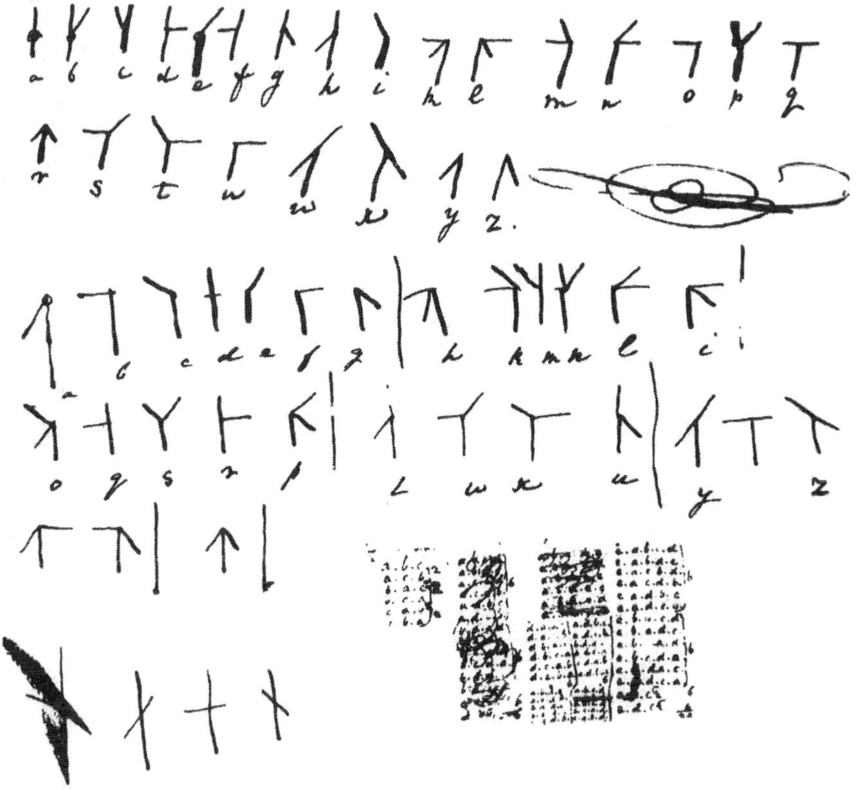

Figure 2.14. Alleged Rosicrucian code found among Jefferson's papers. (Illustration from Arundel, *Everybody's Pixillated.*)

sity of Pennsylvania and Vice President of the American Philosophical Society, who was interested in ciphers. During the later period, he was again in close contact with Patterson, who in 1801 sent him a cipher.

. . . Jefferson's wheel cipher was far and away the most advanced devised in its day. It seems to have come out of the blue rather than as a result of mature reflection upon cryptology.[101]

There also exist claims that Jefferson was an astrologer, although my research has yet to substantiate them.

Over the years there have been implications that Jefferson was a member of the Illuminati.[102] Jefferson's own published criticism of

Illuminism, although based on an imperfect acquaintance with the doctrine, seems sincere and balanced. Concerning the work of Adam Weishaupt (founder of the Bavarian Society of Illuminati) and his critics Jefferson concludes:

> I have lately by accident got sight of a single volume (the 3d.) of the Abbé Barruel's Antisocial Conspiracy, which gives me the first idea I have ever had of what is meant by the Illuminatism against which "Illuminate Morse," as he is now called, and his ecclesiastical and monarchical associates have been making such a hue and cry. Barruel's own parts of the book are perfectly the ravings of a Bedlamite. But he quotes largely from Wishaupt [*sic*] whom he considers the founder of what he calls the order. . . . Wishaupt seems to be an enthusiastic philanthropist. He is among those (as you know the excellent Price and Priestley also are) who believe in the infinite perfectibility of man. He thinks he may in time be rendered so perfect that he will be able to govern himself in every

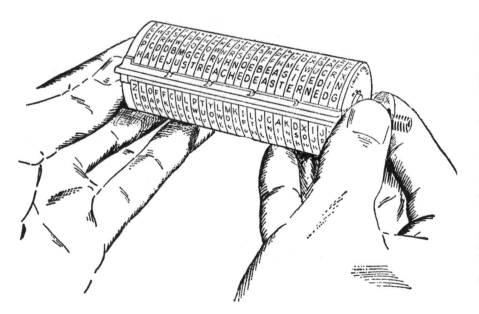

Figure 2.15. The U.S. Army version of Thomas Jefferson's wheel cipher; for its time, it was the most advanced. (Illustration from *M-94 U.S. Army Signal Communications Field Manual.*)

circumstance, so as to injure none, to do all the good he can, to leave government no occasion to exercise their powers over him, and, of course, to render political government useless. This, you know, is Godwin's doctrine and this is what Robison, Barruel, and Morse have called a conspiracy against all government. . . .

The means he proposes to effect this improvement of human nature are "to enlighten men, to correct their morals and inspire them with benevolence." As Wishaupt lived under the tyranny of a despot and priests, he knew that caution was necessary even in spreading information, and the principles of pure morality. He proposed, therefore, to lead the Free Masons to adopt this object. . . . This has given an air of mystery to his views, was the foundation of his banishment, the subversion of the Masonic Order, and is the color for the ravings against him of Robison, Barruel, and Morse, whose real fears are that the craft would be endangered by the spreading of information, reason, and natural morality among men. . . . I believe you will think with me that if Wishaupt had written here, where no secrecy is necessary in our endeavors to render men wise and virtuous, he would not have thought of any secret machinery for that purpose. . . .[103]

This critique would imply that Jefferson was not a member of the Illuminati order, but that didn't stop the accusations. As previously noted, much of this was a last effort of Jefferson's political opponents to regain their strength in the wake of a surge of "liberalism" that was sweeping the nation.

Jefferson was forever under attack because of his refusal to attend the church of the presidents. He was slandered as being an atheist during his political campaign, and the Federalists took advantage of this slur. Jefferson's true religious beliefs were Christian in the broadest and truest sense of the word. Before retiring in the evening, Jefferson observed a daily ritual of reading something moral. For sixteen years he worked on compiling a volume he called *The Life and Morals of Jesus of Nazareth,* now known as *The Jefferson Bible* and more fully discussed in my 1975 and 1985 publications.[104] He confided in few people about his studies, but in 1816 Jefferson wrote to Charles

Thomson: "I too, have made a wee little book . . . which I call the philosophy of Jesus; it is a paradigm of his doctrines. . . . A more beautiful or precious morsel of ethics I have never seen; it is a document in proof that I am a real Christian, that is to say, a disciple of the doctrines of Jesus.[105]

In a letter to Benjamin Rush he notes:

And in confiding it to you, I know it will not be exposed to the malignant perversions of those who make every word from me a text for new misrepresentations and calumnies. I am, moreover, averse to the communication of my religious tenets to the public, because it would countenance the presumption of those who have endeavored to draw them before that tribunal, and to seduce public opinion to erect itself into that inquest over the rights of conscience, which the laws have so justly prescribed. It behooves every man who values liberty of conscience for himself to resist invasions of it in the case of others, or their case may, by change of circumstances, become his own.

To John Adams in 1813, he described his work:

We must reduce our volume to the simple Evangelists; select, even from them. The very words only of Jesus, paring off the amphibologisms into which they have been led, by forgetting often, or not understanding, what had fallen from Him, by giving their own misconceptions as his edicts, and expressing unintelligibly for others what they had not understood themselves. There will be found remaining the most sublime and benevolent code of morals which has ever been offered to man. I have performed this operation for my own use, by cutting verse by verse out of the printed book, and arranging the matter which is evidently his and which is as easily distinguished as diamonds in a dung hill. The result is an octavo of forty-six pages.

Obviously not interested in publishing this compilation for the general public, he wrote in the preface to *The Life and Morals of Jesus* "I not only write nothing on religion, but rarely permit myself to speak on it."[106] The Fifty-seventh Congress published an edition of nine thousand copies in 1904, more than one hundred years after Jefferson first compiled it.

Both Jefferson and Franklin were considered deists, or advocates of a natural religion based on human reason and morality (some went so far as to say they were atheists), and yet they emphasized a utilitarian religion rather than passive dogma. Both men exemplified a religion of service for the brotherhood of man.[107]

One might conclude from Jefferson's rejection of metaphysics that he had no place for visionary experiences, but this is not the case. He, like Franklin and Washington, believed America to have a part in a divine plan. In Jefferson's first inaugural address, he noted that the United States was

kindly separated by nature and a wide ocean from the exterminating havoc of one quarter of the globe; too high minded to endure the degradations of the others; possessing a chosen country, with room enough for our descendants to the hundredth and thousandth generation; entertaining a due sense of our equal right to the use of our own faculties, to the acquisitions of our industry, to honor and confidence from our fellow citizens, resulting not from birth but from our actions and their sense of them; enlightened by a benign religion, professed, indeed, and practiced in various forms, yet all of them including honesty, truth, temperance, gratitude, and the love of man; acknowledging and adoring an overruling Providence, which by all its dispensations proves that it delights in the happiness of man here and his greater happiness hereafter. . . .[108]

Jefferson's visions of America can be translated as expansionist. His Louisiana Purchase was not only a landmark in the development of the American nation but an expression of an "Empire for Liberty" that would manifest in the annexing of Canada and Cuba. From this vantage point the Monroe Doctrine, which Jefferson strongly urged upon President James Monroe, was not as much a separation of America from

Europe as a natural expansion of America's destiny to include the South American continent. In Jefferson's words:

> America, North and South, has a set of interests distinct from those of Europe. . . . While the last is laboring to become the domicile of despotism our endeavor should surely be, to make our hemisphere that of freedom. What a colossus shall we be when the southern continent comes up to our mark! What a stand will it secure as a ralliance for the reason and freedom of the globe![109]

Jefferson's most prized accomplishment, founding the University of Virginia, was based on the traditions of the schools of Athens and Florence and the Alexandrian library: he wanted to ensure freedom from all theological restraint. Jennings C. Wise theorized that within Jefferson's architectural design of the university are hidden the teachings of the mystery schools and secret societies. Realizing that curricula could be altered, Wise suggests, Jefferson embedded the philosophy of the mystical tradition in the bricks and mortar of the university, so that its design would convey a philosophy free from dogma and superstition. Jefferson unites the ancient architectural elements of the rotunda and the rectangular academic hall, which symbolize heaven (the rotunda as used in the Chaldean planet tower called the House of the Seven Spheres) and earth (the four-cornered rectangle). Their use together in one structure symbolizes the union of heaven and earth (figure 2.16).

Wise believed that "the Seer of Monticello" was in fact a mystic of high degree in the same sense as were the great medieval alchemists from Roger Bacon and Dante down to Cardinal Cusa, Paracelsus, and Francis Bacon. "His transcending intellect could envisage Deity in the Jehovah depicted in the Old Testament and foisted on Christendom despite the teachings of Jesus and Paul, no more than Socrates and Evermerus could accept the unmoral Zeus of Olympian Theology as the dictator of human destinies."[110] A thorough analysis of Jefferson's architectural plans of the University of Virginia, his travels in Europe, and his exposure to ancient architecture would be needed to assess Mr. Wise's hypothesis.

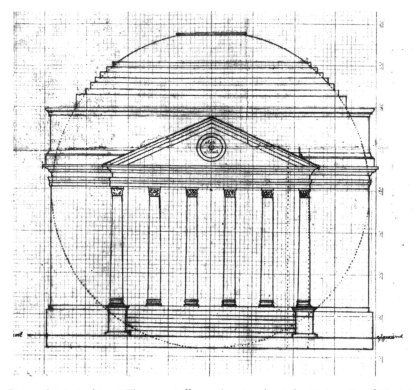

Figure 2.16. Architect Thomas Jefferson's rotunda at the University of Virginia. Jennings C. Wise links the rotunda to the Chaldean planet tower called the House of the Seven Spheres. As in much classical architecture, we have a suggestion of the "sun over the mountain" or the basic symbology of the reverse of the Great Seal, with the circle in this example encompassing the triangle. (Willard Homestead.)

An Astrological Analysis of Jefferson

Jefferson was born on April 13, 1743; his astrological chart reveals that his sun was in Aries (see figure 2.17). The job of the Arian is to align himself with the divine will. The ability to manifest will on the physical plane is shown by the sun in the second house, the house of the material plane. The sun's trine to the planet Mars gives an abundance of energy in the physical world. The sun trine to Saturn gave Jefferson the ability to work slowly, through partnerships, and with those in positions of power and authority. An interesting balance is shown by his sun in square aspect to Uranus, which relates to sporadic revolutionary activity.

Jefferson's sun square with Uranus also shows self-reliance instead of dependence on divine will. Jefferson may have sought a balance between his self and the divine will, between working with those in authority who saw the benefits of his revolutionary ideas and his desire to act immediately regardless of the long-range consequences.

Jefferson's Aquarius rising (symbolizing altruism and brotherhood) indicates that his ultimate motives were geared toward the good of all humankind. Of the three Founding Fathers examined herein, he is the most mysterious. He may have been a member of all three secret societies or perhaps none. He may have had the most profound involvement in the occult sciences, or he may have had few occult leanings.

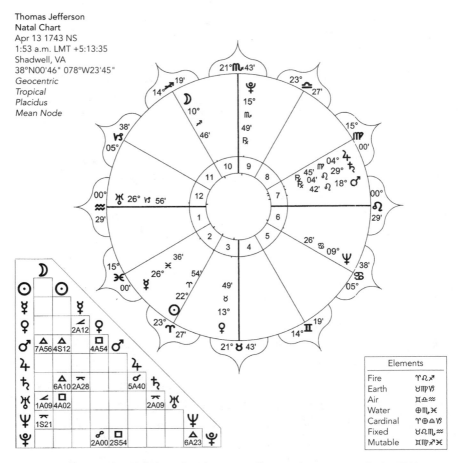

Figure 2.17. Astrological chart for Thomas Jefferson, born on April 13, 1743, 1:53 a.m., in Shadwell, Virginia. (By Margie Herskowitz, CA-NCGR.)

Jefferson's love of science and love of humanity were equal; he believed that science should be used only for the good of all humankind. This is the promise of the Aquarian age just as it was the promise of Thomas Jefferson.

William Barton and Charles Thomson

What is mysterious in the case of Jefferson is clear-cut in the case of two other lesser-known Founding Fathers, the two men directly responsible for the final designs of the Great Seal that will be discussed in the next chapter: William Barton and Charles Thomson. Neither one left any evidence at all of belonging to an esoteric fraternity. Nor is there any evidence that another key contributor to the seal's design, Pierre Du Simitière, was a member of any of these organizations. Of all the known contributors to the Great Seal, only artist Francis Hopkinson is thought to have been a Freemason.

William Barton was a native Philadelphian and the son of Reverend Thomas Barton. He completed his education in Europe and returned to America in 1779. He was an accomplished scholar and writer. Noteworthy topics he wrote about include the nature and use of paper credit and the proper use of coats of arms in the United States.

Another William Barton from Rhode Island was a confirmed Mason, and the two men have sometimes been confused. There is no record that Barton the Great Seal designer was a Mason, although his interests were compatible with Masonic pursuits. In particular, his admiration for his uncle, David Rittenhouse (1732–1796) would imply more than a passing interest in geometry and mathematics in general. Barton published the first biography about his mother's famous brother in 1813, and his regard for this genius instrument maker, astronomer, mathematician, and the first director of the U.S. Mint may have rubbed off. There is no record that David Rittenhouse entered the Masonic Lodge either, but his brother Benjamin Rittenhouse is confirmed to have entered as apprentice Mason in 1786.[111]

Charles Thomson, the first secretary of Congress, was responsible for coordinating the final design of the Great Seal. He befriended and associated with Peter Miller—the mystic and grand master of the

Ephrata Lodge—who translated the Declaration of Independence into several languages, thus making Europe aware of America's independence. It is this association with Miller that has led some—including Harold Preece, writing in the April 1951 *Rosicrucian Digest*—to conclude that Thomson was also a member of the Rosicrucian order.

A Delaware Indian tribe adopted Thomson in recognition of his fairness and integrity and gave him an Indian name meaning "man who tells the truth." He considered both Jefferson and Franklin close friends, the latter being largely responsible for Thomson's political fortunes. Thomson remained firm in his opposition to British policies, actively espousing a radical course from the Stamp Act crisis through the adoption of the Declaration of Independence.

Conclusion

Many authors and students of the esoteric tradition teach and accept the probability that the secret societies had a direct hand in the design of America's seal. A careful analysis doesn't confirm the "obvious." Washington and Franklin were undoubtedly Freemasons and perhaps Rosicrucians. Jefferson cannot be proven a member of any secret society, but many of his habits and stated beliefs could lead one to believe that he was a member in secret, and future research could eventually verify this. Jefferson and Franklin were appointed by Washington to serve on the first committee to design America's seal, but none of their suggestions were accepted. They did, however, eventually approve the seal's final design.

It is the choice of symbols on the reverse of the seal that strongly implicates an influence of the secret societies on its design. Perhaps Franklin and Washington and Jefferson approved our two-sided seal because they were capable of interpreting its symbols as detailing America's secret destiny. An examination of the seal's history and symbols could reveal why so many insist that half of our national seal has occult heritage.

3

THE HISTORY OF
AMERICA'S GREAT SEAL

The colonists' rejection of monarchy as an acceptable system of government represented a major step in the evolution of governmental forms. A republic or democracy had been untried since the Athens of the fourth century B.C.E., even though the British Parliament was, to a limited degree, a representative form of government. America's elected government demonstrated a rejection of its origins and a break with its parent, Great Britain, and that meant a loss of collective and individual security. The mood of our new nation was one of chaos, confusion, and alienation. Greatly needed was a symbol that embodied the identity of the fledgling nation. The traditional form for expressing the individuality of a nation is its coat of arms or seal, and that is what Congress set out to establish in 1776 with the first Great Seal committee.

A seal identifies, authenticates, and documents. Seals predate 4000 B.C.E.; the oldest of them have been found in India, Egypt, and what used to be Babylonia and Assyria. To a largely illiterate population, seals served as signatures. Sealing declined after the fall of the Western Roman Empire in 476 C.E., but it was revived under Pepin the Short during the eighth century. Between the eleventh and thirteenth centuries, the use of seals spread from sovereigns, high clergy, and nobles to craftspeople and tradespeople. The late twelfth century marked the beginning of the great period of seal engraving that culminated in the thirteenth and fourteenth centuries.

The Great Seal of the United States

The term *great seal* may have emerged during the thirteenth-century reign of King John (1199–1216), to differentiate between it and a "privy" or lesser seal, which was used by the sovereign in business and personal matters. Great Seals originated in the seventh century with European royalty. The first English royal pendant seal, that of Edward the Confessor (who ruled between 1042 and 1066), became the model for all future British and American seals. The United States adopted the British tradition of using a Great Seal to authenticate the presidential signature on specific state documents even though it used no lesser seal for other purposes.

America's Great Seal is its national coat of arms, and it symbolizes the United States government. At one time, it was referred to as the Great Seal of the United States, but since 1892 the State Department has referred to it as the seal of the United States.

Pendant seals, including America's, are two-sided. During the years of their greatest use, their obverse (front) and reverse (back) were impressed onto two sides of a wax pendant that served to secure ribbons or cords placed between front and back. Being difficult to affix properly and therefore being costly, pendant seals fell into disuse after 1871.

The First Committee

On July 4, 1776, Benjamin Franklin, Thomas Jefferson, and John Adams were given the task of designing the American seal. Pierre Eugène Du Simitière, a portrait painter with some knowledge of heraldry, acted as a consultant and artist to the first committee.

Esoteric historians frequently exaggerate the contributions and influence of Franklin, Jefferson, and Adams on the seal's accepted design. Many assume that, because Franklin and possibly Jefferson were Freemasons, the design for the reverse of the seal represented a deliberate effort by the esoteric orders to influence our nation's destiny. This stance disregards the fact that none of the suggestions of Jefferson or Franklin were used in the final design. What is revealed in the first committee's designs, however, is the vision each of these three Founding Fathers held for America's birth and destiny.

Franklin's design (figure 3.1) included:

Moses . . . standing on the shore, and extending his hand over the Sea, thereby causing the same to overwhelm Pharaoh who is sitting in an open Chariot, a crown on his Head and a . . . Sword in his Hand. Rays from a Pillar of Fire in the Clouds . . . reaching to Moses . . . to express that he acts by . . . Command of the Deity . . . Motto, Rebellion to Tyrants is Obedience to God.[1]

Jefferson submitted ideas for two sides of the seal (see figure 3.2). For the obverse, he suggested the children of Israel in the wilderness led by a cloud by day and a pillar of fire by night; on the reverse, he suggested Hengist and Horsa, two brothers who were the legendary leaders of the first Anglo-Saxon settlers in Britain.

Jefferson's and Franklin's suggestions were notably similar in their use of biblical and mythological themes instead of heraldic elements. This could have been due either to their rejection of the Old World philosophy behind heraldry or simply to their ignorance of heraldic design.

John Adams turned to Greek mythology for inspiration (see figure 3.3). He proposed an engraving of Hercules resting on his club for the seal's obverse. The moralistic Adams was perhaps enamored of the choice facing Hercules, on one side of whom stands Virtue, exhorting him toward a rocky mountain ascent; on the other stands Sloth, voluptuously enticing

Figure 3.1. An 1856 rendering of the obverse (left) and reverse (right) of the first committee proposal, 1776. (Illustration from Patterson and Dougall, *The Eagle and the Shield*.)

Figure 3.2. Thomas Jefferson's proposals for the first committee, August 20, 1776. The children of Israel in the wilderness for the obverse (left), and Hengist and Horsa for the reverse (right), from the 1903 Benedict realizations. (Illustration from Patterson and Dougall, *The Eagle and the Shield*.)

Figure 3.3. For the seal's obverse, John Adams proposed Gribelin's engraving of Hercules resting on his club. (Illustration from Patterson and Dougall, *The Eagle and the Shield*.)

him—and presumably the United States as well—down the less arduous path of pleasure.

Du Simitière's design for the seal's obverse (figure 3.4) included a shield divided into six sections that represented England, Scotland, Ireland, Holland, France, and Germany. Supporting the shield was the goddess of liberty in a corselet of armor, a spear and cap in her right hand, her left hand resting on an anchor symbolizing hope. On the other side, the shield was held up by a typical American soldier of the day dressed in a hunting shirt of buckskin and equipped with a powder horn and a tomahawk.

With such a remarkable group of men forming the first committee to design our nation's coat of arms, it may be surprising that the only one whose suggestions made it to the final design was the artist brought in as a consultant on the job, Pierre E. Du Simitière. This is a pattern that we shall see repeating itself in the later committees. Patterson and Dougall credit Du Simitière with introducing four of the final elements: the

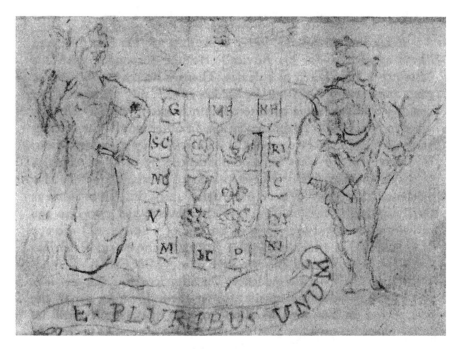

Figure 3.4. Du Simitière's design for the shield's obverse, divided into six sections to represent England, Scotland, Ireland, Holland, France, and Germany. (Illustration from Patterson and Dougall, *The Eagle and the Shield*.)

shield, E Pluribus Unum, MDCCLXXVI, and the eye of providence in a triangle with a glory or rays of light.[2] (See figures 3.1 and 3.4.)

Du Simitière was born in Geneva, Switzerland, on September 18, 1737. Arriving in New York City in 1763, he became a naturalized citizen of the British colony in 1769. He was nearly thirty-nine years old at the time he worked on the seal and had long been acquainted with the other members of the seal's committee. An itinerant collector and researcher of Americana, Du Simitière strove to record the colonies' history, and his collection of pamphlets, newspapers, handbills, and political publications eventually became the basis for the first American museum of history in the United States. In 1781 he was granted an honorary master of arts degree from the College of New Jersey (now Princeton). Perennially impoverished, he died destitute on November 18, 1784, his history of the colonies never written. The principal part of his collection purchased by the American Philosophical Society (of which he had been curator) and the rest of his belongings sold at public auction proved insufficient to pay his debts.

The eye in a triangle and the motto E Pluribus Unum (Out of Many, One) were Du Simitière's most important contributions to the seal design. The source of this lofty motto was probably none other than the *Gentleman's Magazine,* published in London (1731–1922), which carried E Pluribus Unum on its title page and was well known to Du Simitière, a learned lover of books. The Department of State's *The Eagle and the Shield* by Patterson and Dougall contains a detailed account of Du Simitière's various accomplishments.

The Second Committee

In January 1777, Congress rejected the suggestions of the first committee, and a second committee was formed three years later. Serving as consultant was Francis Hopkinson, an artist who had successfully designed the American flag, some currency, and numerous official seals for the Board of Admiralty and the Department of the Treasury.

The second-committee members were Chairman John Morin Scott, a New York City attorney and Yale graduate and member of the Continental Congress (1779–83); James Lovell (b. Oct. 31, 1737), a native of Boston, scholar, teacher, politician, and Harvard graduate, who also served in the Continental Congress for three years; and William

Churchill Houston, a North Carolina native and Princeton graduate and faculty member (1769–83) and member of the Continental Congress in 1779.[3]

Once again, it was the consultant to the committee who made the only lasting contributions to the seal's eventual design. Francis Hopkinson (figure 3.5) was an artist, musician, lawyer, member of the Continental Congress, and signer of the Declaration of Independence. After he graduated from the College of Philadelphia in 1759, he performed and

Figure 3.5. Francis Hopkinson, a Freemason who designed the first American flag and other official seals and currency. His ideas dominated the second committee's report, though the invoices he submitted for his work were never paid. (Illustration from Patterson and Dougall, *The Eagle and the Shield*.)

composed sacred and secular music and claimed to be the first native-born American "who has produced a musical composition." His knowledge of heraldry helped him design the Great Seal of New Jersey and also the American flag adopted by Congress on June 14, 1777.

Hopkinson's ideas dominated the second committee's report. He proposed white and red stripes within a blue background for the shield, a radiant constellation of thirteen stars, and an olive branch (figure 3.6). Hopkinson's most significant contributions to the reverse seal were indirect, however, in that he had used what ended up being the two main elements in his earlier designs for currency. His design for the forty-dollar bill of 1778 contained an eye with rays of light around it, which may have influenced William Barton's use of the same in his 1782 seal proposal. Remember that Du Simitière had also suggested this symbol in the first seal committee. Hopkinson also used the image of an unfinished pyramid on his 1778 fifty-dollar bill (figure 3.7), which was almost certainly the source for Barton's pyramid in the final design of the reverse of the Great Seal.

Of all the contributors whose ideas were eventually incorporated into the finished design for the seal, Hopkinson is the only one who can be verified as having belonged to a secret society, though he is not included in Heaton's list of confirmed Masons because the records of his initiation were lost. Hopkinson's father was a high-ranking Mason, as David Ovason points out, so it "seems unlikely that Hopkinson was not initiated."[4]

The Third Committee

The third committee was formed on May 4, 1782, when Secretary of Congress Charles Thomson commissioned the final committee of three: Chairman Arthur Middleton, John Rutledge, and Elias Boudinot. Middleton was born on June 26, 1742, into a wealthy, distinguished family in South Carolina. He studied law at St. Johns College and Middle Temple, London, served in the South Carolina legislature, was elected to Congress, signed the Declaration of Independence, and served in the militia. Although he was familiar with British and continental coats of arms, seals, and heraldic designs, he ultimately made no contributions to the seal's design and was not instrumental in the committee.[5]

Also from a prominent South Carolina family, John Rutledge was well educated and had lived abroad, but he took no part in the committee

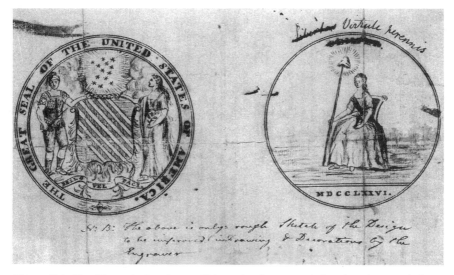

Figure 3.6. Hopkinson's drawings of his revised proposals for the obverse (left) and reverse (right), submitted to the second committee in 1780. (Illustration from Patterson and Dougall, *The Eagle and the Shield*.)

Figure 3.7. The unfinished pyramid first appeared in Hopkinson's design of a 1778 fifty-dollar colonial note.

work and was eventually replaced by Arthur Lee. The latter was from the wealthy and aristocratic Lee family of Virginia, had lived in the British Isles earning two medical degrees as well as an honorary doctorate from Harvard, and was well qualified to serve with his knowledge of coats of arms, seals, and heraldry.

Yet, records indicate that Elias Boudinot gave more attention to the committee than did the other two members. Boudinot was born in Philadelphia on May 2, 1740. An attorney and a cultivated, well-informed gentleman, he served in the New Jersey legislature, was elected to Congress, and served as its president (1782–83). He was familiar with heraldry, coats of arms, and seals and in 1816 authored a book called *A Star in the West; or, A Humble Attempt to Discover the Long Lost Ten Tribes of Israel.*[6]

Secretary of Congress Charles Thomson, Arthur Lee, and Elias Boudinot were the three who enlisted the artist William Barton as consultant. Barton (figure 3.8) was born on April 11, 1754, to a distinguished Philadelphia family. He received honorary master of arts degrees from the University of Pennsylvania (1781) and the College of New Jersey (now Princeton) perhaps because of his forty-page pamphlet, "Observations on the Nature and Use of Paper Credit; and the Peculiar Advantage to be Derived from it, in North America." He attempted to establish The American Heraldic Institution with another pamphlet, "Observations on the Advantages to be Derived from Proper Use of Coats of Arms in the United States." He was a member (1787) and counselor (1790–93) of the American Philosophical Society.

Writing to Thomas Jefferson in August 1790, Barton referred to himself as having "a pretty numerous family" and "a small as well as precarious income," but his attempts to obtain a suitable position in the federal bureaucracy were not fruitful. He published a "Dissertation on the Freedom of Navigation . . ." dedicated to Thomas Jefferson in 1802. He died on October 21, 1817.[7]

William Barton's contributions to the final committee on the Great Seal were pivotal. His suggestions included an eagle for the front and an unfinished pyramid for the seal's reverse (see figure 3.10 on page 94).

By mid-June 1782, Charles Thomson had gathered all the materials from the three committees and, with Barton's help, created a design that was finally approved for the Great Seal. Thomson (see figure 3.9)

Figure 3.8. William Barton served on the third committee. He suggested the eagle (and phoenix) as well as an unfinished pyramid, which Thomson placed in dominant positions on the obverse and reverse of the Great Seal. (Illustration from Patterson and Dougall, *The Eagle and the Shield*.)

was the oldest of those who worked on the final seal's design, born in Ireland on November 29, 1729. He and his five siblings came to New Castle, Delaware when he was ten years old, becoming orphans en route when their father, John Thomson, died during the voyage.

When the seal was completed, Thomson was fifty-two years old and had already served eight of his fifteen years as the first secretary of Congress. He was a teacher, businessman, and politician, as well as a vigorous supporter of the colonies in opposing British measures of repression. John Adams referred to Thomson as "the Sam Adams of Philadelphia, the life of the cause of liberty."[8] Although he did not attend college, live abroad, or travel extensively, he was a scholarly, highly intelligent, well-read, self-disciplined, and morally irreproachable patriot. Thomson completed the first translation of the Greek Septuagint Bible into Latin—a major contribution to religious scholarship. He was referred to as the Soul of Congress.

A man of striking personal appearance, around six feet tall, Thomson had an unusual relationship with the Delaware nation. He was adopted into their tribe as a young man and received the name Wegh-wu-law-mo-end, or Man Who Tells the Truth. It is believed that he was the author of the Northwest Ordinance of 1787, which defined the procedures by which new states could join the union, a law similar to the Great Law of the Iroquois League. "The Ordinance contained an extensive Bill of Rights—a distinctively American idea"—which mirrored the way the Iroquois Great Law of Peace was sensitive to the rights of individuals and the potential abuses of the state.[9]

Figure 3.9. Charles Thomson, the first secretary of Congress, was responsible for coordinating the final design of the Great Seal. A close associate of the German Pietists, and perhaps a Rosicrucian, Thomson had been adopted into an Indian tribe as a young man. (Illustration from Patterson and Dougall, *The Eagle and the Shield.*)

As secretary of Congress for fifteen years, Thomson witnessed the birth and struggle of the new nation and recorded its transactions for posterity. It is possible that the wisdom he gained from the Native Americans and his Rosicrucian friends in the Ephrata community provided him with the insight he needed to establish the final design of America's Great Seal.

The Barton-Thomson Designs

Barton and Thomson borrowed from the designs of the earlier committees and modified each other's designs. Thomson placed the eagle in its dominant position on the seal's obverse and suggested it be a bald eagle, a bird indigenous to America. Manly Palmer Hall and other authors prefer to see the 1782 eagle as the mystical phoenix bird, pointing to the tuft or crest of feathers in the back of its head as evidence (see figure 3.10), along with the fact that William Barton included a phoenix in his early designs for the third committee. Barton had indeed drawn a phoenix in flames, with wings extended, sitting on a golden Doric pillar, as one of three birds (including also the eagle and the dove) in his second design. David Ovason notes that "Barton saw the burning phoenix of his seal design as being emblematic of the expiring liberty of Britain, revived by her descendants in America."[10]

Hall concluded that the tuft on the head of the 1782 eagle was similar to that on the headdress of an Egyptian picture of a kneeling winged god interpreted by English Egyptologist Sir J. Gardner Wilkinson as a phoenix-man. What Hall failed to realize, however, was that Sir Wilkinson had admitted his error in mistranslating as "phoenix-man" an Egyptian term that meant "the pure soul of the ruler."[11] Although it is true that the eagle is related to the phoenix and is sometimes referred to as the fire bird, it is important to note that heraldic eagles often had crests; thus, the tuft on the head of the 1782 eagle in no way makes it a phoenix. Unfortunately, other contemporary authors have perpetuated Hall's unsubstantiated supposition and still claim today that a phoenix appears not only on the original 1782 Great Seal, but also on later dies from 1825, 1841, 1885, and 1904. Twentieth- and twenty-first-century authors on this subject all too often fail to refer to primary documents (as David Ovason meticulously does) and continue to circulate the more picturesque anecdotes, even with little or no evidence to substantiate them.

The report submitted by Barton and Thomson (approved on June 20, 1782) contains their "Remarks and Explanations," the only official record elucidating the symbols in the Great Seal:

The Escutcheon is composed of the chief & pale, the two most honorable ordinaries. The Pieces, paly, represent the several states all joined in one solid compact entire, supporting a Chief, which unites the whole & represents Congress. The Motto alludes to this union. The pales in the arms are kept closely united by the Chief and the Chief depends on that union & strength resulting from it for its support, to denote the Confederacy of the United States of America & the preservation of their union through Congress.

The colours of the pales are those used in the flag of the United States of America; white signifies purity and innocence, Red, hardiness and valour, and Blue, the colour of the Chief signifies vigilance perseverance and justice. The Olive branch and arrows denote the power of peace & war which is exclusively invested in

Figure 3.10. Charles Thomson's drawing for the third committee, 1782, included William Barton's suggestions for an eagle and an unfinished pyramid (the latter used on the seal's reverse, see figure 3.11). (Illustration from Patterson and Dougall, *The Eagle and the Shield.*)

Congress. The Constellation denotes a new State taking its place and rank among other sovereign powers. The Escutcheon is born on the breast of an American Eagle without any other supporters to denote that the United States of America ought to rely on their own virtue.

Reverse. The pyramid signifies Strength and Duration: The Eye over it & the Motto allude to the many signal interpositions of providence in favor of the American cause. The date underneath is that of the Declaration of Independence and the words under it signify the beginning of the new American Era, which commences from that date.[12]

Figure 3.11. Barton and Thomson borrowed from designs of earlier committees to arrive at this proposal for the reverse. (Illustration from Patterson and Dougall, *The Eagle and the Shield*.)

Patterson and Dougall summarized the work of the three committees and what they contributed:

> In all, fourteen men had a part. Each of the three committees—or, more accurately, each of the consultants to those committees—contributed elements to the final design. The various contributions are here identified and summarized—with the reservation that Thomson may have derived his central idea for the obverse (the eagle, with wings spread and a shield on its breast, holding symbols of peace and war in its talons) not from an eclectic study of earlier proposals for the Great Seal device but from entirely different sources.
>
> From the first committee, and specifically from Du Simitière, came the suggestions that resulted in (1) the use of a shield and the motto *E Pluribus Unum* on a scroll in the final obverse, and (2) the eye of Providence in a radiant triangle and the date "MDCCLXXVI" on the final reverse. Du Simitière's shield is here listed because, although a national seal usually bears a coat of arms and a coat of arms usually includes a shield, none of the devices proposed by Franklin, Adams, and Jefferson contained one. Du Simitière's "Imperial Eagle Sable, for Germany," how-

Figure 3.12. The Great Seal today: obverse (left) and reverse (right). The colors are those of the U.S. flag: white signifies purity and innocence; red, hardiness and valor; and the blue color of the chief signifies vigilance, perseverance, and justice. (Illustration from Department of State pamphlet 8868, July 1976.)

ever, is not here listed because it was almost certainly not the inspiration or source for the eagle of the final design.

From the second committee, and specifically from Hopkinson, came the suggestions that resulted in (1) the colors red, white, and blue on the shield, with the red and white as some kind of stripes, (2) the bundle of arrows (from the savage of Hopkinson's first obverse, armed with a bow and arrows), (3) the olive branch, and (4) the radiant constellation of thirteen stars, all on the final obverse.

From the third committee, and specifically from Barton, came the suggestions that resulted in (1) the eagle displayed on the final obverse, and (2) the unfinished pyramid on the final reverse. Subsequently, Barton's paper of June 19 established the thirteen white and red stripes on the shield as vertical and fixed the number of arrows in the eagle's left talon at thirteen.

Thomson contributed a fresh and novel arrangement, using elements from earlier designs, and specifying that the eagle should be of the American or bald species. In his report, which turned out to be the final design, he contributed the two mottoes on the final reverse, *Annuit Coeptis* and *Novus Ordo Seclorum*.

Accordingly, Du Simitière, Hopkinson, Barton, and Thomson each contributed specific items or elements to the final Great Seal design. Actually, the first two recorded a larger score than the last two. For the final design of both the obverse and the reverse, however, major credit must go jointly to Barton and Thomson, who collaborated to combine the elements into a whole device that proved acceptable to Congress.[13]

The Unknown Man and the Seal

Some researchers in the esoteric tradition, including Paul Foster Case, Robert Krajenke, and P. W. Price, suggest that our knowledge of the seal's history and meaning will always remain incomplete because its inspiration was derived from an unseen, hidden, secret, or unknown source.[14] This unknown source has been personified as a secret society, invisible and unverifiable to our physical senses, but represented by the Freemasons, Rosicrucians, and the Illuminati.[15]

The secret origin of the seal has also been mythologized into the form of an "unknown man" or a "stranger" who presented the founders with the design for the reverse.[16] We have been unable to identify the original source of this often-repeated and factually erroneous tale, but we include one example of it here since it illustrates a wish-fulfillment scenario of early Americans seeking divine providence in a risky undertaking. In chapter 5 we will further examine the role of the unknown man or the magician archetype in the history of our nation.

Virginia Brasington relates the story of the mysterious stranger in relation to the design of the Great Seal as follows:

> The Continental Congress had asked Benjamin Franklin, Thomas Jefferson, and John Adams to arrange for a seal for the United States of America. . . . None of the designs they created, or which were submitted to them were suitable. . . .
>
> Fairly late at night, after working on the project all day, Jefferson walked out into the cool night air of the garden to clear his mind. In a few minutes, he rushed back into the room crying, jubilantly, "I have it! I have it!" Indeed, he did have some plans in his hands. They were the plans showing the Great Seal as we know it today.
>
> Asked how he got the plans, Jefferson told a strange story. A man approached him wearing a black cloak that practically covered him, face and all, and told him that he (the strange visitor) knew they were trying to devise a Seal, and that he had a design which was appropriate and meaningful. . . .
>
> After the excitement died down, the three went out into the garden to find the stranger, but he was gone. Thus, neither these founding fathers, nor anybody else, ever knew who really designed the Great Seal of the United States![17]

Conclusion

While our new nation struggled to find an identity, the codesigners of America's Great Seal (Franklin, Jefferson, Adams, Du Simitière, Hopkinson, Barton, Thomson, and all the others on the committees) collaborated over time to create a lasting symbol to unite present and future generations around ideals such as liberty, purity, justice, and virtue. The new country rallied around the front side with its obvious symbols of strength and independence. As we shall see in the next chapter, however, it would take several more generations of identifying ourselves as "Americans" before we could begin to identify with, and embrace, the mysterious reverse of the Great Seal.

4

THE RETURN OF THE REVERSE OF THE GREAT SEAL AND THE DESIGN OF THE DOLLAR BILL

The Reemergence of the Neglected Reverse

The first die of the obverse of the Great Seal of the United States was cut from brass in 1782. Subsequently, new dies were cut as the previous ones became worn—in 1825, 1841, 1877, 1885, and 1902—but each time the reverse went uncut and unused (figure 4.1). The 1841 die, cut by John V. N. Throop in Washington, D.C., caused great controversy because the eagle clutched only six arrows instead of the prescribed thirteen. It was later dubbed the "illegal eagle." By 1884 Tiffany and Company of New York had corrected this and other errors, giving the eagle thirteen arrows. Why did the Throop die use six arrows? Grinde and Johansen remind us that Charles Thomson first preferred five or six arrows for the eagle in his proposal, reminiscent of the League of the Iroquois, but Patterson and Dougall cite the origin of the bundle of arrows as "the savage of Hopkinson's first obverse, armed with bow and arrows."[1]

Until 1877 the State Department escaped controversy about its neglect of the seal's reverse. It was then that John D. Champlin Jr. launched the first assault on the department, claiming that the government's failure to use the reverse was "technically illegal" since the seal had been created by law. Champlin's article aroused public awareness, and in 1882 army officer Charles A. L. Totten requested that a commemoration of the seal showing both sides be struck for the seal's centennial.[2] This commemorative medal represented the first official use of the seal's reverse, it followed an engraving made by James Trenchard in 1786 (see figure 4.2 and figure 5.1a on page 121).

In January 1884, Secretary of State Frederick T. Frelinghuysen stated in letters to the Senate and House Appropriations Committees that by exact interpretation of the law, the seal was not complete without the reverse. On July 7, 1884, Congress appropriated the funds to obtain dies of both sides of the seal. State Department official Theodore Dwight consulted with historical scholars Justin Winsor and Harvard professor Eliot Norton; genealogist William H. Whitmore, author of the only American work on heraldry; John D. Champlin Jr.; and James H. Whitehouse, chief designer of Tiffany and Company. These artists, heraldists, and historians—with the possible exception of Champlin—recommended

Figure 4.1. Impressions of dies cut for the Great Seal in 1782, 1841, and 1885. (Illustration from Patterson and Dougall, *The Eagle and the Shield*.)

against reproducing the seal's reverse, largely on aesthetic grounds. Norton wrote that the reverse was "practically incapable of effective treatment; it can hardly, (however artistically treated by the designer,) look otherwise than as a dull emblem of a Masonic fraternity."[3]

Gaillard Hunt summarized Dwight's decision: "It had undoubtedly been the intention of the Department, when the appropriation was asked for, to cut the reverse; but its purpose was changed after fuller consideration, and it felt at liberty to leave this part of the new law unexecuted, as the law of 1782 remained in part unexecuted for one hundred years."[4]

Patterson and Dougall believe that the neglect of the reverse was not unlawful. They conjecture that Secretary of State Frelinghuysen had been "misled . . . into thinking that the resolution of the Continental Congress of June 20, 1782, *required* or *ordered* the cutting of a die of the reverse, whereas that resolution had simply made available a design for the reverse, to be used if desired to impress the back surface of pendant seals."[5]

As late as 1957 a State Department publication suggested that a die for the reverse might in fact have been cut. In 1973, however, I was told directly by Edwin S. Costrell, the chief of the Historical Studies Division of the State Department, that such a die was never cut.

This scenario was repeated a few years later in a different situation. In 1892 the State Department prepared an exhibit for the Chicago

Figure 4.2. The first official use of the seal's reverse, this commemorative medal was minted in 1882. This medal is not to be confused with an official die of the reverse seal for use on official documents, something that has yet to be cut to this day. (Illustration from Patterson and Dougall, *The Eagle and the Shield*.)

Exposition consisting of two large emblazonments of the seal's obverse and reverse. "The appearance presented by the reverse was so spiritless, prosaic, heavy, and inappropriate that it was never hung."[6]

The Dollar Bill

The first few decades of the twentieth century saw a growing interest in the seal's reverse. Some esoteric writers predicted that the reverse would soon receive fuller recognition.

In 1934, secretary of agriculture and former vice president Henry A. Wallace submitted a proposal to the president to mint a coin depicting the seal's obverse and reverse. Wallace's interest in the seal's reverse had been aroused when he discovered Hunt's 1909 volume on the seal's history. The Latin phrase Novus Ordo Seclorum (New Order of the Ages) struck him as meaning "the New Deal of the ages." President Franklin D. Roosevelt was so impressed with this connection that he decided to place both sides of the Great Seal on the dollar bill rather than a coin. Roosevelt's action brought 153 years of obscurity to an end, and the seal's reverse was officially recognized.

Wallace was interested in esoteric topics and was a friend of the Russian mystic Nicholas Roerich. One theory holds that Wallace undertook the promotion of the seal's reverse for kabbalistic reasons, with Roerich as his guru.

There were some basic similarities between Wallace and Roerich. Both were committed to world federalism; they both opposed the increasing mechanization of modern life, which they thought would threaten individuality; they supported cooperation rather than competition; and they felt that the arrival of a new age was imminent. During this new age humanity would witness the second coming of Christ.

Henry Wallace's daughter, Leslie Douglas, rejected the theory that her father was a devotee of Roerich; indeed, she claimed to possess evidence "quite to the contrary."[7] Earl Rogers, librarian at the University of Iowa, the repository of Wallace's papers, notes that Wallace broke with Roerich in 1935. After that he refused to have further contact with Roerich or any member of his family. Historian and Roosevelt biographer Arthur M. Schlesinger agrees with Rogers on this point.[8]

Wallace and Roosevelt were both Masons and so recognized the eye in the triangle as a Masonic emblem. This fact at least confirms that both individuals had been exposed to the symbol and suggests that they may have had personal motives for its popularization. Needless to say, it was the inclusion of the reverse of the Great Seal on this most popular of items that has done more than anything else to impress it into the American consciousness. A further examination of the design of the dollar bill follows later in this chapter.

Some Possible Reasons
for Suppression of the Reverse

As the currency became available, discussion among scholars opened up. Paul Foster Case took issue with Professor Norton's criticism of the seal's reverse as a "dull emblem of a Masonic fraternity": "A Masonic emblem the design for the reverse of the seal surely is, but he must be ignorant of what it means who calls it dull. It may lack aesthetic appeal, and want finish as a work of art; but as a symbolic statement of the true Americanism it is a marvel of ingenuity."[9]

Not everyone felt that the reverse's mysterious symbols, assumed to originate from secret societies open only to select white men of the upper classes, expressed the essential spirit of America. Manly Hall, the founder of the Philosophical Research Society in Los Angeles, stated that "the reverse was not cut at that time [1782] because it was regarded as a symbol of a secret society and not the proper device for a sovereign State."[10]

The symbols on the seal's reverse *have* been used by various secret societies in their ritual regalia and in their lodges of initiation, but this does not in itself prove that the seal's reverse is an emblem of any such society. The use of these same symbols does, however, provide us with a better understanding of why esoteric historians have linked the reverse seal with secret societies, and perhaps why those who oppose secret orders would be inclined to reject it.

Many authors in the esoteric tradition have attempted to read into the seal's design meanings that originated with the Freemasons, Rosicrucians, and Illuminati. Many have even claimed it as their own. William Carr states that Weishaupt adopted the seal's reverse as the symbol of his new society when he founded the order of the Illuminati on May 1, 1776.[11] H. S. Wyckoff, a prominent instructor in the esoteric tradition, taught that "our beautiful seal is an expression of Freemasonry, an expression of occult ideals."[12]

Although secret societies of the late eighteenth century used the symbols on the seal's reverse, these same symbols were available in books and periodicals found throughout the colonies as well. Since, of the four contributors to the seal's design (Thomson, Barton, Pierre Du Simitière, and Francis Hopkinson), only Hopkinson was a Mason, it's likely that these men were influenced more by the literature of their day than by Masonic culture.

As already mentioned, the most frequent error esotericists have made is to assume that the reverse seal's elements constitute a direct connection to secret societies. They feel that, because at least one and maybe two of the first committee's participants (Franklin and Jefferson) were Freemasons, the reverse seal was a device by which esoteric orders influenced our nation's direction. They contend that the reverse seal in itself is a link to present-day Freemasonry. They ignore the fact that neither Jefferson's nor Franklin's ideas were adopted, except for Jefferson's suggestion of a two-sided seal. This recurring misconception has led to the intermingling of the seal's factual history with "mythological" misinterpretations of its symbols.

The Scary "Satanic" Seal

In the late 1980s and early 1990s President George H. W. Bush began connecting the seal's motto Novus Ordo Seclorum to his policy of launching a "New World Order." This ignited a backlash from Christian fundamentalists already fearful of the Freemasonic influence on the Founding Fathers, an influence that they perceive as satanic. A host of new mistranslations of the Latin motto was the result. The publisher of A. Ralph Epperson's *New World Order* noted on the back cover: "The key to understanding the meaning behind all of those symbols is found in the translation of the Latin phrase 'Novus Ordo Seclorum' *('The New World Order')* found underneath the pyramid on what is known as the reverse side of the seal. Ralph Epperson . . . has discovered that those who designed them committed America to what has been called 'A Secret Destiny.' This future 'destiny' is so unpleasant that those who wanted the change it entails had

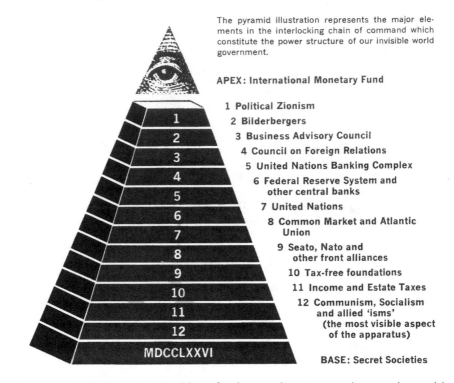

[WHO RUNS THE WORLD?]

The pyramid illustration represents the major elements in the interlocking chain of command which constitute the power structure of our invisible world government.

APEX: International Monetary Fund

1 Political Zionism

2 Bilderbergers

3 Business Advisory Council

4 Council on Foreign Relations

5 United Nations Banking Complex

6 Federal Reserve System and other central banks

7 United Nations

8 Common Market and Atlantic Union

9 Seato, Nato and other front alliances

10 Tax-free foundations

11 Income and Estate Taxes

12 Communism, Socialism and allied 'isms' (the most visible aspect of the apparatus)

BASE: Secret Societies

MDCCLXXVI

Figure 4.3. "Who Runs the World." A fundamentalist view on who runs the world as depicted in the seal's reverse: "This is one sovereign nation to which you can't apply for citizenship, but you are, nevertheless, ITS' [*sic*] SUBJECT."[13] Note how secret societies are identified as the common ground for all the groups allegedly working together toward global domination. (Illustration from Grem, *Karl Marx Capitalist*.)

to conceal that truth in symbols."[14] Figure 4.3 shows an example of how fundamentalists have linked this symbol to their interpretation of secret societies (particularly the nefarious Illuminati) being the common ground for all the groups allegedly working together toward global domination.

Roy Allen Anderson warned his readers, in the title of his book, to beware of *The New Age Movement and the Illuminati 666*.[15] William T. Still's book *New World Order: The Ancient Plan of Secret Societies* claimed: "For thousands of years secret societies have cultivated an ancient plan which has powerfully influenced world events. Until now, this secret plan has remained mysteriously hidden from view. Its primary objective is to bring all nations under one world government—the Biblical rule of the anti-Christ. Today its proponents simply call it the New World Order."[16] Jordan Maxwell asserted the evils of the eye in the triangle and pyramid and enlarged his attack on Freemasonry to include the International Red Cross in his *Matrix of Power:* "The International Red Cross is a Masonic organization. Why is the International Red Cross able to go behind enemy lines in wartime, in conflict? There is a reason. [Their symbol] comes from the Red Cross of Saint George . . . also from a Masonic institution."[17] David Icke in *The Biggest Secret*, remarking on the design of our nation's Capitol (also thought to be heavily influenced by Masons*), wrote: "Capitol Hill is not a political building, it is a temple to the Satanic Brotherhood."[18]

The Rising Popularity of the Reverse

The popular interest that has surfaced since the seal's appearance on the dollar bill has often focused on the apparent occult significance of the eye in the triangle, pyramid, and mysterious mottoes. In the 1960s, the seal's reverse became an emblem of the counterculture, appearing on posters for dance concerts and in underground newspapers, periodicals, and comic books. In August 1970, the image reentered the general cultural consciousness through the cover of *Harper's* magazine. It penetrated scholarly circles in 1974 through its use as a cover device for the *American Quarterly*. Eugene McCarthy employed it in his unsuccessful 1976 bid for the presidency, and even President Ford used it as a theme for a bicentennial speech. The seal's reverse gained an international profile when President Anwar el-Sadat spoke of it as a link between ancient Egypt and modern America in September 1981.[19]

Popular awareness of the symbols on the seal's reverse has continued to expand. In the 1980s Peter Sellers employed the distinctive pyramid-and-eye motif as a tomb in one of his final films, *Being There*. Shirley MacLaine referred to it in her 1984 book, *Out on a Limb,* when she described our Founding Fathers as transcendentalists. The character played by Madonna in the film *Desperately Seeking Susan* had it embroidered on the back of her jacket, and this became an important recurring image.

---

*For more information see Ovason, *The Secret Architecture of Our Nation's Capital.*

Today the image of the pyramid and the eye is regularly used as a graphic background illustration for financial discussions on television, on the web, and in periodicals, since most people connect it exclusively with the dollar bill. The all-seeing eye continues to give people the creeps, as the Department of Information Awareness (formed after 9/11/01 to track suspicions of terrorism) learned quickly, having used it in their initial logo design only to pull it as soon as they realized this logo gave the impression of a "Big Brother" organization monitoring the public's every move.

With the mainstream popularity of books and films like *National Treasure* (2004) and *The Da Vinci Code* (book, 2003; film, 2006), interest in these symbols selected by our Founding Fathers to represent the new nation seems to be at an all-time high. Before this resurgence, many esotericists thought that the reverse's unpopularity meant the time was not yet right for the populace to discern its meaning. Corinne Heline, for example, believed that "altogether its significance is such that it could not be apprehended properly until certain lessons had been learned and realizations acquired such as can come only with approaching maturity. . . . There has not been the consciousness with which to receive it. . . ."[20] Robert Krajenke, a writer on metaphysical subjects, saw this national maturing process in spiritual terms and concluded that "only when there is sufficient understanding of spiritual principles throughout the populace will this emblem ever enjoy wide currency and appreciation."[21]

Considering the choice of the Founding Fathers for a two-sided national seal, we might say their vision of a nation had both a physical (eagle/obverse side) and spiritual (pyramid/reverse side) destiny. Up until now, as a country, we have accepted only our outer image (obverse) and rejected our spiritual identity (reverse). Does this not reflect the values America has come to accept—a commitment to materialism, viewing the earth as an object to conquer or control? Indeed, these very values, along with the rejection of the world of spirit (the reverse), have placed America—and the world—in the precarious position it is in today. In chapter 6 we will examine the theories of synchronicity, similars, and morphic resonance to propose that the rising popularity of the reverse of the Great Seal has paralleled a rising feminine consciousness that is ushering in a growing acceptance of the spiritual half of our destiny.

The Great Seal and the One-Dollar Bill: A Numerological Analysis

The Founding Fathers and some of those who served on the seal's committees were "ardent students of the inner spirit behind heraldry," according to David Ovason.[22] Despite their intentions for a two-sided seal, however, it was not until the one-dollar bill was redesigned in 1935 that most Americans became aware of the reverse. Those responsible for the design of this currency were unquestionably Freemasons, and once again they spoke to us in symbols about the inner truths of the universe. According to David Ovason in his scholarly and highly enjoyable book *The Secret Symbols of the Dollar Bill,* the Great Seal and its use on the dollar bill represent "the most extraordinary example in history of public evolution of a magical design." Ovason notes that both the seal and the dollar bill contain magic symbols for which no public record exists to reveal where they came from or whether those who introduced them recognized their magic or esoteric content.[23]

Ovason makes a superb study of the mottoes on the dollar bill and the symbolic reasons for the selection of each:

E Pluribus Unum. While Du Simitière is given credit for suggesting the use of E Pluribus Unum, Ovason believes that Thomas Jefferson first proffered this motto, which means "Out of Many, One." As noted earlier, the source of inspiration for the motto was likely the title page of the *Gentleman's Magazine* published in London, though Thomson, at least, was aware of other classical sources for this phrase. Virgil used the phrase E Pluribus Unus in his poem "Moretum." De Pluribus Una is found in Horace's *Second Book of Epistles* (epistle 2, line 212), and Ex Pluribus Unum appears in *The Confessions* of St. Augustine (book 4).

Annuit Coeptis. Hunt traced Annuit Coeptis, (He [God] Has Favored Our Undertakings) to Virgil's *Aeneid* (book 9, line 625), as well as to his *Georgics* (book 1, line 40), though in both sources the spelling Annue Coeptis is used. Ovason says that in both instances the phrase was a prayer requesting or invoking aid from the pagan god Jupiter.[24]

Novus Ordo Seclorum. Hunt found Novus Ordo Seclorum, the New Order of the Ages, in Virgil's *Eclogues* (book 4, line 5).[25] Patterson and

Dougall explained the spelling of Seclorum, which had three other permissible options (Saeculorum, Sæculorum, and Seculorum). All three of these choices contained four syllables, which distorted the meter in Virgil's line, so "to preserve the meter the poet resorted to the device known as syncope, dropping the first *u* from the word. . . . The dropping of a vowel or syllable . . . to fit the word into the meter was very common."[26]

Noting its questionable Latin, Ovason points to the seventeen letters in this motto, a number important to both the seal and the dollar bill. He adds these seventeen characters of the motto to the nine characters of the Latin date that appears directly above it, MDCCLXXVI, creating the sum of twenty-six. Divided in half, this gives two groups of 13—the significance of which will be discussed shortly when we hunt for thirteen uses of 13.

In God We Trust. On December 9, 1863, the motto In God We Trust was approved for use on one-cent, two-cent, and three-cent pieces. It had been prescribed for use on coins by an act of January 18, 1837, but no legislation was enacted until 1863. On July 11, 1955, legislation was approved to use In God We Trust on all future coins and currency, and by July 30, 1956, this became our national motto. The House Judiciary Committee, however, recognized that there was widespread acceptance of E Pluribus Unum as a national motto and that this new resolution did not prohibit its continued use as such. In 1963, the Department of State wrote that there is "ample basis both in history and in law for calling 'E Pluribus Unum' a motto of the United States."[27]

In God We Trust was placed on the back of the speaker's rostrum in the House Chamber in 1962, replacing three stars that had been there previously. Ovason suggests that "the motto is designed to link together the two Houses through trust in God."[28] He also elaborates on the magical significance of the orientations of north, south, east, and west, explaining that placement of the speaker's rostrum in the south, where the sun is at its highest and most powerful point, implies that In God We Trust should be regarded as being the most powerful or important of the four official mottoes.[29]

An examination of the four mottoes on the bill provides a strong argument against those who claim that the one-dollar bill has a thoroughly pagan design. Indeed, the fundamentalists and others opposed to Freemasonry are correct in saying the current dollar bill was designed by Freemasons in 1935, but Ovason shows that a tally of the four mottoes reveals a far more Christian leaning than pagan. Annuit Coeptis is the only one of truly pagan origin, coming from Virgil. Novus Ordo Seclorum also originates with Virgil, but even in his day this line was considered deeply spiritual, interpreted by the early Christians as a reference to the coming Christ. E Pluribus Unum has a Christian source, Saint Augustine's *Confessions*, and the most recent addition, In God We Trust, comes out of the Christian tradition. With one motto pagan, one motto originally pagan but having been adopted by Christians, and two mottoes decidedly Christian, Ovason sees the dollar bill's design as inclusive and showing a gradation from the purely pagan right up to the Christian. Christianity at the end of the eighteenth century did seek to embrace other religions, with many of the Founding Fathers being Deists and encouraging freedom of religion.

Much has been made of the repetition of the number 13 in various elements within the Great Seal, and it is likely that even the Latin spellings used were chosen for the number of their letters. According to Ovason the choice and repetition of 13 had more to do with the significance of the number than with the thirteen colonies. He cites Clio Hogenraad's *Names and Numbers: Their Powers and Significance* (1915) to show how the ancient and secret societies linked the number 13 to rebirth and regeneration and considered it to bring luck. "It is a number of evolution and progress . . . a sacred number and a messenger from another world."[30] The fact that there were thirteen letters in E Pluribus Unum was more important than its source. The spellings of Annuit Coeptis and Novus Ordo Seclorum were determined by letter count. There are twelve letters in Virgil's Annue Coeptis, so Hunt and Patterson and Dougall explained that to get to the preferred 13 Charles Thomson used the imperative Annuit in the third person present tense.

Overtly, the number 13 was used to reflect the number of the original colonies. Covertly, however, the number 13 is part of the magical numerology of the dollar bill. David Ovason, numerologist and astrologer, counts a significant thirteen uses of 13 on the dollar as follows:[31]

1) 13 letters in Annuit Coeptis
2) 13 letters in E Pluribus Unum
3) 13 levels of stones in the pyramid

4) 13 stars in the constellation above the eagle
5) 13 horizontal lines on the band on the top of the shield
6) 13 vertical stripes on the shield
7) 13 olive leaves
8) 13 olive berries
9) 13 arrows held by the eagle
10) 13 nodules in decorative leaves to the left of the pyramid roundel
11) 13 nodules in decorative leaves to the right of the eagle roundel
12) & 13) the combination of Novus Ordo Seclorum (remember the questionable use of Latin to arrive at 17 letters) and the Roman date MDCCLXXVI (9 letters) to equal 26, or twice 13.

Some are frightened by the emphasis on the number 13, but Ovason sees its repetition on the dollar bill as a kind of literary symbolization of America's thirteen-in-one. There are many esoteric correlations for the number thirteen, including Christ with the twelve disciples and the twelve signs of the Zodiac traversed and returned to Aries the thirteenth. Acknowledging the thirteen colonies is only seeing the first layer of the intricate symbolism on the dollar bill.

The Secret Geometry of the One-Dollar Bill

Among the Freemasons involved in the design of the 1935 dollar bill were the president of the United States, Franklin D. Roosevelt; the secretary of agriculture, Henry A. Wallace; the secretary of the treasury, Henry Morgenthau; and the actual designer of the reverse of the bill, Edward M. Weeks. Patterson and Dougall record the following other artisans who worked on the dollar bill: Joachim Benzing engraved the reverse of the Great Seal; R. Ponickau engraved the obverse of the Great Seal; Donald R. McLeod, Edward M. Hall, and William B. Wells engraved the lettering.[32]

Edward Mitchell Weeks was born in Riverside, New Jersey, on August 20, 1866. He received his art training at the Spring Garden Institute in Philadelphia, the Pennsylvania Museum and School of Industrial Art also in Philadelphia, and the Cocoran Art School in Washington, D.C., and received his law degree (L.L.B) at George Washington University. In 1925 he became a foreman of letter engravers at the U.S. Bureau of Engraving and Printing and, in 1933, superintendent of engraving. While with the bureau, he did frames and lettering for various U.S. postage stamps and created a steel-engraved facsimile of the Declaration of Independence. He published *Letters Analyzed and Spaced* in 1952 and died in 1959.

Weeks was a member of the Masonic Order (D.C.) and served as a vestryman and superintendent of Sunday school at Saint Albans Episcopal Church (D.C.). He was a Republican and member of the Capitol City Chess Club.

In his *Letters Analyzed and Spaced,* Weeks displays a mind of exacting care and accuracy, allowing a student of geometry to endlessly enjoy the puzzles, tricks, and codes he embedded into his design for the reverse of the dollar. Even those without training in geometry or an appreciation for the meaning of symbols are able to sense the symbolic weight in its design. One of the rewarding things about studying symbols is the ability to approach them on so many different levels. All the world's great religions and various secret societies recognize and employ multitiered levels of meaning in their messages, mottoes, and designs, and apparently Weeks was following the established pattern. In his *Secret Geometry of the Dollar,* Ken McGrath argues that the numbers and proportions in Weeks's design reflect his Masonic membership and religious idealism.[33]

A Mason and surveyor, McGrath uses geometry, the golden ratio, letter/number logarithmic codes, and some of the number theories of nineteenth- and early-twentieth-century pyramidologists to show a striking intricacy in the geometric layout of the design on the back of the 1935 dollar (the side with the Great Seal on it). For example, he found the length of the design on the back, 5.655" (estimating the round one thousandth with a machinist's vernier caliper), multiplied by pi (3.1415927...) equals the date of the Declaration of Independence divided by one hundred (17.7657...) or that date within a few thousandths of an inch. The most important element employed in the design, however, is the use of the divine proportion or golden ratio, which McGrath sees as an important clue left by the designers. "The dollar's secrets were obviously intended to be openly discovered and puzzled-out by the public. There will be many [answers] here that can only have meaning to students of the mysteries. This design may contain messages of a prophetic character, or other messages that careful study may in time reveal."[34]

The mathematical formula or geometric pattern called the golden ratio, or phi, "meant life force to the ancient Egyptians, the principle of dynamic balance to the ancient Greeks, and the principle of beauty to many thinkers in Leonardo Da Vinci's time," says McGrath. "Da Vinci illustrated a book on the golden ratio called *De Divina Proportione,* 'Concerning the Divine Proportion.' The ratio is found all throughout nature, art, music, and science. It is found in ratios of the limbs of the body, the helix of DNA, atomic radiation decay values, and naturally appears in pine-cone seed spiral patterns, spiral sea shells, and tree branching sequences."[35]

The golden ratio, or phi, is called the most perfect number in all mathematics. It is equal to the square root of 5 plus 1 divided by 2, or 1.618033988749895.... The golden ratio is an irrational number, meaning it can't be written as a fraction. However, one way to get a close approximation of phi is by dividing two consecutive numbers in a simple sequence called the Fibonacci series. Fibonacci numbers basically follow the pattern 1, 1, 2, 3, 5, 8, 13, 21, 34, 55... where each number is the sum of the two before it. If one divides any two consecutive Fibonaccis, one will get an increasingly better approximation of phi: 15/8 = 1.625, which is off by 0.006966011 and 55/34 = 1.61764705882..., which is off by only 0.000386929....

According to McGrath, the golden ratio is found in two different visible forms on the back side of the dollar bill. The first form is the outer border rectangle that encloses the entire design. McGrath calls this the large outer rectangle and measures it at 5.655" by 2.160", a ratio which is the square of the golden ratio or 1:2.6180339. The second form appears twice in the filigree design in the center area of the bill, composed of a white rectangle connected at the corners by the four numeral ones. When you fold the dollar in half lengthwise, you can create two golden spirals on either side of the fold within this white inner rectangle.[36] (Figure 4.4.)

Another of the many secrets McGrath believes was deliberately left geometrically encoded in the dollar's design is "an ancient number motif, within this golden ratio form. . . . Carefully incorporated within the special golden ratio shapes and related shapes . . . is a mathematical element based on measurements made from an ancient design offset found throughout the internal alignment of the architecture of the Great Pyramid of Giza." As we'll see in the next chapter, Patterson and Dougall have established that the designers of the Great Seal based their pyramid on what they knew of the Great Pyramid at Giza. McGrath uses the much ignored work of pyramidologist David Davidson, which was in turn dependent upon the pyramid geometry and prophecy theories of Piazzi Smyth and Robert Menzies, to conclude that "the design offset was a choice made by the ancient Pyramid builders to place the central shaft alignment in the Pyramid to the East by somewhat more than 23 feet from its true centerline. . . . The exact, mysterious length . . . of David Davidson's 'Displacement Factor,' or the offset length, of 286.1 Pyramid Inches . . . was encoded into the dollar's design by a very simple arithmetical method that employed scaled lengths in decimal inch units. . . . The length of the dollar can be thought of as a composite number, numerically an approximation of 1,000 times phi then divided into 286.1, making a length rounding to 5.655 inches. At one thousandth of an inch: 1618.033 / 286.102 = 5.655."[37] The number 286.1 had religious significance to Davidson and many others. It is well known to present-day students of the Great Pyramid of Giza lore and may very well have been known to Edward Weeks in 1935.[38]

Rectangle projected *from centerline*

Figure 4.4. The golden spiral superimposed on the dollar bill by Ken McGrath. When you fold the dollar in half lengthwise, you can create two golden spirals on either side of the fold within this inner rectangle. (Based on Illustration courtesy of Ken McGrath.)

Figure 4.5. A slightly different kind of Masonic symbol: the Compass and Square of International Co-Masonry (which accepts both women and men), into which the author was initiated in 1971. Note the G, which stands for *Geometry* (in one level of interpretation).

Conclusion

The secret geometry and the magical history of the symbols in the dollar bill firmly connect it, and therefore the Great Seal, with the Freemasonic and Rosicrucian influences on the Founding Fathers. As a Mason, Weeks would have been quite familiar with the use of geometry to encode secrets. The colonial Masons referred to Providence or first cause (God) as the Great Architect of the Universe, and the G seen between the legs of the compass in the Masonic symbol refers (in one level of interpretation) to Geometry (figure 4.5).

Although it may not have been done with conscious intent, the design of the 1935 dollar, inspired by Masons to include the reverse of the Great Seal, has done more than any other development to elevate this symbol to national public awareness. The reverse of the Great Seal remains woefully misunderstood by fundamentalists, but as we will see in the next chapters, through the law of similars, the return of this symbol into our national consciousness may reflect a shift in how we identify ourselves as Americans. It is my contention that by embracing the hidden side of the seal, we are finally becoming the dual-sided nation intended by our founders; we are finally more open to expressing our destiny on a global scale.

A Symbolic and Mythological Analysis of the Reverse of the Great Seal

The Power of Symbols

When examining the Great Seal, we are looking at how the Founding Fathers embodied their vision of America in symbols. Other volumes could be filled to explain why other powerful symbols (such as the Join or Die serpent or the Betsy Ross flag) had the effect of uniting the early American republic, but this chapter focuses exclusively on the design chosen for the reverse of the Great Seal. This design is primarily made up of two ancient and ubiquitous symbols: the unfinished pyramid surmounted by a radiant eye in a triangle.

In order to truly comprehend what the Founding Fathers were expressing in the reverse of the Great Seal, we must first understand the power of symbols. Behavioristic psychologists see symbols as man-made signs whose meanings are cultural and transitory. Positivists perceive symbols as fables and myths that serve chiefly to entertain. Some critics will even try to belittle a certain aspect of a work as "merely symbolic," treating symbols as unreal and therefore insignificant.

Those in the humanistic tradition, however, see myths, symbols, and archetypes as powerful forces in the psyche, and not mere representations of the objective world or human history. Our contemporary disintegrative state is explained by transpersonal psychology as resulting from the modern West's lack of emphasis on the creation of meaningful myths. The development of a symbolic mythological system is deemed absolutely necessary to a culture's health and stability. Symbols cultivate wholeness and provide a bridge between the conscious and unconscious minds, resulting in the process of individuation and self-realization. Because they contain both conscious and unconscious elements, symbols relate to the entire psychic system and can therefore be assimilated by consciousness with relative quickness.

Carl Rogers wondered if perhaps symbols were even more important than, and possibly responsible for, the self: "Is the self primarily a product of the process of symbolization? Is it the fact that experiences may not be directly experienced, but symbolized and manipulated in thought, that makes the self possible? Is the self simply the symbolized portion of the experience?"[1]

Humanistic psychologists suggest that symbols originate not in the intellect but in the irrational depths of the psyche.[2] "Symbols cannot be produced intentionally," says Paul Tillich. "They grow out of the individual or collective unconscious and cannot function without being accepted by the unconscious dimension of our being."[3] Tillich believes that the symbol is the only vehicle appropriate for conveying our ultimate concerns about being and reality.

Symbols are spontaneous products of the archetypal psyche that cannot be discovered or manufactured. They are often seen as carriers of psychic energy. Without symbolic life, the ego is alienated from its suprapersonal source and falls victim to a kind of cosmic anxiety. The ultimate goal of Jungian psychotherapy is to make the symbolic process conscious.

June Singer cites the power of the symbol to attract and lead the individual on the way to becoming what he or she is capable of becoming.[4] "That goal is wholeness, which is integration of the parts of his personality into a functioning totality. Here conscious and unconscious are united around the symbols of the self."[5] Rollo May regarded the original meaning of symbol as "drawing together," echoing Singer's vision of integration and wholeness.[6] Joseph Campbell believed that a living mythological symbol releases and directs energy to awaken and guide humanity.[7]

Carl Jung was also convinced that the unconscious forms symbols by way of revelation, intuition, and dreams.[8] He thought that slowly evolving symbol formations are responsible for the development of cultural ideas and behavior. Symbols act as the formative agents of communities: they supply the psychological and the organizational foundations of social life.[9]

The "affect image" is a term applied by John W. Perry to a living mythological symbol:

> It is an image that hits one where it counts. It is not addressed first to the brain, to be there interpreted and appreciated. On the contrary, if that is where it has to be read, the symbol is already dead. An "affect image" talks directly to the feeling system and immediately elicits a response. . . . When the vital symbols of any given social group evoke in all of its members responses of this kind, a sort of magical accord unites them as one spiritual organism.[10]

To sum up, symbols play a central role in the integration of the personality. They direct us to the center of our being. They are objects pointing to subjects. Symbols lead us to the missing part of the whole and relate us to our original totality, healing and mending our alienation from life. The lack of affect images and the presence of disembodied images create an existential vacuum. The absence of a symbol system leaves communities without formative agents, without basic foundations, thereby increasing instability and anxiety.

We shall consider a symbolic rendering of the transformative powers of the reverse of the Great Seal as an archetype, talisman, mandala, and myth, but first we must examine the individual symbols that make up the reverse of the Great Seal itself: the single eye, the triangle, the radiant eye in the triangle, and the unfinished pyramid.

The Single Eye

Barton and Thomson in 1782 interpreted the eye in the triangle as "the many signal interpositions of Providence in favor of the American cause" and described the single eye as the "all Seeing Eye of the Deity." The single eye had already been used on the forty-dollar bill in 1778 and served as a well-established artistic convention for an "omniscient Ubiquitous Deity" in the medallic art of the Renaissance. Du Simitière, who suggested using the symbol on the Great Seal, collected art books and was familiar with the artistic and ornamental devices used in Renaissance art.[11]

The single eye, alone or in a triangle, was used extensively by Freemasons and other secret societies, which is one reason why a die for it was not cut in 1884. ("It can hardly . . . look otherwise than as a dull emblem of a Masonic fraternity.")

After Du Simitière first proposed the eye in the triangle for the Great Seal in 1776, it later reappeared in Barton's designs in 1782, and then Charles Thomson gave it final approval. Thomson was a biblical scholar and as such may have been aware of several biblical references to the single eye. For example, Matthew 6:22 states, "If therefore, thine eyes be single thy whole body shall be full of light." An almost identical phrase can be found in Luke 11:34.

Du Simitière, Barton, and Thomson all may have been aware of the single-eye motif in Egyptian symbolism. The seal of 1782 depicted the right eye, but after Benson Lossing submitted his designs in *Harper's New Monthly Magazine* in 1856, the left eye began to be used (see figures 5.1, 3.11 on page 95, and 3.12 on page 96). It is unknown whether the switch was intentional.

To the ancient Egyptians, the right eye symbolized the sun, and the left eye, the moon. The sun was the creative aspect of the Deity, and the eye in the triangle symbolized divine providence to them. There was widespread interest in Egypt and things Egyptian in eighteenth-century America, and this information would have been available to both Hopkinson and Barton. It is therefore possible that Barton's use of the right eye may have intentionally symbolized the sun.

The single eye also has been identified with the third or spiritual eye, and therefore with clairvoyance. The esoteric tradition relates the single eye to the inner light, intuitive power, illumination, and the philosophers' stone.[12] Jung compares the eye to the mandala, the structure of which symbolizes the center of order in the unconscious. Thus, the eye can also represent God.

(a) (b)

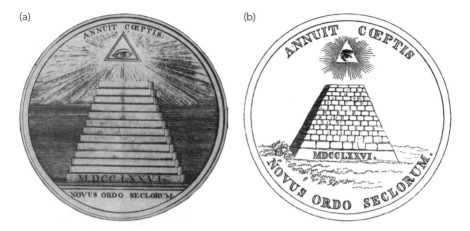

Figure 5.1. (a) The Trenchard Realization of the Reverse. James Trenchard was a Philadelphia engraver who produced full-page engravings of both the obverse and reverse of the Great Seal at an early date. These were printed in *Columbia Magazine*, Philadelphia, in September and October of 1786, just four years after the Great Seal had been accepted by Congress; they were most likely based on Barton's design and prepared with his help. (b) The Lossing Realization of the Reverse. Benson Lossing was an artist and historian who rendered this drawing for an article in *Harper's New Monthly Magazine*, July 13, 1856. Note the switch from the right eye to the left. (Illustration from Patterson and Dougall, *The Eagle and the Shield*.)

The Triangle

The single eye is contained in a triangle. Buckminster Fuller held that the triangle—along with its three-dimensional counterpart, the tetrahedron— is the strongest building structure in the universe, which accounts for the strength in his dome structures.[13]

Many religions possess trinities or triads: for example, Christianity's Father, Son, and Holy Spirit; Judaic Kabbalism's Kether, Chokmah, and Binah; ancient Egypt's Osiris, Isis, and Horus; and Hinduism's Brahma, Vishnu, and Shiva.

There may be a deep-seated tendency to organize temporal or developmental events into threefold patterns. To Freud, psychological development was seen in three states—oral, anal, and genital—while Edward Edinger perceived the development of consciousness as ego, self, and ego-self axis. Alfred North Whitehead distinguished three stages in the natural learning process: romance, precision, and generalization. Hegel under-stood the historical process from the threefold cyclic pattern of thesis, antithesis, and synthesis. This is identical to what Rosicrucians refer to as the "law of the triangle," which states that an action generates a reaction, both on the physical and spiritual planes, resulting in a manifestation (the third point of the triangle).[14]

Other common triune expressions include solids, liquids, and gases; spirit, life, and matter; stability, mobility, and rhythm; mineral, vegeta-ble, and animal; time, space, and measure; past, present, and future.

Jung's individuation process is a unification of consciousness and unconsciousness, creating a third state that broadens the field of con-sciousness and promotes maturation of the personality. Jung linked indi-viduation to self-realization and believed it entailed a lifelong process of growth and healing. Joseph Campbell's monomythic process, discussed in chapter 6, bears many similarities to the individuation process and has its own threefold structure: separation, initiation, and return. Edinger conjectures that the trinity archetype symbolizes the individuation pro-cess, whereas the quaternity stands for its completed state. "Three is the number for ego-hood; four is the number for wholeness, the Self. But since individuation is never truly complete, each temporary state of completion or wholeness must be submitted once again to the dialectic of the trinity in order for life to go on."[15]

Officially, the eye in the triangle symbolized "the many signal inter-positions of Providence in favor of the American cause," as Barton and Thomson noted in 1782. All the aforementioned interpretations are in harmony with this reading. Spiritual vision, illumination, intuitive power, and the philosophers' stone all refer to and describe Providence—or, as the Freemasons would say, "the All-Seeing Eye of God" the "Supreme Great Architect of the Universe."[16]

The Pyramid

According to Barton and Thomson, the pyramid signifies "Strength and Duration." William Barton first suggested a pyramid for the seal's reverse, though, as noted earlier, his interest in paper credit probably made him aware of the Hopkinson design for the fifty-dollar bill of 1778, which also incorporated a pyramid.

Patterson and Dougall reveal why Hopkinson's pyramid resembled the Great Pyramid at Giza:

> . . . In the Library Company of Philadelphia there was a detailed work entitled "Pyramidagraphia" [by John Greaves, published in 1646] which would have been available to both Hopkinson and Barton. This work included a drawing of the "first pyramid" which was stepped, did not come to a complete point, and had an entrance in the center . . . a detail found also in Hopkinson's design.[17]

The designs of Greaves and Hopkinson show obvious similarities (see figure 5.2 and also figure 3.7 on page 89).

John Greaves was an Oxford mathematician and astronomer. In 1638 he tried to establish the dimensions of the planet from measurements of the Great Pyramid. He believed that the Great Pyramid was built to record the dimensions of the earth and to furnish imperishable standard linear measure. Sir Isaac Newton used Greaves's measurements of the Great Pyramid in a rare paper, "A Dissertation upon the Sacred Cubit."

John Greaves's research also gave the mathematical calculations that pyramidologists have used in their systems of interpretation. His work is the basis for kabbalistic interpretations of the pyramid's measurements. A pyramid on the seal's reverse could carry kabbalistic interpretations, for Greaves thought that the Great Pyramid itself contained such meanings.

If Greaves was indeed Hopkinson's source, then the pyramid on the seal's reverse ultimately represents the Great Pyramid of Giza. It is thought to be the oldest and largest in the world, an apt model for the "Strength and Duration" alluded to by Barton and Thomson.

When the Tiffany Company cut a new die for the seal, Theodore F. Dwight, chief of the Bureau of Rolls and Library, inquired of the company: "Is the pyramid drawn to the scale of the Great Pyramid? . . . If I am correctly informed the veritable pyramids of Egypt were finished with smooth lines, and that the steps, or indentations now appear, because the surface stones have been removed, if such is the case your representation need no correction in that respect."

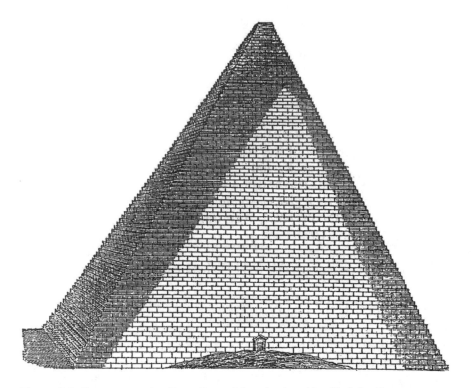

Figure 5.2. Entrance to the Great Pyramid as depicted by Sir John Greaves, the likely inspiration for the use of the unfinished pyramid on colonial currency (1778) and the Great Seal (1782). (Illustration from J. Greaves, *Pyramidographia*.)

Tiffany answered Dwight as follows: "The reverse of the Pyramid is drawn to the scale of the Great Pyramid: the side seen in perspective to the right means the East, this view being desired."[18] Remember that the Seal's designers numerologically or patriotically wanted thirteen rows of bricks in their unfinished pyramid symbol, and thus depicted a rendering of only the truncated top section of the Great Pyramid, which is obviously much taller and wider at the base when viewed in its entirety.[19]

Another similarity between the Great Pyramid and the seal's pyramid is their incompleteness, for neither has a capstone set in place. The seal's capstone is suspended above the pyramid; we do not know whether the Great Pyramid of Giza ever had a capstone. Sometimes the ancients did not complete their temples or monuments to symbolize the imperfection of the mundane world. Another possibility is that a capstone once existed but was stolen or removed, and many theories exist as to what it was used for. The capstone of the Great Pyramid was missing centuries before Greaves, however, so the fact that the pyramid in the Great Seal design of Hopkinson and Barton also has a truncated top further identifies it as the Great Pyramid of Giza.

Ironically, under pressure of public controversy, the Egyptian government canceled its millennial celebration plans to lower a temporary golden capstone by helicopter onto the Great Pyramid at the stroke of midnight ushering in the year 2000. Muslim and Christian fundamentalists feared both the symbol and the secret societies linked to it. Muslims were upset about a rumor that the capping ceremony was part of a black magic spell. Fundamentalist Christian leaders in the United States, notably Texe Marrs of Living Truth Ministries in Austin, Texas, alleged that the Illuminati were planning to hold a black mass in the King's Chamber at midnight, which would "culminate in a visit by their glowing Masonic god of light and magic, Lucifer himself, at exactly the stroke of midnight, December 31, 1999."[20]

Tradition holds that the Great Pyramid was a tomb for the pharaoh Khufu. Although it may have been used as a burial monument, other purposes have also been ascribed to it. For centuries, the treasures it reportedly contained have been of an informational nature only. Contemporary pyramidologists, such as Coville and Nelson, Tompkins, and Valentine, have proposed that the Great Pyramid was a theodolite for surveyors, an almanac of the ages, an astronomical and astrological observatory, and a geodetic and geographic landmark.* There are also many—including Coville and Nelson, Flanagan, Toth and Nielsen, Russell, and Valentine—who believe that the pyramid's shape creates an "energy" generator. They theorize that the pyramid may act as a huge resonating cavity that is capable of focusing the rays of the cosmos like a giant lens, affecting the molecules or crystals of any object in the path of the beam of focused energy.

A significant number of esoteric writers—including Paul Brunton, Manly P. Hall, H. Spencer Lewis, and Peter Tompkins—identify the Great Pyramid as a temple of initiation. In this temple, neophytes

---

*For more information see West, *Traveler's Key to Ancient Egypt* and Schoch and McNally, *Pyramid Quest.*

became aware of the heavenly worlds by undergoing a series of initiations that made them realize their personal and collective unconscious processes.

Research at the Giza plateau in the last two decades employing ground-penetrating radar, sonic-resonance equipment, and robotics has revealed astonishing new discoveries, including passageways or cavities under the Sphinx, doors blocking ventilation shafts, and an entirely new dating system based on geological weather patterns. Several engineers have concluded that the pyramid was originally constructed as a pump for either water or sonic vibrations for healing or energy purposes. The most important work on this subject is *Pyramid Quest* by Dr. Robert Schoch and Robert Aquinas McNally (2005), a veritable encyclopedia of mysteries and research into the Great Pyramid's age and how it was built. Like Schwaller de Lubicz and John Anthony West, Dr. Schoch concludes that there was a more ancient culture (Nabta Playa, ca. 9000 B.C.E.) that developed the Giza plateau's Sphinx and pyramids, incorporating pi, the golden ratio (phi), and the center of the galaxy in its configuration.[21] "Giza isn't the birth of something new. . . . It is the full flower of something old," they conclude. (See appendix 1 for an overview of the new discoveries at the Great Pyramid and how they magnify the relevance of its use in the Great Seal.)

The two central symbols on the seal's reverse, the eye in the triangle and the pyramid, are interpreted differently in historical and esoteric traditions. The historical tradition regards only the views of William Barton and Charles Thomson as having authority, whereas the esoteric tradition accepts a broader range of interpretations. To understand the power of symbols we shall examine archetypes, talismans, mandalas, and myths and consider each of them in light of the reverse of the Great Seal.

The Function of Archetypes

Jung notes that the term *archetype* is not a modern expression. It was in use before the time of Saint Augustine and is reminiscent of Plato's "Idea" which was a primordial image reposited (in a supracelestial place) as an eternal, transcendent form.[22]

Approaching the word *archetype* etymologically, Jolande Jacobi explains that *arch* signifies beginning, origin, cause, primal source, principle, leader, supreme ruler, or a "dominant."[23] *Type* means a blow, as in the striking or the imprinting on a coin. It also means form, image, copy, prototype, model, order, "pattern underlying," or primordial form. *Archetype* would mean, therefore, a primal dominant order or prototype. The form of the archetype has been compared to the axial system of a crystal that preforms the crystalline structure in the mother liquid although it has no material existence of its own.[24]

The seal's reverse is an emblem composed of symbols derived from archetypes. Symbols, born within humanity's personal or collective unconscious, are infinitely variable expressions of the underlying static archetypes.[25] Archetypes are potentialities, while symbols are actualizations conditioned by individual and social situations.[26]

Archetypes mediate the primal chaos in the first stratum of the psyche, in which the psyche and the natural world are fused together in an undifferentiated mass. The archetypes are vehicles through which order is transmitted from the collective unconscious into the personal unconscious. Experiences reappear again and again around the constellating hub or ordering principle of the archetype.

Providing us a means to perceive and experience correlations between larger patterns of the universe and the destiny of the individual, archetypes tend to manifest through the "synchronistic" process.[27]

Jung lists the principal archetypes affecting human thought and behavior as the self, the persona (the role-playing personality), the shadow (the unconscious), the anima (feminine characteristics), the animus (masculine characteristics), the wise old man (spirit who provides guidance in a meaningful direction), the earth mother (who brings forth all life from herself), and the child (the young undeveloped aspect of the personality). The self is the central archetype, the archetype of wholeness. Or, as Ira Progoff regards it, the self is the archetype of archetypes.

The Pyramid and the Archetypal Mountain

In nature, the corresponding symbol for the pyramid is the mountain, and thus the pyramid symbol on the seal's reverse may be derived from the mountain archetype. Frankfort and Frankfort explain the relationship between the mountain and the pyramid: "In Egypt the Creator was said to have emerged from the waters of chaos and to have made a mound of dry land upon which he could stand. This primeval hill, from which creation took its beginning, was traditionally located in the sun temple at Heliopolis, the sun god being in Egypt most commonly viewed as the Creator. . . . Hence the royal tomb was given the shape of a pyramid which is [the] Heliopolitan stylization of the primeval hill."[28]

Mircea Eliade locates the sacred mountain (where heaven and hell meet) at the center of the world and lists some cultural expressions of this cosmology. "According to Indian beliefs, Mount Meru rises at the center of the world, and above it shines the polestar. The Ural-Altaic peoples also know a central mountain Sumeru, to whose summit the polestar is fixed. Iranian beliefs hold that the sacred mountain Haraberezaiti (Elburz) is situated at the center of the earth and is linked with heaven. The Buddhist population of Laos, North of Siam, know of Mount Zinnalo, at the center of the world."[29] In another work, Eliade compares the ziggurat to the cosmic mountain. We can liken the polestar over the mountain to the eye in the triangle over the pyramid. The motif of the eye or sun rising over the mountain can be found worldwide, from ancient Egypt (figure 5.3) to Babylon (figure 5.4) to South America (see figure 5.5). This potent symbol or combination of symbols lends itself to many possible interpretations, including the union of opposites from which a third, or synthesis, is formed.

Erich Neumann's *The Great Mother* provides historical, cultural, and psychological interpretations of the mountain and its meaning to the psyche, relating mountain symbolism to mother symbolism.[30] The central symbol of the feminine is the vessel, which fulfills the function of containing, protecting, and nourishing.

The center of the vessel, or the belly, is linked to the mountain symbol. Below the belly is the womb, which is attached to the cave. The mountain serves to protect the cave, which is connected to a series of related archetypes, one of which is the coffin. The transformation process within the feminine scheme begins in the lowest level—the darkness, night, underworld, the unconscious. It proceeds to the belly, heart/breast, and mouth areas.

The elements of mountain, cave, and coffin symbolism can be traced in the design of the Great Pyramid. We can identify the Great Pyramid

Figure 5.3. The ancient Egyptian eye as Ra (sun) rising above the eastern mountain. The Twenty-first Dynasty interpretation of the seal's reverse. (Illustration from Grimal, *Larousse World Mythology.*)

Figure 5.4. The Babylonian sun above a mountain, another expression of the archetype found on the seal's reverse. (Louvre Museum, Paris.)

with the mountain, the cave with the King's Chamber, and the coffer with the coffin.

Some Rosicrucian and Freemasonic groups assert that the Great Pyramid was used to conduct rites of initiation. The Master Mason's 3rd degree ritual parallels the initiation process the temple neophyte underwent in the Great Pyramid before he became a master of the spiritual plane. The candidate purportedly was placed in the coffer in the King's Chamber for three days, whence he left his physical body to visit the spiritual world, where will and character were tested. If the candidate succeeded, he gained a view of the microcosm and insight into personal destiny. Returning from the spiritual realms, the candidate was reborn into the physical world and set about realizing his potential by rendering service. According to Freemasonry, the highest privilege of the human being is work in the service of the Divine Architect.[31]

Jung connects the mountain symbolism to "the goal of the pilgrimage and ascent, hence it often has the psychological meaning of the self."[32] Ascending the mountain is analogous to the process of knowing oneself—which is becoming conscious of the unconscious, or of uniting opposites.

In the alchemical process it is from the union of opposites that the philosophers' stone emerges. This stone is triune in substance and in part regenerative. The shapes, forms, and symbols used to depict the alchemical process repeat the themes of the mountain, the cave, the coffin, and rebirth. The process of rebirth and transformation is depicted repeatedly and universally by the same symbols, which are thus archetypal in nature.

The Eye and the Archetypal Sun

In many cultures the single eye is linked to the symbol for the sun. Du Simitière, Barton, and Thomson were familiar with Egyptian symbolism through the work of Sir John Greaves, but many archaic societies and ancient civilizations also identified the solar orb as a deity. The solar orb is the archetype from which the eye in the triangle is derived.

The sun and pyramid symbols are closely interrelated in Egyptian mythology. The sun (the father, Osiris) performs the act of creation on the primeval hill (the mother, Isis) in the pyramid (the temple). The eye/pyramid or sun/mountain relationship is a father/mother, husband/wife, brother/sister—that is male/female relationship—from which a son is born. Horus, the result of the act of union, is the self, who avenges his father's death by overcoming his brother, Seth, who is darkness, unconsciousness, and death. Osiris is reborn in Horus. This same sun/mountain archetypal process is repeated in the symbolism of other ancient mythologies around the world.

The early-seventeenth-century prints shown in figures 5.6 and 5.7 are contemporaneous with the sudden appearance of Rosicrucianism in Europe and the publication of *The Chymical Wedding of Christian Rosenkreutz* (1616). Both contain the motif of the sun over the mountain and thus show the importance of these symbols in the esoteric traditions, as well as their archetypal "staying power." Figure 5.6 further illustrates the union of opposites—heaven and earth, male and female—and the alchemical dictum of "As above, so below" found

Figure 5.5. From Quenca, Ecuador, a heavy golden plate with the sun above a thirteen-stepped pyramid with puzzling Proto–North Semitic linear writing at the bottom. A forerunner of the seal's reverse. (Photo by Richard Wingate.)

in the Emerald Tablet attributed to Hermes Trismegistus. The mountain in figure 5.7 is more directly related to alchemy and initiation, portrayed with the four elements, the seven alchemical processes listed on the steps, an alchemist's chamber and athanor, or furnace, the blindfolded aspirant who can't see the hare (symbol of the first matter), the adept who knows to follow the hare "inside," and the planetary metals arrayed on the sides of the mountain with Mercury on its summit.

The Seal's Reverse as an Archetype

Millennia later a new nation, the United States of America, chooses for half of its national emblem symbols that also depict the individuation process. The use of archetypal images, whether intentional or not, expresses humanity's need to identify with the archetypal process of regeneration, rebirth, self-realization, and synthesis. The seal's reverse is a contemporary expression of an ancient archetypal process that

Figure 5.6. "As above, so below," or the unity of microcosm and macrocosm from *Opus Medico-Chymicum, Basilica Chymica*, Frankfort, 1618, by physician Johann Daniel Mylius. This illustration is a reflection of the sun-over-mountain archetypal process. (Illustration from Allen, *A Christian Rosenkreutz Anthology.*)

Figure 5.7. Also reflecting the sun-over-mountain archetypal process, "The Holy Mountain of Initiation," published in *Cabala, Spiegel der Kunst und Natur* by physician Steffan Michelspacher at Augsburg, appeared the same year (1616) as *The Chymical Wedding.* (Illustration from Allen, *A Christian Rosenkreutz Anthology.*)

resolves human fragmentation. Literally depicted in the transformation of Osiris, the need to become whole was just as great to archaic society as it is to contemporary humanity. Wholeness occurs through the union of opposites—basically a creative process—and symbols facilitate this union.

In desperate need of uniting their countrymen and of overcoming the fragmented state of the American colonies, the Founding Fathers ended up agreeing upon a symbol that expressed both their predicament and its resolution.

The Unknown Man as the Magician Archetype

An example of the archetype in the creation story of the Great Seal can be found in the tales of the unknown man or stranger who mysteriously appeared just long enough to pass along the fully formed design. There are several uncorroborated accounts of this story (see chapter 3, pages 97–98), and, although they cannot be factually substantiated, an archetypal examination allows us to explore them in a useful manner. Functioning as an archetype, the unknown man or stranger could be a centering device, restoring meaning and purpose to life, a role formerly filled by ancient myths.[33] The persistence of this unsubstantiated tale also reveals a need in some Americans to find a more unusual or occult origin for the seal's design.

Within the version of the story as told in chapter 3, these notable elements are included: it is set in a dark night in a garden; a black-cloaked stranger appears who is fully aware of the committee's work inside to devise an American seal; he hands Jefferson the completed design as we know it; he vanishes forever, preventing us from ever knowing who really created the Great Seal of the United States.[34]

I would identify the stranger or unknown man as an expression of the magician or wise old man archetype. According to Jung, the magician archetype does not express human or personal qualities, but instead possesses unknown or inhuman characteristics.[35] Jung also warns of the subtle psychic dangers such masculine collective figures can create by inflating the conscious mind. The stranger in this account wore a black cloak "that practically covered him, face and all"—making him, in effect, an invisible source, possessing unknown or inhuman characteristics. He both enters and exits mysteriously without offering to identify himself or discussing where he obtained the seal's design, actions that typify the magician archetype.

Archetypes give birth to symbols and mythological motifs, and with this account Virginia Brasington has inadvertently related a myth or created a mythology.[36] Whether intentionally or unintentionally created, these myths inevitably find a receptive audience in a society that lacks meaningful mythology; despite their irrational nature, their meaning and centering capacities continue to be sought after.

Jefferson's stranger in the garden is not the only one of his kind. Unknown professors, visitors, and speakers are said to have influenced the designs of the American flag, the signing of the Declaration of Independence, and other key elements of our founding.[37] Theodore Heline wrote of an "influential person" known as "the Professor" who was apparently known to both Franklin and Washington and "who submitted to the Cambridge Committee a design for a flag with the notion that if it were accepted, little or no alteration would be necessary when the colonies would secure their independence." Another mysterious man reportedly rallied the Continental Convention at a low point of indecision by closing his "appeal for decisive action with the ringing words: 'God has given America to be free.'"[38] In chapter 2 (pages 48–52) we discussed Washington's experiences with mysterious visitors who granted him visions of our country's future. Yet another story relates a vision experienced by the Civil War general McClellan, in which General Washington appears to him in a dream, warning him of military betrayal and a future World War.[39] All of these visitors can be considered expressions of the magician archetype.

Talismanic Symbols as Transformers

The common definition of a talisman is a "stone, ring, or other object, engraved with figures or characters under certain superstitious observances of the heavens, which is supposed to possess occult powers, and is worn as an amulet or charm."[40] But there is far more to talismanic art and science than the carving of occult symbols and characters on an object under auspicious planetary conjunctions. Random objects are not used for their construction. Material considered "sympathetic" to the desired end or goal that corresponds to a planet improve their effectiveness, and the intention and concentration of the workman is key throughout the propitious time period of its construction.[41]

Ceremonial magic serves as a bridge between the world of symbol and the world of matter. It is in ritual that symbols and talismans may function as transformers of energy. First, the magus attempts to embody the symbol in the world and so lift the objective realm into a symbolic level, spiritualizing the will. Second, he or she strives to call forth or revivify the symbolic images so that energy associated with them will reappear. Ritual can produce the numinosity associated with a symbol and release the desired energy with that symbol's constellation in the psyche of the participant. The psychic field of vision is narrowed through ritual, concentrating the conscious and unconscious forces on the desired ends. The canalization of psychic energy produces the magical numinosity without the appearance of the symbol and, later, the act of willing can replace the ritual. (See appendix 2 for more on the nature of talismans.)

The Seal's Reverse as a Talisman

The elements in the seal's reverse resemble some ancient talismans that employ eyes, triangles with centers, and triangles containing series of letters that resemble the blocks in the pyramid (see figures 5.8, 5.9, 5.10, and 5.11). Although there is no evidence that America's Great Seal was created as a talisman, it is possible that some of the designers had some knowledge about the function of talismans. A lack of talismanic intent in the seal's conception and design, however, would affect its efficiency, as conscious will is needed to create a fully operational talisman.

The underlying image depicted in the seal's reverse is that of two elements in separation. The triangle bearing the eye (center) is one whole, single unit hanging above the pyramid, which is incomplete. The eye in the triangle (capstone) completes the unfinished pyramid, which is composed of many stones. The substance of both elements is different: the capstone is made of light and the pyramid of dense matter.

The two symbols are opposites. The pyramid is larger (macrocosm) but unfinished; it is made up of many smaller units. The eye in the

Figure 5.8. The Abracadabra Invocation of the Holy Name of Jehovah reflects the completed pyramid on the seal's reverse. (Illustration from Pavitt and Pavitt, *The Book of Talismans, Amulets, and Zodiacal Gems.*)

Figure 5.9. Shemhamphorus talisman used to discover buried treasure. Reflects the eye in the triangle on the seal's reverse. (Illustration from Lehner, *Symbols, Signs, and Signets.*)

Figure 5.10. The Sixth Pentacle of the Sun in the Key of Solomon reflects the eye in the triangle on the seal's reverse. This pentacle was meant to serve for the operation of invisibility. The verse is from Psalms 69:23 and 135:16. "Let their eyes be darkened that they see not; and make their loins continually to shake. They have eyes and see not."[42] (Illustration from De Laurence, *The Greater Key of Solomon.*)

Figure 5.11. The Udjat, the right eye of Ra, also identified with Maat, the personification of physical and moral Law. (Illustration from Petrie, *Amulets*.)

triangle (microcosm) completes the pyramid, making it whole. In itself, the eye in the triangle is a miniature three-dimensional pyramid, consisting of one unit (which is centered).

These two opposites are coming together. Diversity (two) is being formed into a unity (both = one). If the seal's reverse had been consciously created as a talisman, its intent would have been the unification of diverse aspects into a whole, or the cooperation between the self and society in furthering the evolutionary development of the human species. This would have mirrored the intention of the Founding Fathers to unite the many colonies into one nation.

The many/one theme reflects the society/individual relationship and the unconscious/conscious aspects of the psyche in the individuation process. The seal's reverse as a talisman would delineate individual and collective wholeness, its basic message being the ultimate unity of all living things and, in particular, humanity. The motto E Pluribus Unum (from the many to the one) found on the seal's obverse is an expression of the ultimate unity in diversity. To esotericists, the many/one concept was an assertion of the New Order of the Ages (Novus Ordo Seclorum) that God favored (Annuit Coeptis).

The seal's reverse could function as a talisman. Its psychic factor (the "message" in the seal's symbols) is parallel to its physical factor (the government). For some students of the American seal, the reverse cultivates and integrates their values and actions. It provides them with a symbol system that helps to resolve their disequilibrium and alienation from national attitudes with which they can no longer identify.

The Mandala: The Mother of All Symbols

The mandala has been described as the mother of symbols and the matrix of symbolic systems.[43] Jung used the mandala to represent the self.[44]

To Jung, the self is the most important and the most central of archetypes, representing wholeness, and is symbolized by the circle and cross, or mandala.[45] The chief quality of the self is the experience of synthesis or the realization of individuality and universality.[46] According to Singer the self is the center of the totality of the psyche.[47] According to May it is the sum total of the individual's capacities.[48] Because the variously named growth experiences are all aspects of a single process, the mandala can be used to describe them all.

Mandala is a Sanskrit word meaning "circle." It denotes circular images that are not only drawn but also painted, modeled, or danced. José Argüelles and Miriam Argüelles suggest that the mandala's basic properties are center, symmetry, and cardinal points.[49]

Found in ancient and contemporary cultures, mandalas are universal. From the sand paintings of the Navajo creation myth to the Tibetan wheel of life, all are methods for entering the world of the gods.[50] The rituals of making or using the mandalas enable their creators to orient themselves to eternal truths.

Everything is related to the mandala's center, which acts as a reference point from which to establish relationships and center the individual. The mandala constitutes an attempt to create order out of chaos. If the individuation process is the goal of psychic development, as Jung believed, and the mandala represents the self, then the mandala could function as the preeminent symbol of our time.

The Great Seal as a Mandala

Many national seals are circular, or mandala-like, perhaps in part because the establishment of a central point to which everything is related creates order, gives definition, and eliminates confusion. In a similar way, governments are constructed by establishing order and by acknowledging or determining the head of state.

There are obvious differences between the two sides of the Great Seal that are made all the more apparent when each is examined as a mandala. According to Jung there were nine formal elements of mandala symbolism.[51] The obverse fills seven of them, while the reverse, only four. See figure 5.12 for a comparison of the seal's obverse and reverse to Jung's nine formal elements of the mandala.

The obverse of the seal contains the basic properties of a center: symmetry and the cardinal (or chief) points are readily established. The center falls in the throat area of the eagle. The seal's obverse reads as a well-defined mandala ordered around a central point, which could have had some bearing on its immediate acceptance and use as the national seal. Early America may have attuned itself to the seal's obverse because it fulfilled a profound need for balance and structure, thus establishing a center that early Americans found meaningful.

The seal's reverse, on the other hand, does not contain as many of the fundamental mandalic elements. It is symmetrical, and the cardinal points of north and south can be established, but east and west are less clear. With some difficulty, the center of the seal's reverse can be imagined near the center of the pyramid.

The seal's obverse could be described as having "embodied" symbols or an affect image. The symbols are grounded in daily existence; they express meanings that give individual satisfaction and reflect the goals of our society. The eagle, shield, arrows, and olive branch speak directly to the feeling system and elicit an immediate response.

The reverse's elements are much less rooted in the American cultural experience, whether colonial or contemporary. The mystery and vagueness of these "disembodied" symbols conceal their meaning. The seal's reverse was simply not comprehensible to the America of the revolutionary period. Its gradual expansion into America's consciousness may indicate that our society is becoming more aligned with the values and goals expressed in the seal, or that the seal's symbols now communicate more directly to our emotions and focalize an element of the American public consciousness. In respect to the mandala's self-healing and centering capacities, the seal's reverse may be initiating a higher

Jung's Elements of Mandala Symbolism	The Obverse of the Great Seal as a Mandala	The Reverse of the Great Seal as a Mandala
1. Circular, spherical, or egg-shaped formation.	1. Circular.	1. Circular.
2. The circle is elaborated into a flower (rose, lotus) or a wheel.	2. Arranged like a wheel.	2. Not patterned after flower or wheel.
3. A center expressed by a sun, star, or cross, usually with four, eight, or twelve rays.	3. Center is the eagle's throat, and the wings, talons, head, tail, and banner can be likened to rays.	3. Center is vague and does not contain a sun, star, or cross.
4. The circles, spheres, and cruciform figures are often represented in rotation (swastika).	4. Elements suggest motion.	4. No evidence of rotation.
5. The circle is represented by a snake coiled about a center, either ring-shaped (uroboros) or spiral (orphic egg).	5. Coiling or spiral-like effect not pronounced but can be visualized.	5. No spiral or coiling shape about the center.
6. Squaring of the circle, taking the form of a circle in a square or vice versa.	6. Squaring of the circle found in the patterning of the eagle's wings and talons.	6. Does not square the circle, but the Great Pyramid does (see pp. 143–45).
7. Castle, city, and courtyard (temenos) motifs, quadratic or circular.	7. No castle, city, or courtyard motifs depicted.	7. Pyramid can be likened to a castle.
8. Eye (pupil and iris).	8. Eagle has an eye.	8. Contains the single eye.
9. Besides the tetradic figures (and multiples of four), there are also triadic and pentadic ones, although these are much rarer.	9. Contains triadic and pentadic figures. The interlaced triangles above the eagle's head double as the top of a triangle with the arrows and olive branch serving as the base. The five-pointed star (pentadic) formation in the crest above the eagle's head is also the top of a pentagram with the eagles wings, olive branch, and arrows serving as the four remaining points.	9. Pyramid has triadic shape.

Figure 5.12. A comparison of Jung's nine formal elements of the mandala with the Great Seal of the United States.

level of integration in the American consciousness, which, according to Jung, fulfills the function of the mandala.

The union of opposites is an important mandalic element. Jung's writings on mandala symbolism include a sketch that contains elements of the sun and a hill or mountain (figure 5.13), which Jung referred to as depicting the individuation process. The similarities to the elements in the seal's reverse are striking and support the contention that the seal's reverse can be seen as a mandala depicting the individuation process. The sun surrounded by a rainbow has the same meaning and basic structure as the eye radiating from the triangle. The mountain represents a natural

Figure 5.13. Sketch by one of Jung's patients depicting the individuation process. The elements bear a striking similarity to those found on the seal's reverse. (Illustration © the Estate of C. G. Jung.)

pyramid formation, and it is located directly below the sun, just as the pyramid appears below the eye in the triangle.

The elements in the seal's reverse exhibit both masculine (eye in the triangle as an active force linked to the sun) and feminine (pyramid as holding, protecting, and nurturing the spirit) values. The New Order of the Ages is a union of masculine and feminine virtues; it is androgynous. In its broadest sense, *androgyny* can be defined as the one that contains two: namely, the male (*andro-*) and the female (*-gyne*). Androgyny may be the oldest archetypal concept of which we have any experience; humans have an innate sense of a primordial cosmic unity existing in oneness before any separation occurred. True change begins primarily within the psychic structure of the individual when the positive/negative or male/female combination separates into two individualities. The seal's reverse represents the archetypal androgyny and, as such, can be understood as a symbolic system, or archetype, delineating the philosophy of the transitional period or the New Age.

The Great Pyramid and Squaring the Circle

Knowing that the seal's designers intended their pyramid to depict the Great Pyramid at Giza may help resolve the difficulty of locating the center of the design of the reverse. Figure 5.14 shows the Great Pyramid's internal structure. About one-third of the way up from its base is the King's Chamber. Although the King's Chamber is not located in the actual center of the Great Pyramid, it is considered the central and most important chamber in the Great Pyramid, for it is the area in which the candidate was "raised" for initiation, during which he transmuted his lower physical nature and became self-realized or whole. Marilyn Ferguson refers to the King's Chamber in the Great Pyramid as the "transcendent center."[52] Also worth noting is the fact that the central vertical meridian going from the top of the Great Pyramid to the center of its base passes through the entrance to the King's Chamber. The pyramid in the seal's reverse is placed at an angle, meaning the site of the King's Chamber in the seal's reverse would be rotated slightly to the right to allow for the angular vantage.

Jung's sixth formal element of the mandala is the squaring of the circle, meaning mandalas very frequently "contain a quaternity or a

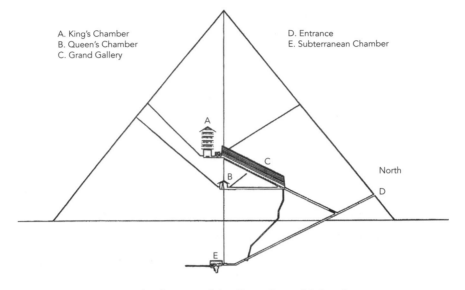

A. King's Chamber
B. Queen's Chamber
C. Grand Gallery

D. Entrance
E. Subterranean Chamber

Figure 5.14. An internal side-view of the Great Pyramid showing passageways and chambers. (Based on illustration from Hancock and Bauval, *Message of the Sphinx.*)

multiple of four, in the form of a cross, a star, a square. . . ." Squaring the circle is one of the most important archetypal motifs, and Jung said that it formed the basic patterns of dreams and fantasies. He called it the archetype of wholeness and said that the "quaternity of the One is the schema for all images of God."[53] June Singer believes that squaring the circle means "enclosing the mystery of nature."[54] In an indirect way, the mandalic squaring of the circle can be identified in the seal's reverse, because the seal's pyramid is identical to the Great Pyramid. Some theorists believe there is a strong connection between true pyramids and the squaring of the circle. Peter Tompkins, for example, argues that the "pyramid is so designed that for all practical purposes it accomplishes the squaring of the circle. The pyramid's base is a square whose perimeter is equal to the circumference of a circle whose radius is the Pyramid's height. Superimpose the square on the circle and you get not only an interesting but an extremely useful diagram consisting of the perimeter of the pyramid and the circumference of the circle it represents."[55] The geometry of the pyramid reveals a knowledge of both phi and pi. If the design of the Great Pyramid does contain the element of squaring

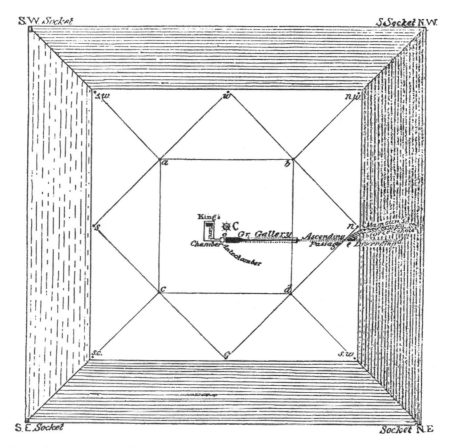

Figure 5.15. An internal top-view of the Great Pyramid showing location of the King's Chamber.

the circle, then its inclusion in the reverse of the Great Seal is one more argument for considering that side as a mandala.

The Impact of Mythology on Society

For the most part the contemporary world identifies myths with fairy tales and legends. The humanistic tradition of psychology sees myths as a significant force in the human psyche rather than as merely valuable from anthropological, intellectual, and sociological perspectives. Indeed, the events and timetables of a myth are often paradoxical and contradictory. The humanistic view of myths places the greatest emphasis not on their historic value, but on their description of humanity's psychological development.

Just as the symbol is a derivative of the archetype, mythological motifs are attributed to the archetypes of the collective unconscious.[56] As illustrated in great works by Joseph Campbell, Rollo May, Erich Neumann, June Singer, and many others, the development of science has paralleled the disintegration of our mythological systems, a shift that has contributed to the alienation and fragmentation experienced in this contemporary period.[57] Campbell notes:

> It may well be that the very high incidence of neuroticism among ourselves follows from the decline among us of such effective spiritual aid [as mythology]. We remain fixated to the unexorcised images of our infancy, and hence disinclined to the necessary passages of our adulthood. In the United States there is even a pathos of inverted emphasis: the goal is not to grow old, but to remain young; not to mature away from mother, but to cleave to her.[58]

Myths refer to humanity's inward spiritual state, according to Jolande Jacobi; or goals to be approached, and efforts to become what we potentially are, according to Erich Neumann.[59] To Jung, "Myth is the primordial language natural to these psychic processes, and no intellectual formulation comes anywhere near the richness, and expressiveness of their imagery. Such processes deal with the primordial images and these are best and most succinctly reproduced by figurative speech."[60] Myths are a product of the unconscious archetype and are therefore symbolic, requiring psychological interpretation.[61]

Joseph Campbell suggests that the following four functions are descriptive of a properly operating mythology. First is the "mystical function," which serves

> to waken and maintain in the individual a sense of awe and gratitude in relation to the mystery dimension of the universe . . . so that he recognizes that he participates in it. . . . The second function of a living mythology is to offer an image of the universe that will be in accord with the knowledge of the time, the sciences and the fields

of action of the folk to whom the mythology is addressed. . . . The third function . . . is to validate, support, and imprint the norms of a given, specific moral order, that, namely, of the society in which the individual is to live. And the fourth is to guide him, stage by stage, in health, strength, and harmony of spirit, through the whole foreseeable course of a useful life.[62]

The seal's reverse fulfills all four of Campbell's functions of a properly operating mythology. The seal's eye in the triangle and pyramid carry out the first mystical function to awaken and maintain awe and gratitude. Their historical and cultural meanings and functions brim with the mysterious. They clearly represent a metaphysical dimension and invite us to participate in it.

The seal's reverse fulfills the second function of mythology by providing an image of the universe that is in accord with contemporary scientific knowledge. The more we see of the diversity of the physical universe (the pyramid, matter, and its many-tiered structure) the more certain we are of an ultimate unifying plan or design at its foundation (eye in the triangle, spirit, unity).

The relationship between the eye in the triangle and the pyramid provides the fulfillment of the third function (to uphold our social norms) and the fourth (to offer guidance throughout life). The guide to health, strength, and harmony is embodied in the vision of setting the capstone on the pyramid, completing its structure, and making it whole.

Myths in Archaic and Modern Society

Archaic society regarded myths as patterns of actions (or rituals) performed by deities, heroes, and ancestors. By imitating the actions of these figures, people found their identity, and human behavior was therefore a ceaseless repetition of gestures initiated by others. The repetition of such gestures allowed the participant to enter the world of gods, heroes, and ancestors in which mundane time did not exist. Any act that was not an "imitation" was meaningless and considered unworthy.[63]

Birth, adolescence, marriage, and death were considered a series of initiations in which human beings experienced the essential oneness of the individual and the group. Individual meaning was found in the group, and the group's meaning was taken from the actions performed by the gods, as described in myths. This dependency on myth and derivative ritual processes was not only significant to the individual, it influenced the development of ancient cities, palaces, temples, and tombs by inspiring the devotion and urge to construct such homages.

Modern society has no exemplary models to follow, for contemporary people associate themselves with the present, material world and not the cosmos. We find the past unworthy of imitation and ritually meaningless. Gods, heroes, and ancestors offer little to identify with as technology has become the center of contemporary man's adulation. Stanley Krippner notes, "Western industrialized, technological societies are marked by a dearth of formal rituals and a tattered mythic legacy. As a result, combat veterans of unsuccessful and unpopular wars [like Vietnam] have had to search for sustaining myths and enact the ensuing rituals alone, without the community support that characterizes similar endeavors in native cultures."[64] With no patterns of behavior to imitate, humanity must turn inward to acquire meaning, destiny, and purpose. A living mythological symbol is needed to awaken and guide the energies of human life, and Krippner and David Feinstein note that "while no one can reliably predict what new myths will come to dominate in the coming decades, a remarkably diverse group of candidates from the 'New Fundamentalism' to the 'New Age' can be seen vying for the cultural spotlight."[65]

The Reverse of the Great Seal as the Solar Journey Myth

Although contemporary society has rejected the ancient myths that once gave archaic societies their relationship with the cosmos, the importance of myths has not been undermined. Instead, myths have been internalized and projected into the human psyche, which then projects them into the cultural environment.[66] As a symbol derived from an archetypal process, the seal's reverse depicts at least three different mythic systems: the solar journey, the binary interpretation, and Joseph Campbell's monomyth.

The sun's presence provided the light and warmth (consciousness) to overcome the chaos of the night (the unconscious). Its physical presence was a gauge by which a society controlled its destiny. The path of the sun through the heavenly worlds, marked by the solstices and equinoxes, completed a cycle that foretold the time of sowing and reaping, allowing humans to exist in the present and project themselves into the future, by understanding the cycles of the past.[67]

Humanity identified its individual growth and evolution (microcosm) with the sun's journey (macrocosm), allowing people to feel whole and united with the cosmos, permitting them to enter the world of "mythological time," and associating with the cycle of the gods, which gave their lives greater meaning and fulfillment.[68] Jacobi summarizes it this way: "The myth of the solar hero is the psyche's spontaneous 'translation' of the sun's course and reflects man's growing awareness of the psychic processes accompanying the physical process. . . . The archetype makes it possible to translate physical factors into psychic factors."[69]

The sun's procreative force is greatest at the midday or the summer solstice. Consciousness is therefore maximized (symbolically) at this position of the day or time of year. The summer solstice is the midpoint of the new year. In other words, it is located at the center of the year, and can be viewed as a time when people center themselves to achieve consciousness of the self. The summer solstice is a season during which agricultural growth flourishes, and human survival needs are met with abundance.

The sun (eye in the triangle) atop the Great Pyramid, as an aspect of the solar journey myth, depicts a point in the process when the earth and humanity receive maximal procreative force. This allows internal and external growth, so that life as we know it continues. It represents an active giving process that is received by the earth and humanity, who benefit from its life force. Our nation was born under this influence (July 4, 1776), and the seal was both accepted and designed almost exactly at its height (June 20, 1782). Its mythical implications are that it provides guidance and awakens and maintains a sense of awe and gratitude. It offers an image of the universe that validates and supports a given specific society in which the individual lives. The solar journey can be read into the elements of the seal's reverse, but it does not utilize all of the reverse's symbols to a significant degree.

Binary Interpretation of Myths and the Reverse of the Great Seal

The binary mythic process utilizes the eye in the triangle (sun) and pyramid (mountain) to a greater degree than the solar journey. The binary interpretation of myths is derived from the techniques of the structural linguist, Roman Jakobson.[70] Its more recent exponent is Claude Levi-Strauss:

> In every myth system we will find a persistent sequence of binary discriminations as between human/superhuman, mortal/immortal, male/female, legitimate/illegitimate, good/bad . . . followed by a "mediation" . . . achieved by introducing a third category which is "abnormal" or "anomalous" in terms of ordinary "rational" categories. Thus myths are full of fabulous monsters, incarnate gods, Virgin mothers. This middle-ground is abnormal, non-natural, holy. It is typically the focus of all taboo and ritual observance.[71]

In the solar myth, the sun is the active element of the spirit or father aspect of the deity, giving life force. Of equal importance to the life cycle of humanity is the earth (mother and matter) upon which it evolves. The mother (the earth or Isis in the Egyptian myth) nurtures, contains, protects, and receives the life force from the father (the sun or Osiris) and provides food and shelter for humanity to survive and grow.

Binary oppositions are intrinsic to the process of human thought, permitting discrimination and the separation of one thing from another. Two has been referred to as the first real number and symbolizes the act of creation.[72] The opposition that is implied in the binary is representative of a state of conflict. This necessary conflict is expressed in the manifestation of the one's (God's) potentiality in the creation of humanity, which is inherently binary—male and female.

The seal's reverse contains two categories, the eye in the triangle (sun, father, spirit, Osiris) and the pyramid (mountain, mother, earth, Isis). The mediation, or third category that is a reconciliation between the opposites, is the process of setting the eye in the triangle (the capstone) on the pyramid, thus making it whole. The mediation or reconciliation between spirit and matter (the creation of a complete pyramid) is "abnormal," "non-natural," and "holy." Sun and earth have joined and produced humanity. The father and mother have joined to create a new being, a son. Spirit and matter have combined to produce soul. Osiris and Isis unite and bear Horus.

The struggle to place the capstone on the pyramid is the intention of becoming conscious (eye in the triangle) of the unconscious (pyramid). The eye in the triangle and the pyramid are opposites (representing spirit and matter), and their unification involves a creative process that results in wholeness and the birth of consciousness of self. This struggle to achieve self-consciousness is an unnatural process, and its successful completion permits entrance into the world of gods. It is a holy process by which humanity realizes its potential, resulting in growth toward a greater integrity, and eventuates in a new being, that is, a conscious self. The unification of the eye in the triangle with the pyramid cannot manifest without effort, because of their polarity.

In the next chapter we shall also discuss how the seal's reverse depicts the monomyth described by Campbell and the Great Story described by Jean Houston.

Conclusion

In summary, the reverse of the Great Seal can be a tool for self-transformation when viewed symbolically. The eye in the triangle symbolizes the sun, consciousness, and the father aspect of the deity. The pyramid or mountain symbolizes the earth, the unconscious, and the mother deity. The sun (eye in the triangle) and earth (pyramid) are separated, as is consciousness from the unconscious. The seal's reverse depicts the relationship between the physical and psychological elements. The pyramid (physical) is unfinished. Its capstone (psychological) is unplaced. When the capstone is set, the pyramid becomes whole and the psyche is then linked with the body. The union of consciousness and the unconscious produces self-consciousness, through which humanity becomes whole, individualized, and self-realized. The Founding Fathers may not have grasped the contemporary psychological terminology, but they almost certainly would have agreed with using the language of symbols to decipher the Great Seal.

6

THE GREAT SEAL AND THE PARADIGM SHIFT

Western culture is experiencing a transitional period that some call the New Age, though I prefer the term "New Paradigm" as more descriptive of what is essentially a shift in perspective. While there are many positive aspects to this new era, it is also viewed—often with concern—as a period of historical discontinuity or a crossroads for the human race. Some people think that Western culture is disintegrating and that we are nearing a climax in human cultural evolution. Calling attention to apocalyptic images of universal destruction, they compare our era to the decline of the Roman Empire.

The Seal's Reverse as Symbol of a New Paradigm

A paradigm is a theoretical pattern or a collective framework of thought.[1] A new paradigm represents not necessarily more knowledge than the old one, but rather a new perspective. When a critical number of people accept a new idea, a collective paradigm shift occurs.

The renewal of interest in the seal's reverse suggests an alteration in American values. A gradual identification with the values represented by the seal's reverse and a shifting away from the seal's obverse might reflect the current theory that American culture is undergoing a paradigm shift.

Marilyn Ferguson believes that we are the "children of transition" and are not fully conscious of the new powers of mind that have been unleashed.[2] She theorizes that we are emerging from an old into a new world paradigm in terms of power, politics, economics, medicine, and education. Characterized by such concepts as centralization, conquest, rationality, and exploitation, the old paradigm is oriented toward symptoms, products, and performance, separating body and mind by using the analytic and linear ("left hemisphere") brain functions. The analytic mind controls speech; it adds, subtracts, measures, compartmentalizes, organizes, names, pigeonholes data, and watches clocks. Linear thinking fits information into patterns and categorizes experience.

With its focus on capitalism, science, and industry, the old paradigm developed economic rationalism, a trend that supported society's move away from religion and toward the tendency to organize activities rationally in utilitarian patterns. Management, optimized efficiency, and economic values became pseudoethics shaping society's choices.

The new paradigm is described as less stable, but more flexible. Decentralized and with an emphasis on partnership, conservation, and cooperation, the new paradigm is rational, intuitive, and process-oriented, and its medicine is cause-oriented and holistic.

So-called right hemisphere thinking (intuitive reasoning) responds to novelty and the unknown. The right brain is more musical and sexual than the left and thinks in images, sees in wholes, and detects patterns.

A key characteristic of the new paradigm is transformation. The new paradigm grows out of the awareness that unlimited technological and economic growth and energy consumption will eventually have to end. The concept of unlimited growth is so deeply embedded in the fundamental assumptions of the old paradigm that it may be answered only if society evolves toward a new guiding paradigm. Willis Harman suggested two guiding ethics to replace the fragmented materialistic ethics: The ecological ethic fosters a sense of total community of humankind, of human responsibility for the fate of the planet. It connects self-interest to the interests of all present and future generations. The self-realization ethic holds that the proper end of all individual experience is the evolution of the human species and that the appropriate function of social institutions is to create environments that foster this evolution. Harman believed that the ecological and self-realization ethics are complementary, not contradictory.[3] Each allows for cooperation, wholesome competition, love, and individuality.

The paradigm shift that Harman foresaw in 1977 has been detected and statistically measured by Paul Ray and Sherry Ruth Anderson. Their groundbreaking research indicates that a subculture of more than a quarter of American adults is already firmly established in this new paradigm.

Calling these people "Cultural Creatives," Ray and Anderson note that they "cross all the demographic demarcations. . . . It's their values and worldviews that define them."[4] These values generally combine a concern for one's inner life with social and environmental activism. After thirteen years of research and more than one hundred thousand responses to questionnaires, they conclude that "these 50 million people are trying to create a new American culture, and to a large extent, they are succeeding." Currently growing at a rate of 1 or 2 percent a year, this population represents $2 trillion in disposable income—in other words, a powerful source for social change.[5]

Most exciting to Ray and Anderson is how quickly this movement could grow globally and exponentially as soon as the group becomes aware of itself as an identifiable group. "As they come to appreciate their numbers," notes Ray, "there's no telling what kind of impact they will have." Adds Anderson, "What we're observing is a great current of change, a change that will fundamentally alter the way humanity relates to itself and our life here on earth. This has been predicted by many seers for many years . . . and it is happening."[6]

The Contemporary Transitional Period: The New Order of the Ages

The difficulties we encounter during any age of transition are reflected in social disruption. As our society integrates the new trends changing our perceptions of marriage, divorce, family, sexuality, education, religion, and technology, many begin to experience a great sense of instability. The result is often confusion, anxiety, estrangement, loneliness, emptiness, disorientation, drug addiction, and meaninglessness.

Many point to modern technological values as responsible for the loss and destruction of humanity's symbolic and mythological systems. A worshiping of objects and a loss of humanism can lead to the view of the individual as an object and to an estrangement of people from their true nature.

Rollo May called attention to an increase in people's inability to feel and an avoidance of close relationships that he linked to a larger cultural shift. "We are called upon to do something new, to confront a no-man's land, to push into a forest where there are not well-worn paths and from which no one has returned to guide us. This is what the existentialists call the anxiety of nothingness."[7]

In this era of transition, many have turned to ancient Eastern methods of problem solving, while others are drawn to psychology. Reflecting Western culture's condition, psychology is also in transition, redefining itself and returning to its primary business of examining consciousness. Turning within and becoming conscious of the unconscious results in individuation. Manifesting one's potential promotes transcendence of the self, otherwise known as self-actualization or self-realization.

Many believe that this emerging change in consciousness in America demands a new type of leadership able to reflect this change. It is possible that this is the very shift in consciousness our Founding Fathers were hoping for when they accepted the final designs for our nation's coat of arms—something they could probably sense would have to take place before the general public would be able to relate to the mystic symbolism on the reverse.

In describing this new era, June Singer could almost be describing the goals of the Founding Fathers to set forth a new nation of liberty and justice for all: "The new era we are entering will require a shift from the exclusively personal viewpoint to one that includes the transpersonal, a shift from an egocentric position toward a universal orientation. The new consciousness is founded in a deeply felt awareness that our being in and of the universe means that the universe is in and of ourselves."[8]

The Synchronicity of the Return of the Reverse of the Great Seal and the New Paradigm

After studying the symbolism of the Great Seal, discussed in the last chapter, I would argue that the seal's obverse represents our country's masculine characteristics (straightforward, comprehensible symbols of strength and vitality) and the reverse represents our country's more reflective or feminine characteristics (with its occult symbols dominated by the pyramid, or mountain, or mother). For thousands of years the world has been guided by the masculine sex, just as the seal's obverse has presided over America's cultural image. We have exemplified masculine tendencies in the sciences, the allopathic approach to medicine, and even outer space travel (with its emphasis on building spaceships as an expression of a mechanical domination of matter, as opposed to a more contemplative approach to discovering our place in the universe). Since the seal's placement on the back of the one-dollar bill by President Franklin Delano Roosevelt (notably a 32nd degree Freemason), and with curiosity about the seal growing stronger in recent decades, there has been a renewal of interest in the seal's reverse and a growing acceptance of its use. During this same period, as the eye in the triangle and the pyramid are literally passed daily from hand to hand on the dollar bill, there has been a steady growth in women's rights and a return to a more reflective perspective as evidenced by the proliferation of Eastern meditation and self-realization techniques practiced in the West today. Is there a connection between the resurgence of the feminine intuitive nature in both male and female humanity and the increased interest in the eye in the triangle and pyramid? Perhaps. Esoteric writers in the early twentieth century certainly thought so. Corinne Heline and Grace Kincaid Morey both linked the opposition to the reverse of the Great Seal to the lack of recognition of feminine consciousness. Writing soon after women gained the right to vote, they believed that only this growing awareness and acceptance of the feminine would convince the patriarchy and the fundamentalists not to fear this symbol.

If such a connection exists, what might happen if America were to recognize the seal's reverse and use it as the Founding Fathers wished, as a seal authenticating official documents? Could we expect to see a corresponding effect in increased sensitivity to feminine values, such as cooperation rather than competition with nature? Because of the law of similars and the theory of synchronicity, I believe so.

Renewed interest in the seal's reverse may stem from the similarities between America's present circumstances and its founding period. As we shift into a new paradigm, the sensations of confusion, loss, and separation from the old paradigm that are common today could be compared to the same sensations experienced by the American colonists after declaring independence from Britain. The two time periods are also linked by the symbol of the reverse of the Great Seal, which was officially created by our founders but has only been coming into its own as a national symbol in the past few decades. As we saw in chapter 5, archetypes manifest synchronistically. The seal's symbols crystallize meaningfulness and draw relevant contents to them. On the reverse seal, the symbols are derivatives of archetypes that express synthesis and wholeness.

Students of symbology look for connections, coincidences, and patterns in time, and when one symbol emerges as meaningful to two different time periods, one might interpret it as a signpost pointing to a relationship between the two. Theories on how to read these connections have been advanced since the time of the ancients.

In today's jargon, one might more easily say that the return of the feminine is the outward manifestation of the inner development or growth depicted on the reverse seal. Essentially all symbols are both masculine and feminine, with one merely predominating over the other, but we could interpret the "going within" process represented on the reverse of the Great Seal as a "feminine" process requiring the reflection, intuition, and nurturance associated with femaleness. The interpretation of the symbols on the reverse of America's Great Seal as discussed in the last chapter is in sympathy with the rise of a feminine consciousness (i.e., supporting, preserving, and cooperating). It may not be a coincidence that this archetypal image is reasserting itself at the same time that there is a regeneration of these feminine values.

The Law of Similars

The ageless wisdom teachings refer to this process as the law of similars. This theory, which evolved in many ancient cultures, held that similars—those things that were identical in design but different in size and magnitude—could never be entirely separated, and dissimilars could never actually be united. This is one explanation for the use of masks in religious ceremonies of the American Indians, the shamans of Siberia, and the ancient Greeks. The wearer of a mask that depicted a god would be bound directly to that god during the ceremony, and the two could never be entirely separated.

It was also believed that there was a magnetic sympathy—a flow of energy—between similars, and a flow of energy downward along channels of similars. Sympathies were thought of as bonds uniting similars. They consisted of vibrations, patterns, designs, colors, numbers, qualities, and quantities tying similars together. Emotional sympathy was referred to as compatibility, while mental sympathy was referred to as mutual understanding. Spiritual sympathy was thought of as the power that binds human consciousness to the divine will.

The Theory of Synchronicity

Carl Jung first proposed the theory of synchronicity, a scientific method of accounting for meaningful coincidences. He explained synchronicity as a coincidence in time of two or more causally unrelated events having the same or similar meaning. Examples of synchronicity could include ESP, oracle-consulting techniques, astrological horoscopes, prophetic dreams, déjà vu, omens, and meaningful series of numbers (like having the winning lottery number match the number of that day's date, which happens to be your birthday and also the number that rolled over on your odometer that day).

An example cited by Jung involved a young woman relating a dream to him in which she received a golden scarab beetle. While listening to her, Jung heard a tapping noise at a closed window. When he opened the window, he was amazed to see a scarab beetle fly in. More dramatically convincing for Jung was an experience he had during a heated conversation with his mentor, Sigmund Freud, when Freud was challenging him on his interest in the paranormal. In Alan Vaughan's retelling, ". . . a loud noise . . . erupted from a bookcase, alarming Freud, who had just said that precognition was 'bosh.' Jung afterward accurately predicted another explosive noise, which alarmed Freud even further. It was a most meaningful coincidence to Jung and made him keenly aware of human involvement in the production of psychic events. He based his synchronicity hypothesis on his theory of the collective unconscious, the archetypes of which manifest through individuals."[9]

Jung described synchronicity as the match of an inner event (such as a dream) with an outer event (such as a murder). Stanley Krippner points to Abraham Lincoln's prophetic dream about his coffin in the East Room of the White House as an example of synchronicity. Lincoln was known to have believed in dreams "and other enigmatic signs and portents,"[10] and a few days before he was assassinated he recounted a disturbing dream to his friend and bodyguard, Ward Hill Lamon, who promptly recorded it. ". . . I heard subdued sobs, as if a number of people were weeping. . . . I kept on until I arrived at the East Room. . . . Before me was a catafalque, on which rested a corpse wrapped in funeral vestments. Around it were stationed soldiers who were acting as guards; and there was a throng of people, some gazing mournfully upon the corpse, whose face was covered, others weeping pitifully. 'Who is dead in the White House?' I demanded of one of the soldiers. 'The President,' was his answer. 'He was killed by an assassin.'"[11]

A few days later, Lincoln was shot by an assassin and his body was lying in state in the East Room of the White House (outer event), just as his dream (inner event) had predicated.

In regards to the reverse of the Great Seal, the inner event was the decision of the Founding Fathers to devise the back (or hidden side) of their national seal using symbols that evoked the individuation process and America's purpose and destiny. The outer event is the reemergence of the reverse seal in an age more receptive to the intuitive (or hidden side) of human nature, which could result in the completion of America's purpose and destiny.

The Theory of Seriality

Much less known is a theory referred to by Austrian biologist Paul Kammerer (in 1919) as the theory of seriality. Kammerer believed that coincidences—singular or in a series—are manifestations of a universal principle in nature that operates independently from physical cause. He believed the law of seriality to be as fundamental as the laws of physics, but as yet unexplained. He theorized that there is an acausal principle active in the universe that tends toward unity. In some respects it is comparable to universal gravity but, unlike gravity, it does not act on all mass indiscriminately, but rather acts selectively. This mysterious force works on forms and functions to bring similar structures together in space and time.[12]

With our mentality based upon cause-and-effect philosophy, the Western mind feels uneasy about synchronicity or seriality or the law of similars. Causal analysis represents linear thinking and delineates general trends or possibilities. Acausal analysis, like synchronistic thinking, is "field thinking." It pulls together seemingly unrelated events having similar meanings that are happening at the same time toward a shared effect or purpose. The Eastern mind embraces synchronistic thinking. To the Chinese, for example, the universe has an ultimate, basic numerical rhythm; and all relationships of things with one another, in all areas of outer and inner life, mirror the same basic number pattern in a form conceived as a rhythm. This philosophy is incorporated into the I Ching or Book of Changes.

Morphic Resonance and Memory

Like synchronicity, seriality, and the law of similars, morphic resonance offers yet another theory for the linking of random, seemingly unrelated events such as the return to popularity of a national symbol coinciding with the rise of certain trends or shifts in consciousness. Biologist Rupert Sheldrake's work on memory and form has resulted in the hypothesis of formative causation, which "suggests that memory depends on morphic resonance rather than material memory stores. Morphic resonance depends on similarity. It involves an effect of like on like. The more similar an organism is to an organism in the past, the more specific and effective the morphic resonance."[13]

Sheldrake's contention is that the memory principle in nature depends on similarity—or the effect of resonance. A dictionary definition of resonance is "a condition in which a vibrating system responds with maximum amplitude to an alternative driving force."[14] Morphic, from the Greek word *morphe,* meaning "form," combined with resonance, creates a hybrid concept called morphic resonance. This phenomenon implies "the form of a system, including its characteristic internal structure and vibrational frequencies, becomes *present* to a subsequent system with a similar form; the spatio-temporal pattern of the former *superimposes* itself on the latter."[15]

Sheldrake asserts that vibratory patterns are themselves maintained by morphic fields that organize atoms, stars, cells, and so on. "The process by which the past becomes present within morphic fields is called morphic resonance. Morphic resonance involves the transmission of formative causal influences through both space and time. The memory within the morphic fields is cumulative, and that is why all sorts of things become increasingly habitual through repetition . . . [w]hen such repetition has occurred on an astronomical scale over billions of years . . ."[16]

Sheldrake's theory of morphic resonance states that evolution is the result of repetition of habit and that the longer something is practiced, known, and realized, the easier it is for others of the species to participate in that knowledge. When the morphic resonance theory is applied to archetypes, it seems evident that the longer an archetype is pointed to through natural and invented symbol systems, the more accessible, through sympathy, is its meaning. Abraham Maslow's "peak experience," in which one achieves Progoff's "numinosity" and is bound to the transcendent, replicates in consciousness what is actually occurring at the cellular and galactic levels of existence. At a certain level of "packaging" of energy units—people, atoms, planets, ideas, and so on—a quantum shift occurs.

The Science of Consciousness and Conscious Acts of Creation

Physicist Bill Tiller sees thoughts as energy units, expressed in waves and particles—and as such, they touch all life, even the immaterial domains of the universe. Being able to control one's mind and emotions is the goal of spiritual practices worldwide, the effect of which some call cosmic consciousness. It is said all becomes one, yet still differentiated. This type of bio-self-management leads to what Ingo Swann calls Biomind-superpowers, or what is shown in classical wisdom teachings and oral traditions to be the key to teleportation, bilocation, healing, and more. Having total control over the faculties of mind and feeling, traditions show us, gives one the ability consciously to be in many realms at once. This may even explain accounts of inter-dimensional beings that seem to pass in and out of our physical dimension.[17]

Tiller and his colleagues are actually proving in the laboratory that human intention can be captured in a simple electronic device that can then meaningfully interact with specific target experiments. He arranges for well-accomplished meditators, highly inner-self-managed individuals, to sit around a table and go into a deep meditative state, and then attempt to imprint a particular intention on a device to influence the experiment, for example, raising or lowering the pH of a solution. Not only have the results demonstrated on a robust scale that this is statistically possible but, even more interesting, they have shown that the thought patterns of the meditators in their laboratory setting have improved the atmosphere of the setting itself. After three or four months of these experiments, he says, "the electrodynamic symmetry state of the space is raised," meaning that repetition of the experiments in given locales can dramatically increase the power of the locales to reproduce the results. They have literally created "sacred space."[18]

To explain his theories, Tiller proposed a higher-dimensional substance called deltrons that can enable an energy exchange between the electric substance and the magnetic substance in the domain of the emotions. According to Tiller's latticelike structures and ideas about reciprocity in nature, we can assemble or disassemble matter with our minds and, in fact, we are doing it all the time. "Our focused attention to something conditions its environment to receive it, an upholding at a higher order." In this sense, our consciousness contains the effects of the past as well as the potentials of the future.[19]

We are approaching a period in which we can now understand and have more choice in the human evolutionary process. However, we must recognize our responsibility in cocreating the world, a huge responsibility that many may wish to deny.

If the reverse of the seal details the process of self-transformation and self-realization, then it could be a meaningful synchronous event that humanity is reexamining the role of feminine consciousness concurrent with this symbol's return to the world stage. By acknowledging the importance of the seal's reverse, we are declaring our intention to more fully cultivate our intuition and our capacity for integration, qualities normally associated with the feminine. A "whole" person (composed of both the masculine and feminine innate talents)—or a "whole" nation or even a "whole" planet—achieves well-being and peace when the two aspects of human soul are in balance with divine will. Because symbols are approachable on many different levels, there is value to be gained by a continued examination of the reverse of the Great Seal, as we will see in contemplating the growth experience.

Growth Experiences and the Reverse of the Great Seal

The reverse of the Great Seal of the United States incorporates the basic ideology of humanistic and transpersonal psychology. It symbolizes the process through which the individual achieves self-realization and wholeness. Its two basic elements, the eye in the triangle and the pyramid, are opposites that are in the process of being transformed into a whole. When these two elements, representing consciousness and the unconscious, are linked, self-consciousness begins to emerge. This result can be seen as epitomizing Maslow's peak experience, in which the dichotomies, polarities, and conflicts of life are transcended or resolved, and movement toward the perception of unity and personal fusion and integration occurs.[20]

Growth processes include self-actualization, peak and plateau experiences, self-realization, individuation, self-transcendence, essentialization, and personalization.[21] All of these share some similarities and represent various aspects of growth experiences.

The ultimate end of all of these processes is the realization of the self as a single homogeneous being, although wholeness cannot be achieved directly and involves pain and struggle.[22] There are degrees of self-actualization, the highest of which manifests as unselfish and universal. It is usually accomplished through a commitment to a task outside of oneself. Self-transcendence, self-realization, and individuation delineate the fulfillment and maturation of the self, or a state of wholeness through which humanity's potential is fully manifested.

The eye in the triangle and the pyramid might also represent, respectively, linear or analytic thought (often associated with the left hemisphere of the brain) and intuitive thought (right hemisphere). Linking the eye in the triangle and the pyramid transforms two foreign and opposite elements into something new—whole-brain knowing. The seal's reverse could thus symbolize this transformational aspect of a new paradigm that furthers the evolutionary development of the human species.

The seal's reverse could be describing the perception of the universe as an integrated and unified whole. It could also express the peak experience and the more advanced stages of integration (self-transcendence, self-realization, and individuation). I believe the seal's reverse represents the unification of the psychological and physical dimensions of being that transforms the "many" (consciousness/the unconscious, male/female, active/perceptive, positive/negative) into "one," fragmentation into wholeness, thus helping to resolve transitional consciousness.

At least on the symbolic level the Founding Fathers may have realized that if America was to succeed it must embody all the characteristics symbolized on the seal's obverse and reverse. Their vision was expressed in the symbols and mottoes of a two-sided national emblem, of which only the one side so far has been used legally and recognized as our coat of arms.

The Monomyth or Hero's Journey

The process that best illustrates the mythological meaning of the seal's reverse is the monomyth of the hero's journey evolved by Joseph Campbell. The monomyth is similar to the ordering principle of the archetypal psyche that analytic psychology uses. Binary interpretation reflects the process of two opposites joining to make a whole or third aspect, following Hegel's dialectic of thesis, antithesis, and synthesis. While the monomyth is also a three-part process, its first two aspects (separation and initiation) are not opposites that are resolved in mediation; instead, the hero completes his journey through a transformation that results in dedication to a task outside of himself.

The three stages of separation, initiation, and return describe the evolution of the hero.[23] During separation, the individual rejects the social order and retreats inward or regresses. He reassesses his beliefs and moves toward the center of his being. The second stage marks a clarification of his difficulties and the encountering of dark and terrifying forces. The candidate is victorious over them and feels fulfilled, harmonized, and whole. In the return, the third stage, the hero is reborn into the physical world and applies the knowledge he has gained to the world in which he lives. He rejects his self-serving and self-centered tendencies and shares his "treasure" (new awareness) with the rest of society. The hero has become self-actualized, and he dedicates himself to a task outside of himself, serving society.

The monomythic process provides a natural way of healing alienation, as do the processes of self-realization, self-transcendence, and individuation. Archaic people learned the individual's essential oneness with the group through the rites of passage. Since contemporary society has rejected the external rites of passage, modern humanity may internalize these, suggesting that the monomyth is essential—as are self-realization, self-transcendence, and individuation—to the continued health of the psyche.

The Seal's Reverse as a Monomyth

The seal's reverse depicts the state of separation in the disconnection of the eye in the triangle from the pyramid. There is not only a separation between the pyramid and its capstone but also a difference in their substance. The pyramid is made of stone and earth—and represents the unconscious. The capstone is made of an immaterial substance—light or spirit—and is conscious.

The pyramid exemplifies the initiation stage of the monomyth. As a tomb, it is the pharaoh's final resting place and the place where he is initiated into the afterlife. As a temple, it is the house of initiation, in which the candidate confronts the world of darkness and enters the world of spirit. By passing the tests of the elements, the candidate is initiated into the realm of higher consciousness, from which he perceives the oneness of all things spiritual and material.

After successfully completing the initiation process, the candidate is reborn or transfigured. The return, in the monomyth process, is represented by the hero's joining the single eye in the triangle—the deity—to the many-tiered pyramid. The one becomes the many, that is, the capstone joins the multiple-stoned pyramid. The capstone is returned to the pyramid through the hero's labor; the successful completion of this task is a service the hero renders to society. The supreme deed of the hero is to make known his experience of perceiving the unity in multiplicity. By sharing his firsthand knowledge and the fruits of his labor, he helps to carry the human spirit forward, restoring meaning and purpose to culture.

The American Revolution itself can also be viewed as a monomyth: the Founding Fathers separated from Great Britain; they received initiation through the war with their mother; they completed their task in setting up a new system of government. By taking the best of the old administration, adding the wisdom gained from the Native Americans, and making something new with the American Constitution, the founders served society by creating a blueprint for independence used thereafter by colonies around the globe. The seal's reverse is an expression of this historical process.

Personal Mythology

Although Campbell's monomyth or hero's journey applies appropriately to our interpretation of the reverse of America's Great Seal, Michael Pieracci questions whether the monomyth is the one true story that we all share. He posits that the hero's journey is more applicable to masculine orientation and achievement than it is to feminine energy and relationship skills, attitudes, and values.[24]

Feinstein and Krippner believe that personal myths do for an individual what cultural myths do for a community: they explain the world, guide personal development, provide social direction, and address spiritual longing.[25] Robert Atkinson sees "personal mythmaking as recognizing and understanding the archetypal images and traditional motifs in one's life story."[26] To Atkinson, the monomyth is a person's quest to become, in essence, who he or she really is, while the personal myth reveals common threads that are shared by all humanity.

According to Feinstein and Krippner there are eight principles by which a personal mythology evolves:

1. During our lifetime, we will pass through a succession of guiding myths.
2. To emerge from being psychologically embedded in one guiding myth and move to a new myth requires a shift in our sense of self.
3. Conflicts—both in our inner life and in external circumstances—are natural markers of these times of transition.

4. On one side of the underlying mythic conflict will typically be a personal myth that has become self-limiting but that once served a constructive function in our development.

5. On the other side of the conflict will be an emerging counter-myth that serves as a force toward expanding our perceptions, self-concept, worldview, and awareness of options in the very areas where the old myth is limiting us.

6. While this conflict may be painful and disruptive, a natural, though often unconscious mobilization toward a resolution spontaneously occurs . . . pushing us toward a new myth.

7. During this process, previously unresolved mythic conflicts will tend to reemerge—with the potential of either interfering with the resolution of our current developmental task or opening the way to deeper levels of resolution in our mythology.

8. When we have successfully formulated a new guiding myth, reconciling it with our existing life structure becomes a vital task in our ongoing development.[27]

The psychotherapeutic literature saw the first use of the term *personal myth* in 1956 by Ernst Kris, but the term *private mythology* was used by Carl Einstein to describe Paul Klee's art in 1926.[28] By 1975 Rollo May was writing that "the individual must define his or her own values according to personal myths. . . . Authentic values for a given patient emerge out of the personal myth of the patient."[29]

The Great Story

Jean Houston writes about the "Great Story," which incorporates a rich mytho-poetic language that propels us away from a personal-particular focus of life into a realm of personal-universal knowledge and expression.[30] "This Great Story contains images that are historical, legendary, mythical, ritualistic, and archetypal."[31] Most important, whereas the monomyth is better experienced by the masculine principle, Houston's sacred psychology incorporates the development of the feminine principle with its focus on relationships and the recovery and deepening of our personal story.

David Feinstein sees the unfolding new guiding myths as surpassing the emphasis on individualism and taking on a transpersonal character that reincorporates community values.[32] Ken Wilbur identifies people who are presently living that new mythology of the coming era as shamans, sages, and saints who are prototypes of self-actualization. Rollo May saw the "green myth," "women's liberation," and "planetism" as correctives that will change the direction of today's hero's journey,[33] but Joseph Campbell believed that one cannot predict the next mythology, because it is experienced in the heart and not projected from the brain.[34]

The Great Story is reflected in the seal's reverse in the relationship between its two disparate symbols. The eye in the triangle as the sun is the masculine, active energy that is in a relationship with the lunar receptive mountain (the truncated pyramid). The feminine mountain protects and nurtures the new being that is created by the interaction between the solar/lunar, masculine/feminine, active/passive energies. That being is born in the hidden place of the womb, or cave in the mountain, or the coffer in the King's Chamber of the Great Pyramid. The individual person's small story is the struggle to join one's singular physical body (the pyramid/mountain) to one's spiritual self (the eye in the triangle), or the process of making oneself conscious of one's soul knowledge. The greater story is that all humans are moving through this process of transformation. The individual "I" is becoming the group "we." This personal and group transformation process eventuates in a community of self-actualized beings, and a new mythology comes into being. The symbols on the seal's reverse are historical, legendary, mythical, ritualistic, and archetypal and thus create the mythic and symbolic drama that Houston identifies as the Great Story.

Conclusion

An understanding of the contemporary cultural transitional condition provides clues as to both why the die for the reverse of the Great Seal was never struck and why this symbol is reemerging today. It is suggested that the elements of the reverse are in sync with processes that fulfill unconscious needs. By delineating growth experiences, reestablishing symbolic and mythological systems, and summoning assistance from a higher force, the seal may function as a talisman. During this transitional period the reverse's symbols can give order through meaning and act as a cohesive force among Americans, promoting growth toward wholeness, and helping to resolve personal and collective dilemmas.

Through the struggle of linking consciousness (the eye in the triangle) and the unconscious (the pyramid), the individual becomes self-realized and centered. The struggle of placing the capstone is symbolic of the internal struggle the psyche undergoes in making order out of chaos. To reach the summit (the center of the universe) and remain there, as the hero does in completing the pyramid, means that the individual has become centered and is at one with the cosmos. The reverse of the Great Seal could provide the centering force for a growing American audience in an age that lacks a coherent symbolic and mythological system.

After the long rejection of the seal's reverse, its 1935 rebirth into America's public consciousness on the dollar bill paralleled the rise of feminine consciousness as manifested in women's liberation, environmental awareness (the green myth), and the concept of one people, one planet (planetism). Developing the so-called feminine traits of nurturing and caring for each other, I believe, is our best chance of surviving the increasing weather changes on this planet and the resulting challenges humanity faces ahead.

There is considerable optimism that humanity will succeed in being able to guide itself through this transitional period. The reverse of the Great Seal is a symbol to rally around as we evolve toward increasing cooperation with each other and with the earth. Campbell concluded: "It is my whole present thesis, consequently, that we are at this moment participating in one of the very greatest leaps of the human spirit to a knowledge not only of outside nature but also of our own deep inward mystery that has ever been taken, or that ever will or ever can be taken."[35] If we listen to the message of the reverse of the Great Seal, we will seek a life of balance, completion, and wholeness—not only for ourselves, but also for our country and our planet.

7

THE BLUEPRINT FOR AMERICA'S VISION AND FULFILLMENT

Ye Are Brethren

The vision of the Founding Fathers can be described in the biblical phrase "Ye are Brethren," which Thomas Jefferson expressed more openly than the other Founding Fathers. As biographer Daniel Boorstin put it, "The fulfillment of Jeffersonian equality was not postponed to a future state when all economic classes would disappear and each would be rewarded according to his needs. Equality was first and foremost a biological fact."[1]

In essence Jefferson was espousing the foundational philosophy of Freemasonry, "the brotherhood of man and the fatherhood of God." Aside from the sexism of the language, all humans are brothers; in effect, we are one world, one people. The symbols and mottoes found on both sides of America's seal also reflect Jefferson's philosophical ideal that all humanity is one.

The front side of the seal depicts the bald eagle holding a scroll upon which is emblazoned E Pluribus Unum, meaning "Out of Many, One." E Pluribus Unum conveys the same meaning as Ye are Brethren. Although the Latin motto was chosen as an allusion to the union of the thirteen colonies into one nation, it can also refer to the manyness of the material world being transcended by the unity of the spiritual world.

Charles Thomson explained the motto Novus Ordo Seclorum as a reference to the new American era that commenced in 1776. This new era was characterized by America's republican form of government, which signaled a new age in the sense that people were becoming more able to rule themselves rather than submit to tyranny. The New Order was the brotherhood of humanity, in which all humans were equal. Annuit Coeptis boldly announces that God favored the founders' vision, and that it had a spiritual dimension.

Esoteric Beliefs about America's Destiny

If some of the Founding Fathers were influenced by the esoteric tradition, then the visions of America's destiny held by the Freemasons, Rosicrucians, and Illuminati are important to consider. While it is difficult to ascertain what esoteric Freemasonry has to say on this subject, the beliefs of the Rosicrucians and Theosophists (whose philosophies and teachings mirror those of Freemasonry) are spelled out in some detail.

Theosophists and Rosicrucians believe that America represents the thirteenth step in evolution.[2] The occult tradition states that man, the prodigal son, is journeying from unconsciousness to cosmic consciousness through a series of root races. By adding up the Lemurian race (originating in the Indian Ocean), the seven subraces of the Atlantean race, and the five present subraces of the Aryan race (originating in India), we come to the number 13 (1 + 7 + 5 = 13). The thirteenth race is expected to mother a sixth subrace that in turn will foster the sixth root race. It is prophecied that by the year 2600 c.e., the seeds of the sixth root race will have germinated, and a great part of America's destiny will have been fulfilled.

As America nurtures the beginnings of the sixth root race, other nations are evolving toward their own destinies. Occultists such as H. P. Blavatsky, Rudolf Steiner, Edgar Cayce, and others believe that Russia is paralleling America's evolution. Russia's spiritual contribution is not expected to manifest until the fourth millennium. They believe that Russia and America will unite in the next two millennia, with earlier attempts being only temporarily successful.

The Theosophical and Rosicrucian traditions hold that every nation has a spiritual destiny guided by a hierarchy of beings using all ethical means of manifesting the divine plan through the will of the nations' leaders. It was England's destiny, for example, to be the mother of nations. Her empire was slowly and painfully disassembled while she learned the lessons of selflessness and service to mankind. America repeats similar lessons in the Near and Far East while she struggles to uphold the aspirations of Thomas Paine's belief that "The world is my country, All mankind are my brethren, To do good is my religion, I believe in one God and no more."[3]

The dawning of a new age is a spiritually potent era. Many of the ideas, beliefs, and hopes for the Aquarian age are being expressed now in their initial forms. The coming decades will see many altruistic endeavors attempted. It is from these beginnings that the seeds will be sown for the New Age.

The emergence of world brotherhood could be expedited in the merging of the Western Hemisphere, the union of America, Canada, and Mexico being the most likely first step. The union of South America with North America would link the whole hemisphere, as Jefferson wished.

The union in the Eastern Hemisphere will take more time, but its success is inevitable. Great Britain and Europe could act as the cement to unite the two hemispheres. The only way the efforts toward world union could remain permanent would be through peaceful negotiations. All methods using force would destroy its longevity.

According to the Rosicrucians and Theosophists, supporting the divine plan are great beings referred to as masters of the physical and spiritual planes. The evolution of America owes much to the seed thoughts of four masters—Kuthumi, El Morya, Rogoczy, and Djwal Kul. Some of the founders of America may have been consciously or unconsciously students of these teachers, just as some contemporary Americans are pupils of these masters. In fact, the motto of the hierarchy of world teachers is identical with America's destiny—the brotherhood of man and the Fatherhood of God.

Most nations may prefer their independence, but wars, economic survival, and environmental problems will inevitably persuade nations to pursue the objective of one world. Having accomplished world union, America's spiritual destiny will have been fulfilled.

A Blueprint for Destiny

The Great Seal of America not only describes the destiny of the American nation and its people, but also refers to all humanity on this planet. The seal's reverse expresses the vision of self-transformation. From the union of spirit and matter, a new being—a transformed being—is created that is more than the sum of its parts and different from either. The seal's reverse could thus symbolize this transformational aspect of a new paradigm that furthers the evolutionary development of the human species. God favors this process (Annuit Coeptis) for it expresses the New Order of the Ages (Novus Ordo Seclorum). Few would see this process or vision as anything but positive, but how can such a vision be realized?

The past several decades have seen the growth of various groups and techniques that encourage self-transformation and self-realization. Their goal is to unite the mortal physical body with its spiritual counterpart, thus producing a higher awareness of the self with respect to the universe. This self-realization process is the foundation for determining individual purpose. In other words, the elevation of consciousness provides a perspective that allows one to glimpse a higher order of things, which, in turn, indicates the role of the individual in society.

America's Great Seal may be seen as a blueprint for the elevation of consciousness. It says, in part, that first we must transform ourselves before we can change the world, and that it is during the process of self-transformation that we can catch a glimpse of what part we are to play in national and global transformation.

Since 1776 America has been the leader in realizing the goal of self-government. The spirit of America has successfully followed the path of initiation toward global vision. America has served not only its people but also the world. America was responsible for regenerating the spirit of "liberty, equality, and fraternity," which became a battle cry for the French Revolution. America had the wisdom to become a nation of various nationalities: its "melting pot" philosophy has been one of its great strengths. We also had the wisdom to engrave In God We Trust and Annuit Coeptis on our currency, suggesting that all the money in the world has no power behind it unless it is supported by divine providence.

Universal acceptance of the reverse of the Great Seal as a blueprint for our destiny has not been achieved, however, with fundamentalists continuing to stand firmly against its recognition. They see the seal's reverse as a great conspiracy of secret societies to control not only America, but the rest of the planet as well. They do not see the "Great Story" or the self-realization process that it depicts. They prefer to interpret its multileveled symbolism in just one way, one that loses sight of matters of spirit.

George Lakoff's *Don't Think of an Elephant: Know Your Values and Frame the Debate* offers an explanation for why anyone would reject this Great Story of spiritual realization.[4] Lakoff uses the term *frames* to mean mental structures that shape the way we see the world. These frames are part of what cognitive scientists call the "cognitive unconscious." Fundamentalists are generally conservatives who value a strict-father model of reality. The obverse of America's Great Seal with its tightly centered and controlled eagle and shield design perfectly expresses that patriarchal model.

On the other hand, the progressive family model is one of nurturance, and it is gender-neutral. The seal's reverse, which contains both masculine (eye in the triangle/sun) and feminine (pyramid/mountain/earth), stresses a balance that allows the feminine consciousness to augment the activity of the masculine energies. Those who have difficulty accepting this vision have framed the seal's reverse as a threat. They cannot accept any other interpretation for America than that of patriarch of the planet. "To be accepted, the truth must fit people's frames. If the facts do not fit a frame, the frame stays and the facts bounce off."[5]

Planetary Regeneration

There are also powers at work within the United States that have debilitated its spirit. These forces dominate American culture today. We see these forces at work daily in the way we poison the earth, water, and air. We cannot continue this wholesale destruction of our nation and planet without the severe consequences we are just beginning to experience with ever-increasing natural disasters and weather changes.

How did we get the environment into this hellish predicament? It is a result of the old paradigm scenario, in which Mother Earth is conquered and dominated, just as the male species has dominated the female for the past few millennia. This belief system rejects the importance of spirit and puts its full confidence in the ledger. But has man "conquered" nature? If he thinks he has, he had better prepare himself for what Mother Earth has in store. Nature will cleanse itself regardless of national boundaries and powerful governments.

Fortunately, there are a growing number of world citizens who do not view the earth as an object to be controlled and conquered. They see the earth as a living entity embodying a spiritual life force that nourishes the physical earth and is responsible for the planet's equilibrium. It is not necessary to confront or conquer this life force: cooperation can bring a more positive response. This philosophy exemplifies the new paradigm in that it embraces the reality of both material and spiritual worlds.

America has led the world into a new age of democratic consciousness. But America has also led the way in industrializing and polluting the planet. This planetary destruction must be curtailed immediately if we are to prevent the total collapse of our planetary life force. Again, America must take the lead in reversing this diabolical predicament.

Doing It Now

But what can we do now? Step one is service to others, or volunteerism. You can help clean up the environment. You can work on legislation to prevent continued pollution. You can lobby for a cleaner earth or even run for office. You can work for more social justice worldwide in one of the many institutions already created to foster this evolution.

As you volunteer your services to transform the earth, you need to decide on the extent of your service (step two). Do you want to work on these problems in your neighborhood, or focus your attention on city and state matters? You may feel the need to venture into a regional problem or one that is national, continental, or global.

It is not enough to undertake a service project. The project must be brought to a successful conclusion (step three). We must struggle to transform our ideals into actualities. Bringing to birth positive changes in the world's ecological systems will enable a physical rebirth or the regeneration of our planet.

The fourth step in this journey is to accumulate wisdom of the process of regeneration, and to live the knowledge that right action under the right circumstances gives birth to a new consciousness leading to global vision.

As Americans we have an important job to do. We must transform ourselves before we can successfully transform our planet. We must take the role of leadership in supporting programs that will return the earth to its former healthy balance. We must set tougher standards and see that they are met. Don't depend on the government to do it. We cannot wait for public officials to suddenly build the character needed to prioritize the life systems on this planet over the needs of the industrial world. Americans, because of our form of government, have the capacity to return the earth to environmental balance and global health. To create change is inherent in our nature, as it is inherent in the very symbol that represents the American nation—the Great Seal.

Whatever you choose to do, do it quickly. The world stands on the brink of global collapse. We can consciously choose an enlightened course ushering in a new age of planetary harmony and peace. The League of the Iroquois chose that course hundreds of years before America's founders took on the vision. America is destined to lay the foundation for world peace and global unity. We can encourage this process by remembering that we are not the people of a city or state. We are not the people from the east or west coasts of America. We are people from the planet Earth. We are Earth people. "Ye are Brethren."

Afterword

Completing the Great Seal of the United States of America

It is my contention that it is absolutely necessary for Americans to complete what our Founding Fathers began and finish our Great Seal. Our founders did not envision a nation based upon material principles only! They knew that such a nation would lose its finest resources. My wife, Zohara, and I lobbied from 1976 to 1986 for the completion of our nation's coat of arms and the cutting of the die of the reverse of the Great Seal. Six years of that decade (1981–86) were devoted to the creation and pursuit of legislation. During the Ninety-seventh Congress (1982) we worked with Senator Charles McC. Mathias (R., Md.) in an effort to get a presidential proclamation passed. Senate Resolution 394 (sponsored by Mathias, and cosponsored with Goldwater, Nunn, and Pell) would have directed the State Department, the Keeper of the Seal, to cut a die of the reverse. The proclamation went through senior staff sign-off on the eve of the Great Seal's bicentennial, June 20, 1982. The Legal Council's Office struck language that was pertinent to the cutting of the reverse die from the document, leaving only the proclamation of the week of June 20, 1982, as Great Seal Week.

One objection to the resolution was that the proclamation would affect a standing law, which, under most circumstances, must be changed by congressional agreement. Title 4 of the United States Code (1934) says that "the seal heretofore used" shall be the seal of the United States (referring only to the obverse). The proclamation was in obvious conflict with this code. The other prohibiting factor cited was that there was no language regarding appropriations ($13,000) for the striking of the die. We learned, with the senators, the hard way. All subsequent legislative efforts were written to amend Title 4 of the United States Code in order to complete the official seal of the United States. Language regarding appropriations for the act was included as well.

During the years following 1982, Senator Mathias successfully sponsored the Great Seal Act of 1983 (Senate Resolution 1177), managing to get unanimous support in the Committee on Foreign Relations where the bill was assigned during the Ninety-eighth Congress. The Great Seal Act passed without objection before the full Senate on August 2, 1984. It failed to be introduced in the House.

Mathias, known for his love of American history, reintroduced the Great Seal Act of 1985 (Senate Resolution 726) to the Ninety-ninth Congress. Waiting for the House action, the Great Seal Act was never brought before the full Senate for a third consideration.

Senator Barbara Mikulski, then Representative Mikulski (D., Md.), introduced a companion bill during the Ninety-eighth Congress. However, it was only in the Ninety-ninth Congress that the bill received a subcommittee hearing as House Resolution 1670, the Great Seal Act of 1985 (Judiciary Committee—Civil and Constitutional Rights). The bill was never reported out to the full judiciary prior to the end of the congressional year. The bill was never brought before the full Ninety-ninth or One Hundredth Congress.

In our recent discussions with Senator Mikulski about responsoring the Great Seal Act and identifying a House sponsor, she focused on the need for grassroots support in order to demonstrate a national interest in the issue.

Both sides of the Great Seal should be used as our founders intended in order to make official the two thousand to three thousand documents every year the obverse is currently impressed upon. According to the State Department in 2003, the Great Seal is used to seal proclamations and ratifications of treaties and other international agreements;

appointments of commissions of ambassadors, foreign service officers, cabinet officers, and all other civil officers appointed by the president whose commissions are not required by law to issue under another seal; and assignment commissions for consular officers. The seal is also affixed to the envelopes that contain letters accrediting and recalling ambassadors and other ceremonial communications from the president to heads of foreign governments. The design of the obverse of the Great Seal is used by the government on coins, postage stamps, stationery, publications, flags, military uniforms, public monuments, public buildings, and passports and is displayed above the doors to all U.S. embassies, consulates general, and consulates throughout the world.

Completing the Great Seal would mean more than turning national attention to its reverse. As we absorbed the symbolism of its all-seeing eye and Great Pyramid, we would be reawakening the archetype, drawing it from the unconscious to the active consciousness of our nation. We could expect an American self-realization, a quantum awakening, a recognition of America's spiritual destiny. Imagine the global impact it could have if the reverse of America's Great Seal were embraced and used officially as the other half of our national identity.

THE GREAT PYRAMID, SYMBOL OF MYSTERY

The focus of this book is the lesser-known influences upon the creation of our government as read through the symbols that were chosen for America's Great Seal. Since one-half of our country's coat of arms is dominated by a real Egyptian pyramid, a closer examination of this mysterious landmark is called for to understand its attraction for the early American leaders. This appendix is intended to summarize the discoveries made at the Giza plateau since the first publication of this book in 1989, as we inch our way toward comprehending the purpose of these monuments.

Redating the Sphinx

In May 1991, *21st Century Radio* was the first to interview geologist Dr. Robert Schoch on his theories that would proceed to rock the Egyptological and archaeological communities for the rest of the decade. Tellingly, Schoch's geological colleagues have not found any faults with his measurements and conclusions; only the Egyptologists have tried to challenge his new dates.

Schoch teamed up with maverick Egyptologist John Anthony West, a proponent of the symbolist school, who asked him to apply his training to the age of the Sphinx. Schoch examined the weathering and erosion patterns and was surprised to realize that the only thing that could have caused the deep erosion, especially at the rear of the Sphinx, was torrential rainfall. The last time the Sahara Desert had experienced torrential rainfall was five thousand to seven thousand years ago—which is about a thousand years before the existence of the Egyptian dynasty that is supposed to have built the Sphinx.

Secret societies, particularly the Rosicrucians, have always held that their orders originated in some ancient, forgotten time, long before the advent of recorded history; wisdom from that time was handed down and inherited by the Egyptians, who later handed it down to them. West was inspired by the symbolist school of Egyptology, whose interpretation of ancient Egyptian culture was advanced by the French scholar and philosopher R. A. Schwaller de Lubicz (1891–1962). West's *Traveler's Key to Ancient Egypt* and his Magical Egypt Tours have inspired many of the contemporary writers stirring up debate on Egypt, such as Graham Hancock and Robert Bauval. They testify that West's tours allow one to see Egypt without the filters that cut out all of the magic and mystery.[1]

Traditional Egyptologists, however, led by Dr. Zahi Hawass and his colleague Dr. Mark Lehner (formerly the archeologist for the Association for Research and Enlightenment and currently in charge of the Giza Plateau Mapping Project), have repeatedly debated Schoch's redating theory on the Sphinx. While the majority of geologists examining the evidence are convinced that only heavy rains could have been responsible for the deep erosion, Hawass and Lehner hold to the theory that moisture in the sand that had covered the Sphinx for hundreds of years was the cause of the erosion, a claim that most geologists reject.

The Orion Theory

Although he had published as early as 1983, Robert Bauval's Orion theory did not gain prominence until his 1994 book, *The Orion Mystery,* which he coauthored with Adrian Gilbert.[2] Bauval and Gilbert have demonstrated that the constellation of Orion is reflected on the ground by the three pyramids of Giza, representing Orion's belt. They also believe that the Sphinx represents the constellation Leo. Using archaeoastronomy, Bauval and Gilbert have shown that when diagrams of the star maps are superimposed over the Giza plateau until these astronomical points match up with their corresponding points on the Giza plateau, the date that is embedded in the message of their layout is approximately 10,400 B.C.E., that is, when the vernal point was in Leo, which, as the sign opposite Aquarius, is half of a precessional cycle of twenty-six thousand years ago. This is a period the Egyptians called the First Time, when they believed the god Osiris ruled the earth.

The Giza monuments are also pointing to a region of the sky called the Duat, which according to Graham Hancock reveals the primary function of the pyramids. The Egyptians' quest for immortality and passion about the afterlife are revealed in their books written to guide the soul "through the Duat as a place of initiation into this deep spiritual mystery. This is to be achieved through knowledge, not only through faith. We know that the ancient Egyptians created enormous texts which served almost as guide books to the afterlife realm. I'm absolutely satisfied that the monuments at Giza necropolis are three-dimensional models of that afterlife realm through which it was believed that the soul would journey after death. This afterlife realm was located in the sky and it was associated with specific constellations."[3]

Author Robert Temple, on the other hand, believes that there is evidence linking the layout on the Giza plateau to the star Sirius, saying the pyramids are arranged so the "ventilation shafts" in the sides align with this and other stars at specific times. Temple also disagrees that the Sphinx was carved to represent a lion, believing instead that the body more resembles that of a dog; he believes it represents Anubis, the guardian of the earth and the underworld.[4]

Controversy in the 1990s

After some startling discoveries that have yet to be explained, the 1990s exploded in controversy between establishment Egyptologists and archaeologists on one side and anomaly hunters on the other. Allegations of fraud and cover-up and conspiracy dominated newspaper headlines and late-night radio around the world. Although the possibility of unknown chambers in the Great Pyramid was reported in 1977, and in 1987 a Japanese team from Waseda University in

Tokyo discovered an open anomaly chamber, it was not until March 22, 1993, that a discovery sufficient to grab the world's imagination took place. On that morning the robot camera designed by German engineer Rudolf Gantenbrink, working under contract to clean out the shafts in the Queen's Chamber, encountered an 8-inch-square door blocking its progress through the southern shaft. The mysterious little door with unusual metal fittings was encountered approximately 200 feet up in the 240-foot shaft. Speculation was rampant about what might be beyond that door. Could it be another secret chamber? To this day, we do not know. Speculations as to why the Egyptian authorities have delayed finding out for more than twelve years have filled several books, most notably engineer Robert Bauval's *Secret Chamber* in 1999 (which argues that greed and protection of the status quo and of the reputations of the old-paradigm Egyptologists were among the many reasons).[5]

In September 2002, National Geographic presented a live television documentary as a team of explorers led by Zahi Hawass, secretary general of Egypt's Supreme Council of Antiquities, drilled through the door to see what lay behind it. What they found was another door, or at least another stone block.

> On September 10, with Hawass and television viewers watching, the robot sent a camera through a small hole drilled in the block only to encounter another stone blocking the way. Hawass, head of the Egyptian Supreme Council of Antiquities and a National Geographic explorer-in-residence, was excited nonetheless.
>
> "We can see another sealed door," he said over the shrieks of his team members and television crew crowded into the chamber. "It looks to me like it is sealing something. It seems that something important is hidden there. This is one of the first major discoveries in the Great Pyramid in some 130 years, and now what we need is time for further analysis," he said.
>
> Archaeologists had speculated that the shaft might contain valuable artifacts such as papyrus, builders' tools, or perhaps even a statue of Pharaoh Khufu, the pyramid's builder.[6]

Shortly afterward, the team sent a robot into the northern shaft of the Queen's Chamber and discovered a third door. This one is apparently identical to the one in the southern shaft, with the same handlelike metal fittings. The doors are equidistant (208 feet) from the Queen's Chamber. Explorations in these shafts are set to continue with the help of researchers at Singapore University, who are preparing a new robot for the study.

The conflict of various personalities and millennium fever contributed to the controversies throughout the 1990s. Almost simultaneous with Gantenbrink's initial discovery in 1993, Dr. Zahi Hawass was fired after a conflict with the president of the Egyptian Antiquities Organization, Dr. Mohamad Bakr. Several months later Hawass was reinstated when Bakr himself was fired, claiming as he left that he was trying to expose an official "mafia" responsible for widespread theft of antiquities and financial malpractice. Many were quick to spot a conspiracy in his allegations, and charges and countercharges were made claiming secret tunnels linking Hawass's office to the Great Pyramid, from which the secret rooms were being looted.[7]

Rudolf Gantenbrink found himself in trouble when it was revealed that he did not have permission either to make a commercial film of the discovery, which he did, or to capitalize on it through the print and electronic media. Robert Bauval, who assisted him in making his discovery public, had been unaware that Gantenbrink didn't have permission. After the planetary media broke the story, Gantenbrink was prevented from continuing his work in the Queen's Chamber.

In April 1996 another controversial expedition got underway, this one headed by Dr. Joseph Schor, a member of the Association for Research and Enlightenment (A.R.E.), which is based on the readings of a famous psychic, the late Edgar Cayce. A substantial portion of Cayce's readings dealt with Egypt, and his proponents eagerly follow developments there hoping to validate his predictions about discoveries of chambers full of ancient records—most notably that a Hall of Records would be uncovered by 1998. (As of yet there has been no public disclosure of such a discovery.) Schor's expedition involved a search for passageways underneath the Giza plateau using the same ground-penetrating radar that NASA uses. Based on earlier seismic tests indicating a cavity below one paw of the Sphinx, their hope was to locate this passageway and record its opening on film. According to the late filmmaker Boris Said, they identified a 26-by-40-foot room with roughly 30-foot ceilings about 35 feet below the Sphinx. This corresponded to the 1991 findings of geologist Robert Schoch with seismologist Thomas Dobecki, who had identified a large rectangular chamber concealed in the bedrock approximately 20 feet below the left front paw of the Sphinx. In addition, according to Said, the Schor team discovered a hidden passageway running underneath all three of the little pyramids, continuing on to the funerary temple on the east side of the Great Pyramid, and then going underneath it and vanishing under the Great Pyramid. Unfortunately, when Said passed away the public was left hanging without conclusion to this research; as to this date, no film or book has been released about this expedition.

Tom Danley, a sonics expert and consultant to NASA, has applied his training to testing the sonic resonance of the Great Pyramid. Also accompanying Danley was filmmaker Boris Said, who recounted that the researchers started out by lying down and humming in the King's Chamber sarcophagus—which was cut from a single piece of granite—knowing that certain notes would sound louder and more resonant. They put sensors all over the pyramid, including the five chambers above the King's Chamber. When the speakers and amplifiers were activated in the King's Chamber, all of the sensors resonated. Even if the passages were closed, the pyramid as a whole would resonate with certain fundamental tones. The more power and energy, the louder the tones. When Danley and his crew returned to their laboratory to analyze their recordings, they found that there was sound present in the King's Chamber even when they were not making any noise. The sounds were below the audible range, about half a vibration per second, or half a hertz. When they raised the tone enough to hear it, they discovered it was always in the key of F-sharp. According to Said, early Egyptian texts suggest F-sharp as the harmonic of the earth. Many Native American sacred flutes are also tuned to F-sharp.[8]

Some speculate that sonic resonance was used in the pyramids to raise consciousness and for healing. As discussed in chapter 5, Rosicrucians and Freemasons believe that the Great Pyramid was used to conduct rites of initiation.

All Things Are Vibration

The latest neurological research has shown that classical music can be used to assist in healing, during surgery, and in analysis.[9] Danley and Said showed that the Great Pyramid emits a tone or vibration all its own, though the intentions of its creators in this regard remain a mystery. Others have speculated that the pyramid may have been constructed specifically to effect extraordinary changes of consciousness over wide spaces. Richard Hoagland points to the resonant characteristics of the trillions of tons of limestone underneath the Great Pyramid "stretching a quarter of a way around the planet to Indonesia" and surmises that the pyramid builders may have known that they could "change the resonant characteristics of Planet Earth itself if you pumped enough energy into the pyramids [serving] as machines at their precise latitude." If you excite the calcium carbonate limestone crystal that makes up the Great Pyramid by amplifying a tone inside it, "the result is the entire pyramid, all six million tons, will vibrate; it will resonate," with an effect so powerful, according to Hoagland, that even space and time could be twisted to create extraordinary changes of consciousness.[10]

Engineer Christopher Dunn sees the Giza pyramid as a power plant constructed by master builders and scientists to tap into a renewable energy source that would provide an unlimited supply of energy, while also relieving the earth of seismic stress.

> The Great Pyramid is a coupled oscillator that responds to the earth's vibration. The dimensions and geometry of its interior spaces are specifically designed to maximize the collection and amplification of vibration and transmission of sound. The power center, commonly known as the King's Chamber, has a distinct fingerprint that indicates an advanced knowledge of nonlinear acoustics where sounds of various wavelengths mix in a way that captures and amplifies the energy. In a unique and sophisticated use of chemistry and microwave technology, hydrogen gas created in the so-called "Queen's Chamber" and filling the interior space, is stimulated by a microwave signal that comes from atomic hydrogen in the uni-

verse and enters the King's Chamber through a shaft that is 8.4 inches wide and 4.8 inches high. The incoming microwave has a wavelength of 21 cm or 8.309 inches. . . . The energized hydrogen that fills the "King's Chamber" is stimulated to release that energy, which becomes entrained with other packets of energy. Multiplying billions of times over and at the speed of light, a powerful microwave beam exits the chamber through the Southern Shaft and is directed to the outside of the pyramid where it is used for peaceful purposes.[11]

As Dunn's theories gain attention, it will be interesting to see how the engineering community reacts to them as compared to the Egyptology community. We suspect that his work will be like Robert Schoch's work on redating the Sphinx, which is seriously considered and scientifically debated by his fellow geologists while Egyptologists are intent solely on debunking it.

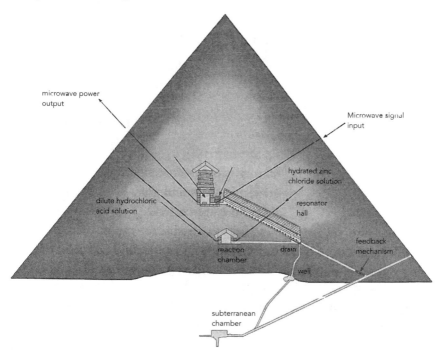

Figure A.1. The Giza power plant. (Illustration from *The Giza Power Plant* by Christopher Dunn.)

The Land of Osiris

Independent Egyptologist and Rosicrucian Stephen Mehler has also concluded that the Great Pyramid was constructed as a machine to generate, transform, and transmit energy. Mehler was led to a master of oral traditions of Egypt and wisdom keeper, Abd'El Hakim Awyan, who told him it was the ancient Khemitians (Khemit is the original name for the land, not the Greek-derived Egypt) who carved the Great Sphinx more than fifty thousand years ago, and constructed the Great Pyramid more than twenty thousand years ago. According to Abd'El Hakim Awyan, the ancient Khemitians drilled miles of tunnels through limestone bedrock in order to bring water from the west to the Nile Valley from an ancient river that today is all desert. This water was used in the Great Pyramid to produce energy using harmonic acoustical vibrations in resonance with the earth itself. A grid line of more than twenty-five square miles known to the ancients as the Land of Osiris contained numerous stone masonry pyramids, including the Great Pyramid, and temples made from igneous rock, such as granite, basalt, and alabaster, and sedimentary rock, such as limestone. Pointing to the work of Victor Schauberger on "verticular dynamics" to describe the swirling, flowing actions of water and its ability to convert potential energy into kinetic energy, Mehler contends that all of the Land of Osiris pyramids were laid out in a geometrical pattern to form what has been called a golden spiral based on the concept of phi. The monuments were connected by a series of water tunnels on a curved line, meaning they would produce tremendous amounts of energy.[12]

The Extraterrestrial Connection

As far afield as their own theories may be from traditional Egyptology, most of the researchers into anomalous Egypt will not entertain the possibility that the Great Pyramid was built by anything other than terrestrial people. Zecharia Sitchin will. Sitchin is a member of the American Association for the Advancement of Science (AAAS), the American Oriental Society (AOS), the Middle East Studies Association of North America, and the Israel Exploration Society (IES). In his series of books known as *The Earth Chronicles,* Sitchin applies his insight and translations of Sumerian clay tablets and other ancient texts to interpret the tales from antiquity as records of actual events. To him, the Giza pyramids represent a link in a chain of monuments and events that began long before the Great Flood, going all the way back to the arrival on Earth of astronauts from another planet, the biblical Nephilim.

These extraterrestrials, which the Sumerians called the Anunnaki, had established a mission control center at Nippur that was destroyed when the deluge known to us from the Bible swept over the lands and destroyed it and much of humanity. The Anunnaki selected the Giza plateau as the site to re-create their space facilities, and there, according to Sitchin's interpretation, they built and equipped the Great Pyramid with guidance and communication instruments, the fate of which he describes in *The Wars of Gods and Men*.[13] Sitchin is certainly not alone in his theory of extraterrestrial origins of the Great Pyramid, but he is probably the best at being able to document his research with primary sources.

Whether these monuments are laid out to match up with Sirius or Orion or to flow like a Fibonacci spiral; whether the Great Pyramid was designed as a pump or a power plant or an initiation chamber for access to the afterlife, it seems clear that this mysterious monument was far more than a tomb for a vainglorious pharaoh. It also seems clear that the American Founding Fathers found this structure just as intriguing as we still do today.

THE NATURE OF
TALISMANS

Even though the Founding Fathers may have been familiar with talismans, there exists no evidence, to my knowledge, to support the idea that the Great Seal was created as a talisman. It is possible, however, to interpret it as a talisman even if it was not intentionally conceived and designed as one. If that is the case, its effectiveness would certainly be limited, for conscious will and intent are needed to create an efficiently operational talisman.

The suggestion that the seal of the United States could act as a talisman necessitates our inquiry into the nature of amulets and their modus operandi.

Charlotte Bühler states that "psychology is the science of behavior, inner experiences, and the resulting products or creations."[1] I shall examine the talisman in this respect to determine the nature of its attributes in regard to its inscriptions and material substance. I shall investigate the manner whereby the talisman functions with respect to its creator and the object produced. I shall also discuss the various methods employed or omitted that may support or deter the talisman's operative performance, using the seal's reverse as an illustration.

The *American College Dictionary* refers to a talisman as a "stone, ring, or other object, engraved with figures or characters under certain superstitious observances of the heavens, which is supposed to possess occult powers, and is worn as an amulet or charm,"[2] but there is far more to talismanic art and science than the carving of symbols upon an object under auspicious planetary conjunctions. Most important are the creator's will and intention, which activate the talisman. Following the laws of sympathy and similars, the pattern, color, number, or quality of the talisman will bind to the user the desired effect. An interesting parallel can be drawn between the talisman and the "architecture" of a living cell, a structure whose pattern is intelligently conceived as if modeled after some existing plan or archetype, or a reflection of the macrocosm in the microcosm.

Talismanic Symbols

Wallis Budge suggests that the origin of the word *talisman* can be found under the Arabic forms *tilasm* and *tillasm,* which mean "to make marks like a magician."[3] The root of *magician* is *magus,* or "wise man." Talismans are a wise manner in which to make marks.

Earlier authorities are more specific about the components of an effective talisman. Random objects were not used for their construction. Material considered "sympathetic" to the desired end or goal, which corresponded to a planet, improved their effectiveness. Emile Grillot de Givry found that they must also be created by a

workman whose mind is settled and fixed upon his work, and at the end of this work without being distracted or dissipated in other unrelated thoughts; on the day and at the hour of the planet; in a fortunate place; during fair calm weather and when the planet is in best aspect that may be in the heavens the more strongly to attract the influences proper to an effect depending upon the power of the same on the virtues of its influences.[4]

The talisman's objective was to attract to it a desired end or goal, and symbols were selected that embodied the intended effect. These symbols were chosen from the macrocosm of the heavens and were carved into, inscribed upon, or in some way embedded in an object that was in sympathy with its ultimate purpose. Astrological symbols acted as guides to the depiction of psychological states being embodied in the physical world. The making of a talisman was accomplished by a workman whose mind was consciously attuned to his immediate work. As de Givry noted, concentration was a key to the successful creation of a talisman, as were timing, location, and weather conditions.

In addition to the object, its symbolism, and the force of the magus's consciousness, a verbal vehicle was employed for the effective operation of the talisman. The magus utilized a phrase or sentence as an invocation to a higher force (macrocosm) to come to the aid of the bearer (microcosm). Some authors refer to this as the "commemoration" and suggest that in the past, as in present times, the deity answered to the needs of the supplicant, as specified by the invocation.[5] The words selected for the commemoration most often originated from the Old and New Testaments. More recent feeling is that all sacred literature is source material, along with words or phrases arousing great emotion and devotion.[6]

Most important to the construction of the talisman was not so much the system of symbols, objects, and commemorations, but the amount of so-called psychic energy that was "absorbed" by the talisman. It is the magician's will that modifies and activates the talisman's inactive components. Without this human ingredient, that is, without the channeling of the magus's psychic energy into the object, the talisman remains largely ineffective. According to Israel Regardie, "rituals and talismans and all ceremonial magic become effective not only because of the employment of the trained will and imagination, but primarily by virtue of the effective arousal of which he is capable. Enthusiasm or divine frenzy is the primary productive factor."[7]

The magus's emotional state was an essential factor in the creation of an effective talisman. The magician embedded his or her will into an object that acted as a carrier for his or her energies. This was accomplished at a propitious time and place with the correct ritual or meditation. Aleister Crowley defines the talisman as "something upon which an act or will (that is, of magick) has been performed in order to fit it for a purpose. Repeated acts of will in respect of any object consecrate it without further ado."[8]

Such repeated acts of will were believed by others to be all that was necessary to transfer psychic energy into an object acting as a talisman. Eventually there was no need for ritual, for the proficiency of harnessing the psychic energy and transferring it to the talismanic form by the magus in a state of mental and emotional concentration accomplished the task. The talisman acted as a transformer of energy, and as its use and effectiveness increased, it recharged itself by the "principle of universal sympathy to attract a flow of similar energy from the universe. This means that while a talisman is using up its energy in furthering the cause to which it was dedicated, it is also drawing into itself sufficient new energy to continue that function."[9]

A talisman was thus a carrier and transformer of energy created to attain a desired goal or end. Concentration of thought appears to be a key in the transference of psychic energy into the physical object. The magus determined the purpose or the desired goal, selected those symbols that best enacted the desire or purpose, consciously set them in order in a meaningful way (ritual), and commemorated the symbols through words found in a sacred text that carried with them emotional content. It was thus the use of the magus's will and imagination (image-making process) that served as the tools through which a physical object was created to convey meaning or purpose. The process of creating a talisman was one of crystallizing the desires and emotions giving meaning and attaining a desired end or goal.

Sympathy and Similars

The ancients' understanding of how a talisman functioned was based upon the belief of a sympathy that flowed through similars. Sympathy existed in pattern, design, color, number, quantity, and quality. Briefly stated, this theory can be explained as follows:

All forms are masks. Each bears witness to some universal geometrical pattern, and the pattern binds a quality of energy to itself by a bond of sympathy based upon similarity. . . . Bodies differ from each other in magnitude and in design. Magnitude is an ascending order of greatness which proceeds in octaves. Design is an arrangement of parts, and proceeds in mathematical sequence. Similars are those natures which agree in design although they may differ in magnitude. The energies flow downward through magnitudes along channels of similars. All similars, therefore, are bound together regardless of magnitude. To understand this formula is to grasp the full import of the doctrine of the Macrocosm and Microcosm.[10]

With respect to the talisman, the similars were found in its astrological timing and symbols. Those selected represented and were symbolic of (or similar to) the desired goal. For example, if a talisman was created to attract harmony, balance, and peace, one used the symbols associated with the planet Venus, along with its appropriate color (green) and a motto to convey the desired purpose. The commemoration was a verbal communication and acted as an emotional stimulus that bound the emotion to the object. This emotional stimulus proved to be an important ingredient. It was believed by Albertus Magnus that

> a certain power to alter things indwells in the human soul and subordinates the other things to her, particularly when she (the soul) is swept into a great excess of love or hate or the like. When therefore the soul of a man falls into a great excess of any passion, it can be proved by experiment that it (the excess) binds things (magically) and alters them in the way it wants. . . . I found that the emotionality of the human soul is the chief cause of all these things, whether because, on account of her great emotion, she alters her bodily substance and the other thing towards which she strives, or because, on account of her dignity, the other, lower things are subject to her, or because the appropriate hour or astrological situation or another power coincides with so inordinate emotion, and we (in consequence) believe that what this power does is then done by the soul. . . . Whoever would learn the secret of doing and undoing these things must know that everyone can influence everything magically if he falls into a great excess . . . and he must do it at an hour when the excess befalls him, and operate with the things which the soul prescribes. . . . The soul . . . seizes on the more significant and better astrological hour which also rules over the things more effective and more like what comes forth.[11]

Goethe, too, lends support to Magnus: "We all have certain electric and magnetic powers within us and ourselves exercise an attractive and repelling force, according as we come into touch with something like or unlike."[12]

"Similarity" was best expressed in the hermetic axiom "as above, so below"; in other words, the microcosm equals the macrocosm. Similarity was also tantamount to the Platonist's view of the archetypal world: all things were in all; or, there was a mutual attraction of related objects or an elective affinity among certain things. Engraving symbols and phrases upon an object in a willful and ritualistic manner in a state of great emotional "excess" bound the small world (microcosm) to the greater (macrocosm) and transformed the wish or desire of the individual (smaller) into the whole (greater). The transference of energy of one flowed into the other so that for the moment "all things were in all." We can understand that the talisman was the vehicle through which the higher world manifested in the lower or through which the macrocosm (great world) was crystallized in the microcosm (smaller world). It was this flow of similarities, according to tradition, that gave the talisman its capacity to act as a conductor of energies.

Synchronicity

The process by which the greater world (macrocosm) was manifested in the smaller world (microcosm) can be examined through the concept of synchronicity. If we consider the talismanic object to be the microcosm, its effects were experienced in the physical environment (macrocosm). The talisman was created for the express purpose of acting as a facilitator through which a desire or wish manifested itself. Although the concept of synchronicity did not emerge totally from the work of Carl Jung, he contributed much to our comprehension of it. Synchronicity, according to Jung, meant "the simultaneous occurrence of a certain psychic state with one or more external events which appear as meaningful parallels to the momentary subjective state. . . . [It is] a coincidence in time of two or more causally unrelated events which have the same or similar meaning. . . ."[13] Jung postulated the acausal principle of synchronicity to explain "coincidences" that were connected by simultaneity and meaning.[14]

Using the talisman as our reference, the psychic image that the magus embedded in its formation was expected to manifest in the physical world; that is, the magus's purpose or desire in creating the talisman was to draw to the magus a specific objective goal. The psychic meaning in the microcosm of the talisman in some way determined its physical manifestation in the macrocosm. Thus, the co-occurrence of a psychic and a physical factor were consciously established by the talisman's creator. The talismanic process and synchronicity are related; they express a meaningful co-occurrence of a psychic and physical function. The talisman manifests synchronistically, as does the archetype.

Meaning

As noted above, one of the primary attributes of the talisman is "engraved . . . figures or characters," usually symbols derived from astrological and kabbalistic sources. These symbols act as references to meanings. The symbols and glyphs used to represent the various deities and states of consciousness constitute a system of communicating metaphorically. As Schwaller de Lubicz put it,

> the symbol serves equally well for the objectification of thought as for a system of references; but in its esoteric sense it will act as a psychological synthesis evoking the functions, thus the unobjectifiable qualitative relationships that its specific form synthesizes. . . . The symbol, as synthesis, evokes—through its static concrete nature—the functional and qualitative whole from which it arises; that is, it vitally evokes its nonlocatable definition.[15]

Symbols are thus synthesizers of information and "carriers of psychic energy."[16]

The power operating through the symbols in the talisman was meaning; the talisman was created to effect a desired end. Meaning was prerequisite to its function. From his or her psyche the magus channeled will, desire, purpose, or meaning into the talisman, and its symbols conveyed the intention for which the talisman was designed. Meaning or purpose were objectified and canalized through the talisman, transforming psychic elements into physical factors. This process was not haphazard. It was accomplished through ritual, order, and concentration.

Meaning may be more than a subjective state of the psyche. Jung suggested that "we are so accustomed to regard meaning as a psychic process or content that it never enters our heads to suppose that it could exist outside the psyche. . . . We have absolutely no scientific means of proving the existence of an *objective* meaning which is not just a psychic product."[17]

Victor Frankl also supported this view: "the striving to find a meaning in one's life is the primary motivational force in man. . . . Will to meaning is in most people fact, not faith."[18]

The magi relied upon "objective meaning" and depended on it for the success of their work. Meaning directed and sustained the power of a talisman. Talismans crystallized the fluidic state of desires, just as archetypes crystallized meaning. The magician's intentions were impressed in the talisman, which acted as a carrier of his or her will. It was the intention of magicians and their confidence and ability to focus their wills into a form that made the talisman effective. The magi concentrated their thoughts and desires upon a form (through ritual and symbol) with such emotional intensity that they relinquished their hold upon their mental functions. They withdrew from the mental world and redirected their energy on the emotional level, thereby lowering their mental level and creating an emotional imbalance within their psyches. This was the "excess" referred to by Albertus Magnus. It was the directing of this excess into the emotional level of the psyche that allowed the mind to withdraw—"mental *abaissement*"—permitting the emotions to focus on the intended goal. Progoff states that as "the 'lowering of the mental level' increases the sensitivity of the psyche to the reflections of the pattern, the individual becomes capable of perception or cognition that goes beyond space and time in our usual causalistic sense."[19]

At the psychoidal level, the psyche and the natural world are fused together in an undifferentiated mass. It is much like the self conceived as cosmos, or as primal chaos, and corresponds with the primal chaos of the universe. Jung suggests that the psychoidal process is the source of magical effects, which when conscious and articulated creates a numinous experience allowing the microcosmic universe (psychic) to experience the macrocosmic universe (physical).[20]

Mental abaissement creates the numinosity that is an expression of great psychic intensity, which catapults the viewer into a higher awareness of the macrocosm as he perceives its reflection in his psyche (microcosm).

From the psychoidal level, where instinct and archetype are fused, the numinous experience crystallizes by allowing the macrocosm (universe) to be focused into the microcosm (psyche), and an archetype (the constellating hub, axial system, ordering principle) is consciously experienced—it can be symbolized in the conscious mind and articulated into words. Thus, the psychic factor of meaning or purpose is channeled into the physical world.

Protoplasm

When Victor Frankl proposed that the striving to find meaning in one's life was the primary human motivational force, and that will to meaning was in most people fact, he was describing the objectification of meaning.[21] The search for meaning or purpose could have had its origins in the cell structure, the foundation of life. Some researchers have suggested that within the protoplasm of the cell lies the key to understanding of meaning and purpose in life. Edmond Sinnott proposes that "the cell is a chemical compound but more significantly, a type of biological organization; the whole organism is not a mere aggregate, but an architecture."[22] Harold Burr agrees:

> The cytoplasm of a living cell is not a formless conglomeration of chemical substances, but is an integrated and co-ordinated system. It is impossible to conceive a cytoplasm as a haphazard arrangement of molecules. A definite pattern of relationships must exist. We possess a modicum of knowledge of these relationships at any one moment, but we have no adequate theory of the mechanism which maintains that pattern through the rapidly changing flux in living systems.[23]

From this we surmise that the cell is an organization. It cannot exist in chaos. It is organized in such a way that it carries on the organic processes of growth, adaptation, reproduction, and death. It is an "architecture," a structure whose pattern is intelligently conceived as if modeled after some existing plan or archetype.

Protoplasm provides the cell organization and structure. Sinnott conceives of protoplasm as a process by which the cell functions.[24] He notes that protoplasm builds organisms; it does not grow indeterminate formless masses of living stuff.[25]

The process by which the cell builds an organism may be essential to the discovery of the origins of meaning and purpose. Sinnott would have us believe that the ultimate physical purpose of humanity is the will to survive. Survival would be possible only if the correct organization of chemicals were patterned in a functional manner and provided for the organic processes of growth, adaptation, and reproduction. Organization is another key to the understanding of the life process. Sinnott believes that "organization as one sees it in living things is a very real fact. . . . In any problem dealing with life it must be taken into account. . . . In the regulatory and organizing processes in protoplasm lies the foundation of what are called the psychological or mental activities in animals and especially in man."[26]

The purpose of the cellular organization is to survive, and Sinnott proposes that "if the primitive purpose to survive is the basis of all psychical behavior . . . such behavior, and thus all mental life, is anchored in the general regulatory activity of living stuff [protoplasm], whether this is in behavior or in development."[27] Sinnott's thesis is that "biological organization (concerned with organic development and physiological activity) and psychical activity (concerned with behavior and thus leading to mind) *are fundamentally the same thing.*"[28]

If the fundamental purpose of cellular organization is survival, then survival itself becomes a system for creating a developmental or physiological equilibrium within the organism and in its relation to the environment in which it functions. In effect, organization may control rather than arise from matter. Sinnott concludes with the following observation:

> A continuous progression exists from the biological goals operative in
> the development and behavior of a living organism to psychological

facts of desire and purpose. What reason is there to exclude from this progression these highest desires? . . . Even the highest spiritual qualities of man are all manifestations of the organizing capacity of protoplasm which shows itself also in the biological phenomena of bodily development and physiological regulation.[29]

Therefore, organic matter undertakes shape and form and organizes itself in a specific "architecture" in order to survive. The psyche also assumes patterns with the intention of survival.

Protoplasmic Images

What is the process by which the protoplasm transfers the pattern needed for survival? Ultimately we must focus upon the genetic structure, or genes, which provide the intelligence factor that directs or organizes the cell's activities. In some cases cells can regenerate lost parts, suggesting that the purpose and function of each gene varies depending upon internal and external conditions. Each gene has many roles, but directs its functions according to the needs of the cell. This inner-direction, or inner-orderedness, progresses unconsciously, unknowingly, but with sure intention. An organism struggles to accomplish what its intelligence requires it to do in order to survive. Images may be the method by which the genes communicate to the organic structure.[30] Images appear to be omnipresent in the psyche (just as relationships and patterns are ubiquitous in the genes). There seems to be a constant flow of images at several levels of the psyche that underlie consciousness. "The imagery of the psyche is constantly in movement. . . . The processes of the psyche are expressed in imagery. Imagery in movement is the essence of the psyche, and of all the processes by which it reaches fulfillment."[31]

Image-making may be considered the psychological side of the life process. The term used by Progoff for images in protoplasm is "protoplasmic images." They are conveyors of life processes.

[Protoplasmic images] are the links by which the processes of life continue themselves. . . . [They] draw life forward unknowingly, but with sure direction. The organism strives to do what its nature requires it to do, and to the degree . . . it succeeds . . . it connects itself to the ongoingness of the life process, helps to carry it forward, and is itself sustained by it. [If the task] . . . can be carried out, the image will be able to express itself concretely . . . and in expressing itself, it will be able to grow and fulfill its possibilities.[32]

The success that the organism experiences in having the cell structure mirror the pattern contained within the protoplasm determines several things. It allows the organism to continue to grow and live, and it connects it with the larger ongoingness of the life process. This sounds very similar to the process by which the talisman successfully mirrors the desires and goals of its creator or wearer, connects one to the ongoing life process, and is thereby strengthened and sustained by it. The talisman succeeds when the physical objective mirrors the symbolic images (psychical intent) found within its physical makeup. Concrete expression therefore encourages growth and fulfills latent possibilities. The outcome of this process is also important, for it allows the organism to survive and grow. Survival is based upon the success of an image expressing itself concretely. The completion of this goal connects the organism with the unity of life. The patterns passed through the protoplasm and into the structure of the cell allow the organism to survive. These patterns have been referred to as "survival forms," and by definition such forms function as "a symbolic connection with the ongoing unity of life."[33]

When the inner direction in the protoplasm of the cell manifests in the cell structure, the microcosm (protoplasm) is mirrored in the cell's organic structure (macrocosm). This realization (microcosm/macrocosm) unites the protoplasm of the cell with the universal life stream, encouraging growth and sustaining it. With this mirroring, or reflecting, numinosity and vast emotional intensity are experienced, decreasing the energy flow into the mind, facilitating mental abaissement. This process activates the unconscious depths of the personality, allowing it to mirror, through images, the goals inherent in its protoplasm. In the talismanic process, emotional intensity is of fundamental importance. Albertus Magnus believed it to be the "basic prerequisite for a magical effect."[34]

Strata of the Psyche

Jung's work is helpful in determining the origins of the patterns that function on the unconscious level and their effect upon external behavior. Jung's proposed "strata" of the psyche provides us with a vehicle through which arises an inner-directedness determining the preformed patterns that are born out of the protoplasm and transformed into the cell structure.[35] As mentioned above, Sinnott proposes that protoplasm is essentially a system moving toward goals and that it provides the basis for understanding survival.[36] The tendency to work toward goals is the function of the mind. This tendency functions unconsciously and is spawned at the lowest (psychoidal) stratum of the psyche. The image passes from the psychoidal (the primal chaos) level, where instincts and archetypes are fused, to the level of the collective unconscious or the transpersonal, whose structuring agent is the archetype, which expresses itself in metaphors and which exists as a preformed pattern of thinking. Archetypes crystallize meaning by acting as a constellating hub, an axial system, ordering principle, and centering process. The image resolves itself in the conscious mind and is expressed in word and idea.

To Jung, archetypes are effective factors that bring about processes of change at profound levels in the human psyche.

Archetypes and Talismans

Archetypes are not causal agents. They are, rather, factors of inner cohesion and integration, drawing relevant contents together within the psyche in terms of their meaningfulness. "It is *via the archetypes* that the encompassing pattern that traverses a moment of time is cohered and separated into minor patterns that relate to the life of the individual person."[37]

Archetypes parallel similars, which were discussed earlier. Similars act as agents through which the talisman objectifies the sympathy that flows through similars. The archetypes manifest through the synchronistic process. "Synchronicity provides a means by which we can perceive and experience the correlations between the large patterns of the universe and the destiny of the individual. The medium for this is the depth of the psyche, and the vehicle for it is the archetype."[38]

The synchronistic process reflects the ancient axiom "as above, so below," (the microcosm = macrocosm). This axiom describes the process by which the talisman is used to objectify a psychological factor.

The process of becoming conscious of the archetype is parallel to the magician's method of constructing a talisman that acts to objectify a psychic intention. The talisman functions as an archetype. The magus creates an "excess" in his or her psyche and experiences numinosity, facilitating a transcendent state and entering the universal life flow. The numinous experience is one in which the influence of an imperceptible presence causes a particular alteration of consciousness.[39] Becoming conscious of an archetype produces a state of alienation. "Something is added to the individual's consciousness which ought really to remain unconscious, that is separated from the ego."[40] Ferguson adds that "an image held in a transcendental state may be made real."[41]

"The Archetype also has a positive numinosity."[42] Thus, both the archetype and the talisman share the numinous experience, allowing entrance to transcendent states of consciousness, perceiving "meaningful coincidences" that exist in synchronistic relationship.

The "experience of an archetypal symbol results in a sense of relationship to the interior workings of life, a sense of participation in the movements of the cosmos."[43]

The transcendent experience (i.e., becoming conscious of the archetype) is a cohesive one. The interior workings of life are seen in the movements of the cosmos (microcosm = macrocosm), which triggers an awareness of an "imperceptible presence" or numinosity that facilitates an alteration of consciousness.[44] The "excess" embedded into the talisman by the magus also triggers a continual flow of energy through it:

> The manifestation of the macrocosm in the microcosm means that something of the world's divinity has been individualized. When a personality experiences this and participates in it, the experience serves as a link between the human being and God. Since this is so, the sense of numinosity and the intimations of spiritual transcendence that go with it are essentially correct.[45]

To the magus, the talisman is also a link between humanity and God and, when it is successfully activated, an aspect of the divine will materializes.

The Cell and the Talismanic Process

There exists a correspondence between the cell's development, growth, and equilibrium, and the modus operandi of the talisman. Both the magus and the cell structure are goal driven. The magus evolves toward a wholeness (the psycho-physical parallelism), while the cell develops into a unit. The purpose of both the magus and the cell is to maintain equilibrium and transform obstructions and problem areas into situations promoting growth and balance. The ultimate purpose behind either's actions is survival. Within the magus, imbalance is manifested in the need to attain a desired end or goal. Within the cell, protoplasm transmits the psychic factor (the end of the goal) into the physical factor (the cell's structure). The cell's inner direction (microcosm) attempts to manifest in the cell's structure (macrocosm), while the will of the psyche (microcosm) of the magus strives to manifest in the physical world (macrocosm).

Both the magus and cell use patterns and images to accomplish an inner-directed psychic need. Within the cell, protoplasmic images are created that act as directive agents giving an organizing pattern or cellular structure. The pattern carried by the genes is mirrored in the cell's structure. The genes' pattern (microcosm) is reflected in the cell structure (macrocosm), and growth and equilibrium are maintained. The protoplasmic image is parallel to the symbol or engraved image used by the magician. Both talisman and protoplasmic images act as carriers of psychic energy.

The process by which the talisman is created—the conscious choosing of its components—mirrors the cell's maintenance of growth and equilibrium. The pattern projected into the protoplasmic images is an organization or architecture. The magus also uses order, organization, and ritual to create a talisman. Magic rituals are organizing processes that create the architecture and organization needed at the cellular level. Cell development cannot be sustained in a haphazard manner.

Another common feature of the magus, the talisman, and the cell's life process is the numinous experience. Numinosity is said to occur when an excess of psychic energy is created by the lowering of the mental processes and the identification with the "ongoing life process." Thus, a fragment of divinity is allowed to individualize. Within the cell, numinosity is thought to occur when its genetic pattern is successfully mirrored in its structure. This is believed to result in further growth, and the creation of new patterns and images within the genetic structure, permitting an identification with the ongoing life stream.

Identification with the continuing life stream is suggested to be the process by which the mental functions are eclipsed (mental abaissement) and during which psychic energy flows into images within the unconscious. Becoming conscious of an archetype is also thought to bring about a unification with the movements of the cosmos. Both cell and talisman may be a part of the ongoing evolution of biological goals and could eventuate in the psychological facts of desire and purpose.

The psychology of the talisman may be identified with the biological goals inherent in the cellular organism. The cell's life process and the talismanic process are believed to utilize images, order, and purpose to sustain equilibrium. Growth is said to occur during each experience, providing a glimpse into the cosmic. The identification with the ongoing unity of life appears to be the method whereby both cellular and human evolution progress. Both express the drive in living matter to perfect itself.[46] In order to achieve appointed goals, the magus presumably identifies himself with the method through which the cell survives and grows. Whether or not the ancient magi were conscious of their imitation of natural processes is a matter for continued research. Being unconscious of the process would not prevent its actualization, although becoming conscious of it would encourage its manifestation.

NOTES

Chapter 1: The League of the Iroquois and the Great Law of Peace

1. Mann and Fields, "A Sign in the Sky: Dating the League of the Haudenosaunee," 105–63.
2. Parker, *An Analytical History of the Seneca Indians*; Wallace, *The White Roots of Peace*.
3. Johansen, *Forgotten Founders*, xiv.
4. Morgan, *League of the Ho-de-no-sau-nee or Iroquois*.
5. Wallace, *The White Roots of Peace*, 8.
6. Parker, "The Constitution of the Five Nations," 11.
7. Hewitt, "A Constitutional League of Peace in the Stone Age of America: The League of the Iroquois and its Constitution."
8. Pound, *Johnson of the Mohawks*. Quoted in Johansen, *Forgotten Founders*, 11.
9. F. Cohen, "Americanizing the White Man."
10. Johansen, *Forgotten Founders*, 48.
11. Ibid., 65–66.
12. Grinde and Johansen, *Exemplar of Liberty*, 164.
13. Benjamin Franklin, "Journal of the Proceedings held at Albany," 5–74.
14. "Proceedings of the Commissioners . . . to . . . the Six Nations, August 25, 1775 at Albany, New York," Continental Congress Papers, 1774–89, National Archives (M247, Roll 144, Item No. 134).
15. Bork, *Slouching towards Gomorrah*, 307.
16. Biolsi and Zimmerman, eds., *Indians and Anthropologists*.
17. Paine, "Agrarian Justice" (1797), in Foner, ed., *The Complete Writings of Thomas Paine* (New York: Citadel Press, 1945), 1:610. Quoted in Grinde and Johansen, "Sauce for the Goose," 630.

18. Jefferson to Edward Carrington, Jan. 16, 1787, in Boyd, ed., *The Papers of Thomas Jefferson*, vol. 11 (Princeton, 1955). Quoted in Grinde and Johansen, "Sauce for the Goose," 632.

19. Jefferson to Adams, Jan. 21, 1812, in Cappon, ed., *The Adams-Jefferson Letters* (Chapel Hill: University of North Carolina Press, 1959), 2:291. Quoted in Grinde and Johansen, "Sauce for the Goose," 630.

20. Jefferson to Madison, Jan. 30, 1787, in Boyd, ed., *The Papers of Thomas Jefferson*, vol. 11 (Princeton, 1955), 92–93. Quoted in Grinde and Johansen, "Sauce for the Goose," 632, 630.

21. *The Bagatelles from Possy* (New York: Eakins Press, 1967), 34. Quoted in Grinde and Johansen, *Exemplar of Liberty*, 199.

22. Adams, *Works from Adams* 4:296. Quoted in Grinde and Johansen, *Exemplar of Liberty*, 200.

23. Grinde and Johansen, *Exemplar of Liberty*, 200.

24. Madison to Jefferson, June 6, 1787, in Boyd, ed., *The Papers of Thomas Jefferson*, vol. 11 (Princeton, 1955), 401–2. Quoted in Grinde and Johansen, *Exemplar of Liberty*, 200.

25. Grinde and Johansen, *Exemplar of Liberty*, xxiii–xxv.

26. Johansen, personal correspondence with the author, July 7, 2005.

27. American Indian Heritage Foundation, Washington, DC, Falls Church, VA, press release, 3 August 1990.

28. Downs, "We, The Iroquois," *Perspectives*, 272–76.

29. Quoted in Johansen and Grinde, "Reaching the Grassroots," 79–80.

30. Quoted in Johansen and Grinde, "Reaching the Grassroots," 80.

31. Quoted in Biolsi and Zimmerman, *Indians and Anthropologists*.

Chapter 2: Secret Societies and the Founding of a Nation

1. Hall, *America's Assignment with Destiny*.

2. Heaton, *Masonic Membership of Our Founding Fathers*.

3. W. Carr, *Pawns in the Game*.

4. Heckethorn, *The Secret Societies*.

5. Leadbeater, *The Hidden Life in Freemasonry*, 260.

6. Sora, *Secret Societies of America's Elite*, 178.

7. Mackey, *Revised Encyclopedia of Freemasonry*.

8. W. A. Brown, *Facts, Fables, and Fantasies of Freemasonry*.

9. Mackey, *Revised Encyclopedia of Freemasonry*.

10. J. Anderson, *New Book of Constitutions*.

11. W. A. Brown, *Facts, Fables, and Fantasies*, 17.

12. Harman, "Creative/Intuitive Decision-Making: A New Thrust for IONS," 20–22.

13. Morse, *Freemasonry in the American Revolution*, 110.

14. Quoted in McGavin, *Mormonism and Freemasonry*, 175.

15. Ibid., 174.

16. Ibid., 176–77.
17. Arthur C. Parker, *American Indian Freemasonry* (Albany, NY: 1919), 7–22. Quoted in McGavin, *Mormonism and Masonry*, 181.
18. Denslow, *Freemasonry and the American Indian.*
19. Charles W. Moore, *History of Freemasonry* (1829), 242. Quoted in McGavin, *Mormonism and Masonry*, 182.
20. Chornenky, "Freemasonry and Native American Traditions," 6.
21. *Oregon Freemason,* reprinted in *California Freemason.* Quoted in Chornenky, "Freemasonry and Native American Traditions," 2.
22. James William S. Mitchell, *The History of Freemasonry.* Quoted in McGavin, *Mormonism and Freemasonry*, 162.
23. Gordon, *Before Columbus.*
24. Fell, *America, B. C.;* Fell, *Saga America.*
25. Joseph, *The Lost Treasure of King Juba.*
26. Schoch with McNally, *Voyages of the Pyramid Builders.*
27. Sora, *The Lost Colony of the Templars*, 58.
28. Ibid., 59.
29. Pinkham, *Guardians of the Holy Grail*, 6.
30. Sora, *Lost Colony of the Templars*, 110.
31. Ibid., 106–11.
32. Robinson, *Born in Blood*, xviii.
33. Spence, *Encyclopedia of Occultism*, 340.
34. Lewis, *Rosicrucian Questions and Answers.*
35. Allen, comp. and ed., *A Christian Rosenkreutz Anthology;* Heckethorn, *The Secret Societies.*
36. Pike, *Morals and Dogma of the Ancient*, 289.
37. Spence, *Encyclopedia of Occultism*, 340.
38. French, *John Dee*, 14.
39. Yates, *The Rosicrucian Enlightenment.*
40. Mackey, *Revised Encyclopedia of Freemasonry;* Waite, *Brotherhood of the Rosy Cross;* Wittemans, *History of the Rosicrucians.*
41. Hall, *America's Assignment with Destiny;* Perkins, *Masonry in the New Age.*
42. Wittemans, *History of the Rosicrucians*, 93.
43. Quoted in Yates, *The Rosicrucian Enlightenment*, 118.
44. Ibid., 119.
45. Yates, *The Rosicrucian Enlightenment*, 119.
46. French, *John Dee*, 14.
47. Yates, *The Rosicrucian Enlightenment*, 221.
48. Mackey, *Revised Encyclopedia of Freemasonry*, vol. 1.
49. Robison, *Proofs of a Conspiracy 1798;* Carr, *Pawns in the Game;* Webster, *Secret Societies and Subversive Movements.*
50. Hall, *Adepts in the Western Esoteric Tradition: Masonic Orders of Fraternity*, 79.
51. Mackey, *Revised Encyclopedia of Freemasonry;* Spence, *Encyclopedia of Occultism.*

52. Robison, *Proofs of a Conspiracy 1798;* Webster, *Secret Societies and Subversive Movements.*

53. Heckethorn, *The Secret Societies,* 306.

54. A. Robbins' comments from radio interview by Dr. Bob Hieronimus, *21st Century Radio,* February 22, 2004.

55. Orlandi, ed., *Life and Times of Washington,* 13.

56. Aldridge, *Benjamin Franklin and Nature's God,* 156.

57. Mackey, *Revised Encyclopedia of Freemasonry,* 2:1093.

58. Ibid., 1095.

59. Steinmetz, *The Royal Arch,* 67.

60. Mackey, *Revised Encyclopedia of Freemasonry,* 2:1095.

61. Sachse, *Washington's Masonic Correspondence.*

62. Mackey, *Revised Encyclopedia of Freemasonry,* 2:1095.

63. Hall, *America's Assignment with Destiny;* Case, *The Great Seal of the United States.*

64. Morse, *Freemasonry in the American Revolution,* ix.

65. Hall, *America's Assignment with Destiny;* Case, *The Great Seal of the United States.*

66. Clymer and Ricchio, *The Brotherhood of the Rosy Cross,* attributed to George Lippard, in *Our Story of Atlantis; or, The Three Steps,* 59.

67. Sparks, *The Writings of Washington,* 377.

68. C. Heline, *America's Invisible Guidance.*

69. T. Heline, *America's Destiny,* 8–9.

70. Bradshaw, *National Tribune.*

71. Barton, *The Bulletproof George Washington.*

72. Ibid., 13–14.

73. Arundel, *Everybody's Pixillated,* 1.

74. Sachse, *Benjamin Franklin as a Freemason.*

75. C. Heline, *America's Invisible Guidance,* 35.

76. Mackey, *Revised Encyclopedia of Freemasonry,* 1:374.

77. Sachse, *Benjamin Franklin as a Freemason,* 33.

78. C. Heline, *America's Invisible Guidance,* 40.

79. Franklin, *The Autobiography of Benjamin Franklin,* 82–85.

80. Heindel, *The Rosicrucian Cosmo-Conception,* 601–6.

81. As quoted in Orval Graves, "Benjamin Franklin as a Rosicrucian," 181.

82. C. Heline, *America's Invisible Guidance,* 32.

83. Disher, *Rosicrucian Digest* (November 1960): 420.

84. Van Doren, *Benjamin Franklin,* 124.

85. Franklin, *The Autobiography of Benjamin Franklin,* 27.

86. Ibid., 46.

87. C. Heline, *America's Invisible Guidance,* 39.

88. Van Doren, *Benjamin Franklin,* 107.

89. Preface to 1733 *Poor Richard's Almanac.*

90. C. Heline, *America's Invisible Guidance,* 38.

91. Graves, *Rosicrucian Digest,* 181.

92. Arundel, *Everybody's Pixillated,* x.

93. C. Heline, *America's Invisible Guidance,* 33.

94. N. Cousins, *In God We Trust,* 18.

95. Aldridge, *Benjamin Franklin and Nature's God,* 25.

96. Patton, *Jefferson, Cabell, and the University of Virginia,* 265.

97. *Holy Bible. Red Letter Edition. Masonic Edition.*

98. Herndon, "Mr. Jefferson," 126.

99. Herndon, *Rosicrucian Digest,* 128.

100. Daniels, personal correspondence with the author, March 14, 1974.

101. Kahn, *The Codebreakers,* 192–94.

102. Stauffer, *New England and the Bavarian Illuminati,* 253.

103. Ibid., 312.

104. Hieronimus, "Were Our Founding Fathers Occultists?"; Hieronimus, *E Pluribus Unum.*

105. Jefferson, *The Life and Morals of Jesus of Nazareth,* x.

106. Ibid., xi.

107. Hieronimus, "Were Our Founding Fathers Occultists?"

108. Boorstin, *Lost World of Thomas Jefferson,* 232.

109. Ibid.

110. Wise, *The Legacy of Jefferson,* 11.

111. Sachse, *Old Masonic Lodges of Pennsylvania,* vol. 1, 234.

Chapter 3: The History of America's Great Seal

1. Patterson and Dougall, *The Eagle and the Shield,* 14.

2. Ibid., 22.

3. Ibid., 32–33.

4. Ovason, *Secret Symbols of the Dollar Bill,* 181.

5. Patterson and Dougall, *The Eagle and the Shield,* 44–48.

6. Tanner, "Where Did Joseph Smith Get His Ideas for the Book of Mormon?" 1.

7. Patterson and Dougall, *The Eagle and the Shield,* 53–55.

8. Ibid., 72.

9. Grinde and Johansen, *Exemplar of Liberty,* 194.

10. Ovason, *The Secret Symbols of the Dollar Bill,* 138.

11. Ibid., 136–37.

12. Patterson and Dougall, *The Eagle and the Shield,* 84–85.

13. Ibid., 92–93.

14. Case, *Great Seal of the United States;* DeVos, *Unfinished Work of the United States;* Fox, *Historical Destiny of the United States;* Krajenke, *Psychic Side of the American Dream;* Price, *The Great Seal.*

15. Case, *Great Seal of the United States;* Doreal, *Symbolism of the Great Seal;* Hall, *Secret Destiny of America;* C. Heline, *America's Invisible Guidance;* Lannin, *Great Seal of Our Nation;* Morey, *Mystic Americanism;* Mosley, *Great Seal of the United States;* Spenser, *Cult of the All-Seeing Eye.*

16. Carey, *13: The Mystery of the Divine Number Revealed,* 5; Carey and Perry, *God-Man,* 133–34; Brasington, *Flying Saucers in the Bible,* 42–43.
17. Brasington, *Flying Saucers in the Bible,* 43.

Chapter 4: The Return of the Reverse of the Great Seal and the Design of the Dollar Bill

1. Grinde and Johansen, *Exemplar of Liberty,* 247; Patterson and Dougall, *The Eagle and the Shield,* 92–93.
2. Champlin, "The Great Seal of the United States," 691–94.
3. Patterson and Dougall, *The Eagle and the Shield,* 256.
4. Hunt, *The History of the Seal of the United States.*
5. Patterson and Dougall, *The Eagle and the Shield,* 245.
6. Hunt, *The History of the Seal,* 61.
7. Leslie Douglas, personal correspondence with the author, December 17, 1973 and February 12, 1974.
8. Schlesinger, *The Age of Roosevelt.*
9. Case, *The Great Seal of the United States,* 23.
10. Hall, *The Secret Destiny of America,* 180.
11. W. Carr, *Pawns in the Game,* xiii.
12. Wyckoff, "The Great American Seal," 56–62.
13. Grem, *Karl Marx Capitalist,* back cover.
14. Epperson, *The New World Order,* back cover.
15. R. A. Anderson, *New Age Movement and the Illuminati 666.*
16. Still, *New World Order,* back cover.
17. Maxwell, *Matrix of Power,* 6–7.
18. Icke, *The Biggest Secret,* 363.
19. Anwar el-Sadat, personal meeting with the author, September, 1981.
20. C. Heline, *America's Invisible Guidance,* 123.
21. Krajenke, *The Psychic Side of the American Dream,* 43.
22. Ovason, *The Secret Symbols of the Dollar Bill,* viii.
23. Ibid., ix.
24. Quoted in Hunt, *The Seal of the United States.*
25. Ibid.
26. Patterson and Dougall, *The Eagle and the Shield,* 90.
27. Ibid., 520.
28. Ovason, *Secret Symbols of the Dollar Bill,* 90.
29. Ibid., 89.
30. Quoted in Ovason, *Secret Symbols of the Dollar Bill,* 177.
31. Ovason, *Secret Symbols of the Dollar Bill,* 121–22.
32. Patterson and Dougall, *The Eagle and the Shield,* 407.
33. McGrath, *Secret Geometry of the Dollar.*
34. Ibid, ii.
35. McGrath's comments from radio interview by Dr. Bob Hieronimus, *21st Century Radio,* July 10, 2005.

36. McGrath, *Secret Geometry of the Dollar,* 18.
37. McGrath, personal correspondence with the author, August 5, 2005.
38. McGrath, *Secret Geometry of the Dollar,* ii.

Chapter 5: A Symbolic and Mythological Analysis of the Reverse of the Great Seal

1. C. R. Rogers, *Client-Centered Therapy,* 497.
2. Read, *Icon and Idea.*
3. Tillich, *Dynamics of Faith,* 43.
4. Singer, *Boundaries of the Soul.*
5. Ibid., 385.
6. R. May, *The Courage to Create,* 153.
7. J. Campbell, *Myths to Live By.*
8. Jung, *Mandala Symbolism.*
9. Jung, *Synchronicity;* Odajnyk, *Jung and Politics.*
10. Quoted in J. Campbell, *Myths to Live By,* 89–90.
11. Patterson and Dougall, *The Eagle and the Shield,* 85, 531.
12. Hall, *Man.*
13. Fuller, *Operating Manual for Spaceship Earth.*
14. Lewis, *Rosicrucian Questions and Answers.*
15. Quoted in J. Campbell, *Myths to Live By,* 193.
16. *Holy Bible. Red Letter Edition. Masonic Edition.*
17. Patterson and Dougall, *The Eagle and the Shield,* 531.
18. Ibid., 253.
19. Ovason, *Secret Symbols of the Dollar Bill,* 95–96.
20. Marrs, *Power of Prophecy,* June 1999.
21. Schoch and McNally, *Pyramid Quest.*
22. Jung, *Archetypes and the Collective Unconscious.*
23. Jacobi, *Complex Archetype.*
24. Jung, *Four Archetypes.*
25. Jung, *Synchronicity;* Tillich, *Dynamics of Faith.*
26. Clift, "Symbols of Wholeness in Tillich and Jung," 45–52.
27. Progoff, *Jung, Synchronicity, and Human Destiny.*
28. Frankfort and Frankfort, "Myth and Reality," 30–31.
29. Eliade, *Cosmos and History,* 12.
30. Neumann, *The Great Mother.*
31. Harman, "Creative/Intuitive Decision-Making."
32. Jung, *Four Archetypes,* 97.
33. Eliade, *Cosmos and History.*
34. Brasington, *Flying Saucers in the Bible,* 42–43.
35. Jung, *Two Essays on Analytic Psychology,* 91.
36. Jung, *Flying Saucers;* Neumann, *The Great Mother;* Singer, *Boundaries of the Soul.*
37. R. A. Campbell, *Our Flag.*

38. T. Heline, *America's Destiny*, 7–8.
39. Hall, *The Secret Destiny of America*.
40. *American College Dictionary*, 1960, s.v. "Talisman."
41. De Givry, *Picture Museum of Sorcery, Magic, and Alchemy*, 338.
42. De Laurence, *The Greater Key of Solomon*, 72.
43. Argüelles and Argüelles, *Mandala*.
44. Jung, *Mandala Symbolism*.
45. Jung, *Symbols of Transformation*.
46. Assagioli, *Psychosynthesis*.
47. Singer, *Androgyny*.
48. R. May, *The Meaning of Anxiety*.
49. Argüelles and Argüelles, *Mandala*.
50. Eliade, *Cosmos and History*.
51. Jung, *Mandala Symbolism*, 77.
52. Ferguson, *The Aquarian Conspiracy*, 81–82.
53. Jung, *Mandala Symbolism*, 4.
54. Singer, *Boundaries of the Soul*.
55. Tompkins, *Secrets of the Great Pyramid*, 197.
56. Jung, *Flying Saucers*; Neumann, *The Great Mother*; Singer, *Boundaries of the Soul*.
57. J. Campbell, *Myths to Live By*; Eliade, *Cosmos and History*; Kerényi, "Prolegomena"; R. May, *The Courage to Create*; Neumann, *The Great Mother*; Singer, *Androgyny*.
58. J. Campbell, *The Hero with a Thousand Faces*, 11–12.
59. Jacobi, *Complex Archetype*; Neumann, *Art and the Creative Unconscious*.
60. Jung, *Psychology and Alchemy*, 25.
61. Jung, *Two Essays on Analytic Psychology*; *Psyche and Symbol*; *Synchronicity*.
62. J. Campbell, *Myths to Live By*, 221–22.
63. Eliade, *Cosmos and History*.
64. Krippner, foreword to *Walking the Point*, iv.
65. Feinstein and Krippner, *Personal Mythology*, 219.
66. J. Campbell, *Myths to Live By*; Eliade, *Cosmos and History*; Jung, *Flying Saucers*.
67. Eliade, *Cosmos and History*; Jacobi, *Complex Archetype*; Neumann, *The Great Mother*.
68. Eliade, *Cosmos and History*.
69. Jacobi, *Complex Archetype*, 47.
70. Leach, "Genesis as Myth."
71. Ibid., 4.
72. Edinger, *Ego and Archetype*.

Chapter 6: The Great Seal and the Paradigm Shift

1. Kuhn, *The Structure of Scientific Revolutions*.
2. Ferguson, *The Aquarian Conspiracy*, 51.

3. Harman, "The Societal Implications and Social Impact of Paranormal Phenomena."
4. Comments by Ray and Anderson from radio interview by Dr. Bob Hieronimus, *21ˢᵗ Century Radio,* January 3, 2001.
5. Ibid.
6. Ibid.
7. R. May, *The Courage to Create,* 2.
8. Singer, *Androgyny,* 266.
9. Vaughan, *Incredible Coincidence,* 188.
10. *The New Encyclopedia Britannica,* 1983, s.v. "Abraham Lincoln."
11. C. Robbins, "Lincoln's Dream," 408.
12. Koestler, *The Roots of Coincidence.*
13. Sheldrake, *The Rebirth of Nature,* 116.
14. Pitt, ed., *Penguin Dictionary of Physics.*
15. Sheldrake, *A New Science of Life,* 96.
16. Sheldrake, *The Presence of the Past,* xix.
17. Tiller, *Conscious Acts of Creation.*
18. Tiller's comments from radio interview by Zohara Hieronimus, *Future Talk,* March 16, 2002.
19. Ibid.
20. Maslow, *Religious Values and Peak Experiences,* 65–66.
21. Self-actualization (Maslow, *Motivation and Personality;* Rogers, *Client-Centered Therapy*), peak and plateau experiences (Maslow, *Religious Values; Further Reaches of Human Nature*), self-realization (Assagioli, *Act of Will;* Maslow, *Motivation and Personality*), individuation (Edinger, *Ego and Archetype;* Jacobi, *Complex Archetype;* Jung, *Mandala Symbolism;* Progoff, *Death and Rebirth*), self-transcendence (Frankl, "Self-Transcendence"; Fromm, *Revolution of Hope*), essentialization (Tillich, *Systematic Theology*), and personalization (De Chardin, *Future of Man*).
22. Jung, *Two Essays on Analytic Psychology.*
23. J. Campbell, *The Hero with a Thousand Faces; Myths to Live By.*
24. Pieracci, "The Mythopoesis of Psychology," 212.
25. Feinstein and Krippner, *Personal Mythology: Our Epic Journey, a Workbook.*
26. Atkinson, "Life Stories and Personal Myth-Making," 205.
27. Feinstein and Krippner, *Personal Mythology.* Summary provided by Carlos Adrián Hernández, personal correspondence with the author, August 3, 2005.
28. Krippner, "Personal Mythology: An Introduction to the Concept," 137–42; "Introduction: Some Perspectives on Myth," 122–33.
29. Krippner, "Introduction," 130.
30. Houston, *The Search for the Beloved,* 92–93.
31. Dubin-Vaughn, "Stories from World Mythology," 192.
32. Feinstein, "How Mythology Got Personal," 162–75.
33. Ibid.
34. J. Campbell, *The Inner Reaches of Outer Space.*
35. J. Campbell, *Myths to Live By,* 255.

Chapter 7: The Blueprint for America's Vision and Fulfillment

1. Boorstin, *The Lost World of Thomas Jefferson*, 105.
2. Heindel, *The Rosicrucian Cosmo-Conception*; T. Heline, *America's Destiny*.
3. Quoted in N. Cousins, *In God We Trust*, 394.
4. Lakoff, *Don't Think of an Elephant*.
5. Ibid., 17.

Appendix 1: The Great Pyramid, Symbol of Mystery

1. West, *The Traveler's Key to Ancient Egypt*.
2. Bauval and Gilbert, *The Orion Mystery*.
3. Hancock's comments from radio interview by Dr. Bob Hieronimus, *21st Century Radio*, April 26, 1998.
4. Temple, *The Sirius Mystery*.
5. Bauval, *Secret Chamber*.
6. Gupton, "Ancient Egyptian Chambers Explored."
7. Hunter and Knott, *Project Gateway to Orion*.
8. Said's comments from radio interview by Dr. Bob Hieronimus, *21st Century Radio*, March 8, 1998.
9. D. Campbell, *The Mozart Effect*.
10. Hoagland's comments from radio interview by Dr. Bob Hieronimus, *21st Century Radio*, March 8, 1998.
11. Dunn, condensed description of *The Giza Power Plant*, personal correspondence with the author, April 20, 2005.
12. Mehler, *The Land of Osiris*.
13. Sitchin, *The Wars of Gods and Men*.

Appendix 2: The Nature of Talismans

1. Bühler, quoted in Krippner, *Song of the Siren*, 209.
2. *American College Dictionary*, 1960, s.v. "Talisman."
3. Budge, *Amulets and Talismans*, 13.
4. De Givry, *Picture Museum of Sorcery, Magic, and Alchemy*, 338.
5. Regardie, *How to Make and Use Talismans*.
6. Ibid.
7. Ibid., 33.
8. Crowley, *Magick*, 249.
9. Conway in S. B. Preston, "From Radionics to Electronic Talismans," 40.
10. Hall, *The Philosophy of Astrology*, 69–70.
11. Quoted in Jung, *On the Nature of the Psyche*, 32.
12. Ibid., 33.
13. Ibid., 25.
14. Krippner, "The Cycle in Deaths among U.S. Presidents," 145–53.
15. Schwaller de Lubicz, *Symbol and the Symbolic*, 52, 68.
16. Edinger, *Ego and Archetype*, 110.

17. Jung, *On the Nature of the Psyche*, 66–67.
18. Frankl, *Man's Search for Meaning*, 154–55.
19. Progoff, *Jung, Synchronicity, and Human Destiny*, 115.
20. Jung, *Synchronicity*.
21. Frankl, *Man's Search for Meaning*.
22. Sinnott, *Cell and Psyche*, 21.
23. Burr, *Blueprint for Immortality*, 31.
24. Sinnott, *Cell and Psyche* and *Biology of the Spirit*.
25. Sinnott, *Cell and Psyche*.
26. Ibid., 42.
27. Ibid., 62.
28. Ibid., 48.
29. Ibid., 96, 103.
30. Progoff, *Depth Psychology and Modern Man* and *Jung, Synchronicity, and Human Destiny*.
31. Progoff, *Depth Psychology and Modern Man*, 165.
32. Ibid., 161.
33. Ibid., 222.
34. Progoff, *Jung, Synchronicity, and Human Destiny*, 125.
35. Jung, *Synchronicity*.
36. Sinnott, *Cell and Psyche*; Sinnot, *Biology of the Spirit*.
37. Progoff, *Jung, Synchronicity, and Human Destiny*, 135.
38. Ibid., 148–49.
39. Singer, *Boundaries of the Soul*.
40. Ibid., 81.
41. Ferguson, *The Aquarian Conspiracy*, 183.
42. Singer, *Boundaries of the Soul*, 81.
43. Progoff, *Jung, Synchronicity, and Human Destiny*, 83.
44. Singer, *Boundaries of the Soul*.
45. Progoff, *Jung, Synchronicity, and Human Destiny*, 84.
46. Albert Szent-Gyorgi in Ferguson, *The Aquarian Conspiracy*.

Bibliography

Akweks, Aren. *Monuments to Six Nation Indians*. Hogansburg, NY: Akwesasne Mohawk, Counselor Organization, n.d.

Akwesasne Notes, trans. *Kaianerekowa Hotinonsionne: The Great Law of Peace of the Longhouse People (Iroquois League of Six Nations)*. White Roots of Peace, Mohawk Nation at Akwesasne, 1971.

Aldridge, Alfred Owen. *Benjamin Franklin and Nature's God*. Durham, NC: Duke University Press, 1967.

Allen, Paul M., comp. and ed. *A Christian Rosenkreutz Anthology*. New York: Rudolph Steiner Publications, 1968.

Anderson, James. *New Book of Constitutions of the Ancient and Honorable Fraternity of Free and Accepted Masons*. N.p.: C. Ward and R. Chandler, 1738.

Anderson, Roy Allen. *The New Age Movement and the Illuminati 666*. N.p.: Institute of Religious Knowledge, 1983.

Argüelles, José. *Time and the Technosphere*. Rochester, VT: Bear & Co., 2002.

Argüelles, José, and Miriam Argüelles. *Mandala*. Boulder, CO: Shambhala, 1972.

Arundel, Russell M. *Everybody's Pixillated: A Book of Doodles*. Boston: Little, Brown & Co., 1937.

Ashe, Geoffrey. *The Ancient Wisdom*. London: Macmillan, 1977.

Assagioli, Roberto. *The Act of Will*. New York: Viking Press, 1973.

———. *Psychosynthesis*. New York: Viking Press, 1965.

Atkinson, Robert. "Life Stories and Personal Myth-Making." *The Humanistic Psychologist* 18 (2) (1900): 199–207.

———. Review of *Your Mythic Journey: Finding Meaning in Your Life through Writing and Storytelling*, by Sam Keen and Anne Valley-Fox. *The Humanistic Psychologist* 18 (2)(1900): 230–31.

Baigent, Michael, and Richard Leigh. *The Temple and the Lodge*. New York: Arcade Publishing, 1989.

Baigent, Michael, Richard Leigh, and Henry Lincoln. *The Messianic Legacy*. New York: Henry Holt & Co., 1986.

Barry, John W. *Masonry and the Flag*. Washington, D.C.: Masonic Service Association of the United States, 1924.

Barton, David. *The Bulletproof George Washington*. Aledo, TX: Wallbuilder Press, 1990.

Bauer, Henry H. *Fatal Attractions: The Troubles with Science*. New York: Paraview, 2001.

———. *Science or Pseudoscience*. Chicago: University of Illinois Press, 2001.

———. *Scientific Literacy and the Myth of the Scientific Method*. Chicago: University of Illinois Press, 1992.

Bauman, Robert F. "Claims vs. Realities: The Anglo-Iroquois Partnership." *Northwest Ohio Quarterly* 32 (2) (1960): 87–101.

Bauval, Robert. *Secret Chamber: The Quest for the Hall of Records*. London: Century, 1999.

Bauval, Robert, and Adrian Gilbert. *The Orion Mystery: Unlocking the Secrets of the Pyramids*. New York: Crown Publishers, 1994.

Beauchamp, William M. *A History of the New York Iroquois, Now Commonly Called the Six Nations*. Port Washington, NY: I. J. Friedman, 1962.

The Bible. King James Version.

Bindrim, P. "Facilitating Peak Experiences." In *Ways of Growth*, edited by H. A. Otto and J. Mann. New York: Viking Press, 1969.

Biolsi, Thomas, and Larry J. Zimmerman, eds. *Indians and Anthropologists: Vine Deloria, Jr. and the Critique of Anthropology*. Tucson: University of Arizona Press, 1997.

Bird, Christopher. *The Divining Hand: The 500-Year-Old Mystery of Dowsing*. New York: E. P. Dutton, 1979.

Boorstin, Daniel. *The Lost World of Thomas Jefferson*. Boston: Beacon Press, 1963.

Borg, Walter R., and Meredith D. Gall. *Educational Research*. 3rd ed. New York: Longman, 1979.

Bork, Robert H. *Slouching towards Gomorrah: Modern Liberalism and American Decline*. New York: Regan Books, 1996.

Boudinot, Elias. *A Star in the West; or a Humble Attempt to Discover the Long Lost Ten Tribes of Israel*. Trenton, NJ: D. Fenton, S. Hutchinson, and J. Dunham, 1816.

Bradshaw, Wesley. *National Tribune* 4 (12) (December 1880).

Brasington, Virginia F. *Flying Saucers in the Bible*. Clarksburg, WV: Saucerian Books, 1963.

Breasted, James Henry. *The Dawn of Conscience*. New York: Charles Scribner's Sons, 1968.

Brown, Dan. *The Da Vinci Code*. New York: Doubleday, 2003.

Brown, Jessie Louise P. *A Bibliography of the Iroquois Indians*. New York: Columbia University, 1903.

Brown, William A. *Facts, Fables, and Fantasies of Freemasonry*. N.p.: William Adrian Brown, 1968.

Brunés, Tons. *The Secrets of Ancient Geometry and Its Use*. 2 vols. Copenhagen: Rhodos, 1967.

Brunton, Paul. *A Search in Secret Egypt*. London: Arrow Books, 1965.

Budge, E. A. Wallis. *Amulets and Talismans*. New York: University Books, 1961.

———. *Egyptian Magic*. New York: Dover Publications, 1971.

Bühler, Charlotte. "Basic Theoretical Concepts of Humanistic Psychology." *American Psychologist* 26 (1971): 378–86.

Burnett, E. C. "Charles Thomson." In *Dictionary of American Biography* Vol. 12 New York: Charles Scribner's Sons, 1933: 481–82.

Burr, Harold S. *Blueprint for Immortality*. London: Neville Spearman, 1972.

Campbell, Don. *The Mozart Effect: Tapping the Power of Music to Heal the Body, Strengthen the Mind, and Unlock the Creative Spirit*. New York: Perennial Currents, 2001.

Campbell, Joseph. *The Hero with a Thousand Faces*. Bollingen Series 17. Princeton, NJ: Princeton University Press, 1972.

———. *The Inner Reaches of Outer Space: Metaphor as Myth and as Religion*. New York: Alfred van der Marck Editions, 1986.

———. *Myths to Live By*. New York: Bantam Books, 1973.

Campbell, Robert Allen. *Our Flag or the Evolution of the Stars and Stripes*. Chicago: H. E. Lawrence, 1890.

Carey, George W. *13: The Mystery of the Divine Number Revealed*. Los Angeles: Health Research, n.d.

Carey, George W., and Inez E. Perry. *God-Man: The Word Made Flesh*. Los Angeles: Chemistry of Life Co., 1920.

Carpenter, B., and Stanley Krippner. "The Interplay of Cultural and Personal Myths in the Dreams of a Balinese Artist." *The Humanistic Psychologist* 18 (2) (1990): 151–61.

Carr, Lucien. *The Social and Political Position of Women among the Huron-Iroquois Tribes*. Salem, MA: Salem Press, 1884.

Carr, William G. *Pawns in the Game*. Glendale, CA: St. George Press, 1970.

Case, Paul Foster. *The Great Seal of the United States: Its History, Symbolism and Message for the New Age*. Santa Barbara, CA: J. F. Rowny Press, 1935.

Champlin, John D., Jr. "The Great Seal of the United States: Concerning Some Irregularities in It." *The Galaxy* 23 (May 1877): 691–94.

Child, Irvin L. *Humanistic Psychology and the Research Tradition: Their Several Virtues*. New York: John Wiley & Sons, 1973.

Chornenky, Dennis V. "Freemasonry and Native American Traditions." Annual California Masonic Symposium, 2004.

Cigrand, Bernard J. *Story of the Great Seal of the United States or History of American Emblems*. Chicago: Cameron Amberg, 1903.

Clark, Rosemary. *The Sacred Magic of Ancient Egypt*. St. Paul, MN: Llewellyn Publications, 2003.

———. *The Sacred Tradition in Ancient Egypt*. St. Paul, MN: Llewellyn Publishers, 2000.

Clark, R. T. Rundle. *Myth and Symbol in Ancient Egypt*. New York: Grove Press, 1960.

Clift, Wallace B. "Symbols of Wholeness in Tillich and Jung." *International Journal of Symbology* 7 (2) (1976): 45–52.

Clymer, E. M., and P. P. Ricchio. *Our Story of Atlantis; or, The Three Steps.* Quakertown, PA: Beverly Hall Corp., 1972.

Cobb, William Holmes. *The American Challenge.* Beverly Hills, CA: Published by author, 1943.

Cohen, Felix. "Americanizing the White Man." *American Scholar* 21 (2) (1952): 177–91.

Cohen, Lucy K., ed. *The Legal Conscience: Selected Papers of Felix S. Cohen.* New Haven, CT: Yale University Press, 1960.

Colden, Cadwallader. *The History of the Five Indian Nations Depending on the Province of New York in America.* Ithaca, NY: Cornell University Press, 1958.

Costrell, Edwin S. Personal correspondence with the author, June 14, 1973.

Cousins, James. *Two Great Theosophist Painters: Jean Delville, Nicholas Roerich.* Adyar, India: Theosophical Publishing House, 1925.

Cousins, Norman. *In God We Trust.* New York: Harper & Bros., 1958.

Cross, J. L. *The Masonic Textbook.* New York: A. S. Barnes, 1857.

Crowley, Aleister. *Magick.* New York: Samuel Weiser, 1974.

Cusick, David. *Ancient History of the Six Nations.* Lockport, NY: Niagara County Historical Society, 1824.

Daniels, Rex. Personal correspondence with the author, March 14, 1974.

Davidovits, Joseph, and Margie Morris. *The Pyramids: An Enigma Solved.* New York: Hippocrene Books, 1988.

Davidson, David, and H. Aldersmith. *The Great Pyramid: Its Divine Message.* Vol. 1. 9th ed. London: Williams & Norgate, Ltd., 1941.

Davis, David Brion. "Some Themes of Counter-Subversion: An Analysis of Anti-Masonic, Anti-Catholic, and Anti-Mormon Literature." In *Conspiracy: The Fear of Subversion in American History,* edited by R. O. Curry and T. M. Brown. New York: Holt, Rinehart & Winston, 1972.

De Chardin, Pierre Teilhard. *Future of Man.* Translated by N. Denny. New York: Harper & Row, 1964.

Decter, Jacqueline. *Nicholas Roerich: The Life and Art of a Russian Master.* Rochester, VT: Park Street Press, 1989.

Dee, Dr. John. *The Rosie Crucian Secrets.* Wellingborough, Northamptonshire, Great Britain: Aquarian Press, 1985.

De Givry, Emile Grillot. *Picture Museum of Sorcery, Magic, and Alchemy.* Translated by J. C. Locke. New York: University Books, 1963.

De Laurence, L. W. *The Greater Key of Solomon.* Hackensack, NJ: Wehman Bros., 1914.

———, ed. *Raphael's Ancient Manuscript of Talismanic Magic.* Chicago: De Laurence Co., 1916.

Denslow, William R. *Freemasonry and the American Indian.* St. Louis: Missouri Lodge of Research, 1956.

DeVos, Cornelius *The Unfinished Work of the United States of America.* Coopersville, MI: New Age Publishing, 1921.

Disher, Joel. "Ben Franklin, part III, Thomas Denham, Mentor." *Rosicrucian Digest* (1960).

Dockstader, Frederick J. *The American Indian in Graduate Studies: A Bibliography of Theses and Dissertations.* New York: Museums of the American Indian, Heye Foundation, 1957.

Dolphin, Lambert T. Personal correspondence with the author, April 2, 1979.

Dolphin, Lambert T., and Ali Helmi Moussa. *Applications of Modern Sensing Techniques to Egyptology.* Menlo Park, CA: SRI International, 1977.

Doreal, M. *Symbolism of the Great Seal of the United States.* Sedalia, CO: Brotherhood of the White Temple, n.d.

Douglas, Leslie. Personal correspondence with the author, December 17, 1973 and February 12, 1974.

Downs, Hugh. *Perspectives.* Atlanta: Turner Publishing, 1995.

Dubin-Vaughn, Sarah "Stories from World Mythology and the Growth of Individual Consciousness." *The Humanistic Psychologist* 18 (2) (1990): 188–98.

Duncan, Malcolm C. *Duncan's Masonic Ritual and Monitor.* Philadelphia: Washington Publishing, n.d.

Dunn, Christopher. *The Giza Power Plant.* Rochester, VT: Bear & Co., 1998.

Edinger, Edward F. *Ego and Archetype.* Baltimore, MD: Penguin Books, 1973.

Edwards, E. E. "The Contributions of the American Indians to Civilization." *Minnesota History* 15 (3) (1934): 255–72.

Eliade, Mircea. *Cosmos and History.* Translated by W. R. Trask. New York: Harper & Row, 1959.

Epperson, A. Ralph. *The New World Order.* Tucson, AZ: Publius Press, 1990.

Feinstein, David. "How Mythology Got Personal." *The Humanistic Psychologist* 18 (2) (1990): 162–75.

———. "Personal Mythology as a Paradigm for a Holistic Public Psychology." *American Journal of Orthopsychiatry* 49 (2) (1979): 198–217.

Feinstein, David, and Stanley Krippner. *Personal Mythology.* Los Angeles: Jeremy P. Tarcher, 1988.

———. *Personal Mythology: Our Epic Journey, a Workbook.* Ashland, OR: Published by authors, 1985.

Fell, Barry. *America, B.C.* New York: Wallaby, 1976.

———. *Bronze Age America.* Boston: Little, Brown & Co., 1982.

———. *Saga America.* New York: Times Books, 1980.

Fenton, William N. "A Calendar of Manuscript Materials Relating to the History of the Six Nations, or Iroquois in Depositories Outside Philadelphia 1750–1850." *Proceedings,* American Philosophical Society 97 (5) (1957): 578–95.

———. "Collecting Materials for a Political History of the Six Nations." *Proceedings,* American Philosophical Society 93 (3) (1949): 141–58.

———, ed. *Parker on the Iroquois.* Syracuse, NY: Syracuse University Press, 1968.

Ferguson, Ida M. *Heraldry and the U.S.A.* Vancouver: Association of the Covenant People, 1965.

Ferguson, Marilyn. *The Aquarian Conspiracy.* Los Angeles: Jeremy P. Tarcher, 1980.

Fisher, Paul A. *Behind the Lodge Door*. Rockford, IL: TAN Books & Publishers, 1988.

Flanagan, G. Patrick. *Pyramid Power*. Glendale, CA: Pyramid Publishers, 1973.

———. *Pyramid Power 2: Scientific Evidence*. Flagstaff, AZ: Flagstaff Vortex Industries, 1981.

Folger, C. F., and A. L. Snowden. *Relative to Striking a Medal Commemorative of the Adoption of the Great Seal of the United States*. Philadelphia: William E. Murphy's Son, 1885.

Forbes, Jack D. *The Indian in America's Past*. Englewood Cliffs, NJ: Prentice-Hall, 1964.

Fosdick, Sina. Director of the Agni Yoga Society, founded by Nicholas Roerich. Personal correspondence with the author, January 11 and February 5 and 14, 1974.

Fox, Emmet. *The Historical Destiny of the United States*. New York: Church of the Healing Christ, 1937.

Frachtenberg, Leo J. "Our Indebtedness to the American Indian." *Wisconsin Archeologist* 14 (2) (1915): 64–69.

Frankfort, Henri, and H. A. Frankfort. "Myth and Reality." In *Before Philosophy*. Baltimore, MD: Penguin Books, 1963.

Frankl, Victor E. *Man's Search for Meaning: An Introduction to Logotherapy*. New York: Washington Square Press, 1965.

———. "Self-Transcendence as a Human Phenomenon." *Journal of Humanistic Psychology* 6 (2) (1966): 97–106.

———. *The Will to Meaning: Foundations and Applications of Logotherapy*. New York: New American Library, 1969.

Franklin, Benjamin. *The Autobiography of Benjamin Franklin*. New York: Macmillan, 1967.

———. "Journal of the Proceedings Held at Albany." In *Massachusetts Historical Society Collections,* Third Series, 5 (1754): 5–74.

———. *Poor Richard's Almanac for 1850*. New York: John Doggett, Jr., 1849.

French, Peter. *John Dee: The World of an Elizabethan Magus*. London: Routledge & Kegan Paul, 1972.

Friedman, Maurice. "Aiming at the Self: The Paradox of Encounter and the Human Potential Movement." *Journal of Humanistic Psychology* 16 (2) (1976): 5–34.

Fromm, Erich. *The Revolution of Hope*. New York: Harper & Row, 1974.

Fuller, R. Buckminster. *Operating Manual for Spaceship Earth*. New York: Pocket Books, 1970.

Fuson, Robert H. *The Log of Christopher Columbus*. Camden, ME: International Marine Publishing Co., 1987.

Gardiner, Alan. *Egypt of the Pharaohs*. Oxford, UK: Oxford University Press, 1961.

Genzmer, G. H. "Peter Miller." In *Dictionary of American Biography*. New York: Charles Scribner's Sons, 1933.

Gilbert, Adrian. *Signs in the Sky*. New York: Three Rivers Press, 2000.

Goldman, Jonathan, and Andi Goldman. *Tantra of Sound.* Charlottesville, VA: Hampton Roads Publishing, 2005.

Goodavage, Joseph F. *Astrology: The Space Age Science.* New York: Signet Books, 1966.

Goodman, Jeffrey. *American Genesis.* New York: Summit Books, 1981.

Goodwin, S. H. *Mormonism and Masonry.* Washington, DC: The Masonic Service Association of the U.S., 1924.

Gordon, Cyrus. *Before Columbus.* New York: Crown Publishers, 1971.

Goswami, Amit. *Physics of the Soul.* Charlottesville, VA: Hampton Roads Publishing, 2001.

Graves, Orval. "Benjamin Franklin as a Rosicrucian." *Rosicrucian Digest* (June 1938).

"The Great Seal: The Law of Heraldry—the New Die—Valuable Review." *The Daily Graphic,* 14 May, 1885, 591.

Greaves, John. *Pyramidographia: The First Book on the Pyramids.* 1646. Reprint, Baltimore: The Maryland Institute Press, 1992.

Grem, June. *Karl Marx Capitalist.* Oak Park, IL: Enterprise Publications, 1972.

Griffin, G. Edward. *The Capitalist Conspiracy.* Thousand Oaks, CA: American Media, n.d.

Grimal, Pierre, ed. *Larousse World Mythology.* New York: G. P. Putnam's Sons, 1965.

Grinde, Donald A., Jr. *The Iroquois and the Founding of the American Nation.* San Francisco: The Indian Historian Press, 1977.

Grinde, Donald A., Jr., and Bruce E. Johansen. *Exemplar of Liberty: Native America and the Evolution of Democracy.* Los Angeles: American Indian Studies Center, 1991.

———. "Sauce for the Goose: Demand and Definitions for 'Proof' Regarding the Iroquois and Democracy." *The William and Mary Quarterly* 53 (3) (July 1996).

Guinness, Desmond, and Julius Trousdale Sadler Jr. *Mr. Jefferson, Architect.* New York: Viking Press, 1973.

Gupton, Nancy. "Ancient Egyptian Chambers Explored." *National Geographic News,* http://news.nationalgeographic.com/news/2002/09/0910_020913_egypt_1.html.

Haberman, Frederick. *America's Appointed Destiny.* St. Petersburg, FL: Kingdom Press, 1942.

———. *Armageddon Has Come.* St. Petersburg, FL: Kingdom Press, 1940.

Hall, Manly Palmer. *The Adepts in the Western Esoteric Tradition: Masonic Orders of Fraternity.* Part 4. Los Angeles: Philosophical Research Society, 1950.

———. *America's Assignment with Destiny: The Adepts in the Western Esoteric Tradition.* Part 5. Los Angeles: Philosophical Research Society, 1951.

———. *Man: The Grand Symbol of the Mysteries.* Los Angeles: Philosophical Research Society, 1947.

———. *The Philosophy of Astrology.* Los Angeles: Philosophical Research Society, 1947.

———. *The Phoenix.* Los Angeles: Philosophical Research Society, 1968.

———. *The Secret Destiny of America*. Los Angeles: Philosophical Research Society, 1972.

Hallowell, A. Irving. "The Backwash of the Frontier: The Impact of the Indian on American Culture." In *The Frontier in Perspective*. Madison: University of Wisconsin Press, 1957.

———. "The Impact of the American Indian on American Culture." *American Anthropologist*, New Series 59 (2) (1957): 201–7.

Hamaker, John D., and Donald A. Weaver. *The Survival of Civilization*. Burlingame, CA: Hamaker-Weaver Publishers, 1982.

Hancock, Graham. *Fingerprints of the Gods*. New York: Crown Publishers, 1995.

———. Interview by Dr. Bob Hieronimus. *21ˢᵗ Century Radio,* radio program, 26 April 1998, www.21stCenturyRadio.com.

Hancock, Graham, and Robert Bauval. *The Message of the Sphinx*. New York: Crown Publishers, 1996.

———. *Talisman: Gnostics, Freemasons, Revolutionaries and the 2000-Year-Old Conspiracy at Work in the World Today*. London: Element, 2004.

Hancock, Graham, Robert Bauval, and John Grigsby. *The Mars Mystery: A Tale of the End of Two Worlds*. London: Michael Joseph, 1998.

Harley, Lewis R. *The Life of Charles Thomson*. Philadelphia: George W. Jacobs, 1900.

Harman, Willis. "Creative/Intuitive Decision-Making: A New Thrust for IONS." *Institute of Noetic Sciences Newsletter* 1 (Summer 1979): 20–22.

———. "Education for a Transforming Society." *Association for Humanistic Psychology Newsletter* (July 1987): 19–22.

———. *Global Mind Change*. Indianapolis, IN: Knowledge Systems, 1988.

———. "The Societal Implications and Social Impact of Paranormal Phenomena. In *Future Science,* edited by J. White and S. Krippner. New York: Anchor Books, 1977.

Harris, Alex. "William Barton." In *Biographical History of Lancaster County*. Lancaster, PA: Elias Barr & Co., 1872.

Hayes, Carlton J. H. "The American Frontier: Frontier of What?" *American Historical Review* 51 (2) (1946): 199–216.

Heaton, Ronald E. *The Masonic Membership of our Founding Fathers*. Silver Spring, MD: Masonic Service Association, 1965.

———. *Masonic Membership of the Founding Fathers*. Silver Spring, MD: Masonic Service Association, 1997.

———. *Masonic Membership of the General Officers of the Continental Army*. Silver Spring, MD: Masonic Service Association, 1959.

———. *Masonic Membership of the Signers of the Constitution of the United States*. Silver Spring, MD: Masonic Service Association, 1986.

Heckethorn, Charles W. *The Secret Societies of All Ages and Countries*. Vol. 1. New York: University Books, 1965.

Heckewelder, John. *History, Manners, and Customs of the Indian Nations Who Once Inhabited Pennsylvania and the Neighboring States*. New York: Arno Press, 1971.

Heindel, Max. *The Rosicrucian Cosmo-Conception.* Oceanside, CA: Rosicrucian Fellowship, 1956.

Heinicke, Milton H. *Heinicke's History of Ephrata.* 11 booklets. Adamstown, PA: Historical Society of the Cocalico Valley, 1975.

Heline, Corrine. *America's Invisible Guidance.* Los Angeles: New Age Press, 1949.

Heline, Theodore. *America's Destiny: A New Order of Ages.* Oceanside, CA: New Age Press, 1941.

Herndon, S. M. "Mr. Jefferson." *Rosicrucian Digest* (April 1961).

Hewitt, J. N. B. "A Constitutional League of Peace in the Stone Age of America: The League of the Iroquois and Its Constitution." Washington, DC: National Anthropological Archives, Smithsonian Institution, 1918.

———. "The Founding of the League of the Five Nations by Deganawidah." Washington, DC: National Anthropological Archives, Smithsonian Institution, n.d.

Hieronimus, Robert. *America's Secret Destiny.* Rochester, VT: Destiny Books, 1989.

———. *E Pluribus Unum.* Baltimore, MD: AUM Center, 1985.

———. *The Growth Experience Depicted in the American Seal's Reverse.* Baltimore, MD: AUM Center, 1982.

———. "An Historical Analysis of the Reverse of America's Great Seal and Its Relationship to the Ideology of Humanistic Psychology." Unpublished doctoral thesis. San Francisco: Saybrook Institute, 1981.

———. *Mythologies Expressed in the American Seal's Reverse.* Baltimore, MD: AUM Center, 1982.

———. *Psychology of the Talisman.* Baltimore, MD: AUM Center, 1982.

———. "Symbols: Agents through Which Consciousness Is Expressed in Art." *Saybrook Review* 5 (2) (1985): 47–54.

———. *The Two Great Seals of America.* Baltimore, MD: Savitriaum, 1976.

———. *The 200th Anniversary of America's Great Seal.* Baltimore, MD: AUM Center, 1982.

———. "Were Our Founding Fathers Occultists?" Parts 1 and 2. *Gnostica News* 4 (9) (1975); (11) (1975).

Hieronimus, Robert, and Zohara M. Hieronimus. "As Above, So Below." *Hieronimus and Co. Journal #15–16* (1998). Owings Mills, MD.

Hoagland, Richard. Interview by Dr. Bob Hieronimus. *21st Century Radio,* radio program, 8 March 1998, www.21stCenturyRadio.com.

Hoffman, Edward. *The Right to Be Human: A Biography of Abraham Maslow.* Los Angeles: Jeremy P. Tarcher, 1988.

Holland, Thomas. *Freemasonry from the Great Pyramid of Ancient Times.* London: R. Folkard & Son Printers, 1885.

Holy Bible. Red Letter Edition. Masonic Edition. Cyclopedic Indexed. Chicago: John A. Hertel Co., 1960.

Houston, Jean. *The Search for the Beloved.* Los Angeles: Jeremy P. Tarcher, 1987.

Hunt, Gaillard. *The History of the Seal of the United States.* Washington, DC: Department of State, 1909.

———. "The Seal." In *The Department of State of the United States: Its History and Function.* New Haven, CT: Yale University Press, 1914.

———. *The Seal of the United States: How It Was Developed and Adopted*. Washington, DC: Department of State, 1892.

Hunter, Larry D., and A. Knott. *Project Gateway to Orion: An Analysis of the Orion Pyramid Theory*. Los Angeles: Published by authors, 1997.

Huntington, Ellsworth. *The Red Man's Continent: A Chronicle of Aboriginal America*. New Haven, CT: Yale University Press, 1921.

Icke, David. *The Biggest Secret*. Valencia, CA: Bertelsmann Industry Services, 1999.

Israel House of David. *Washington's Vision, Strange Forecast of the Destiny of the American Nation*. Benton Harbor, MI: Israel House of David, n.d.

Jacobi, Jolande. *Complex Archetype: Symbol in the Psychology of C. G. Jung*. Princeton, NJ: Princeton University Press, 1974.

Jahn, Robert G., and Brenda J. Dunne. *Margins of Reality*. New York: Harcourt Brace Jovanovich, 1987.

James, Geoffrey, ed. *The Enochian Magick of Dr. John Dee*. St. Paul, MN: Llewellyn Publications, 1994.

James, George Wharton. *What the White Race May Learn from the Indian*. Chicago: Forbes & Co., 1908.

Jefferson, Thomas. *The Life and Morals of Jesus of Nazareth*. New York: World Publishing Co., 1942.

Jenkins, John Major. *Galactic Alignment*. Rochester, VT: Bear & Co., 2002.

Johansen, Bruce E. *Forgotten Founders*. Boston: Harvard Common Press, 1982.

———, comp. *Native American Political Systems and the Evolution of Democracy: An Annotated Bibliography*. Westport, CT: Greenwood Press, 1996.

———. "Notes from the 'Culture Wars': More Annotations on the Debate Regarding the Iroquois and the Origins of Democracy." *American Indian Culture and Research Journal* 23 (1999): 165–75.

Johansen, Bruce E., and Donald A. Grinde Jr. "Reaching the Grassroots: The Worldwide Diffusion of Iroquois Democratic Traditions." *American Indian Culture and Research Journal* 27 (2) (2003): 77–91.

Johnson, Melvin M. *The Beginning of Freemasonry in America*. Kingsport, TN: Southern Publishers, 1924.

Johnston, Charles M., ed. *The Valley of the Six Nations*. Toronto: University of Toronto Press, 1964.

Jones, S. G. "George Washington As a Master Mason: A Rediscovered Portrait by Emanuel Leutze." *Studies in Iconography*. Vols. 7–8. Highland Heights: Northern Kentucky University, 1981–82.

Joseph, Frank. *The Lost Treasure of King Juba: The Evidence of Africans in America Before Columbus*. Rochester, VT: Bear & Co., 2003.

Jung, Carl Gustav. *The Archetypes and the Collective Unconscious*. Edited by H. Read et al., translated by R. F. C. Hull. Bollingen Series 20, vol. 9 (pt. 1). Princeton, NJ: Princeton University Press, 1975.

———. *Flying Saucers*. Translated by R. F. C. Hull. New York: New American Library, 1969.

———. *Four Archetypes: Mother, Rebirth, Spirit, Trickster*. Translated by R. F. C. Hull. Bollingen Series 20, vol. 9 (pt. 1). Princeton, NJ: Princeton University Press, 1970.

———. *Mandala Symbolism*. Translated by R. F. C. Hull. Bollingen Series 20, vol. 8. Princeton, NJ: Princeton University Press, 1973.

———. *On the Nature of the Psyche*. Translated by R. F. C. Hull. Bollingen Series 20, vol. 8. Princeton, NJ: Princeton University Press, 1973.

———. *Psyche and Symbol*. Edited by V. S. de Laszlo. New York: Doubleday, 1958.

———. *Psychology and Alchemy*. Bollingen Series 20, vol. 12. Princeton, NJ: Princeton University Press, 1953.

———. *Symbols of Transformation*. Edited by H. Read et al., translated by R. F. C. Hull. Bollingen Series 20, vol. 5. Princeton, NJ. Princeton University Press, 1967.

———. *Synchronicity*. Translated by R. F. C. Hull. Bollingen Series 20, vol. 8. Princeton, NJ: Princeton University Press, 1973.

———. *Two Essays on Analytic Psychology*. Edited by H. Read, M. Fordham, and G. Adler, translated by R. F. C. Hull. Bollingen Series 20, vol. 7. Princeton, NJ: Princeton University Press, 1953.

Kahn, David. *The Codebreakers*. New York: Macmillan, 1967.

Kennedy, Archibald. *The Importance of Gaining and Preserving the Friendship of the Indians to the British Interest Considered*. New York: James Parker, 1751.

Kerényi, Karl, and Carl G. Jung. "Prolegomena." In *Essays on a Science of Mythology*. Translated by R. F. C. Hull. Bollingen Series 22. Princeton, NJ: Princeton University Press, 1969.

Kieffer, Gene. *The Secret Teachings*. Greenwich, CT: Bethel Publishers, 2000.

Kimm, Silas C. *The Iroquois: A History of the Six Nations of New York*. Middleburgh, NY: P. W. Darforth, 1900.

Knight, Christopher, and Robert Lomas. *The Hiram Key*. Rockport, MA: Element, 1997.

Koestler, Arthur. *The Roots of Coincidence*. New York: Vintage Books, 1973.

Krajenke, Robert K. "Edgar Cayce and the Metaphysical Bicentennial." *The A.R.E. Journal* 11 (3) (1976): 1–4.

———. *The Psychic Side of the American Dream*. Virginia Beach, VA: A.R.E. Press, 1976.

Krippner, Stanley. "The Cycle in Deaths among U.S. Presidents Elected at Twenty Year Intervals." *International Journal of Parapsychology* 9 (1967): 145–53.

———. "Introduction: Some Perspectives on Myth." *The Humanistic Psychologist* 22 (2) (1994): 122–33.

———. "Personal Mythology: An Introduction to the Concept." *The Humanistic Psychologist* 18 (2) (1990): 137–42.

———. *Song of the Siren*. New York: Harper & Row, 1977.

———. Foreword to *Walking the Point*, by D.S. Paulson. New York: Paraview, 2005.

Krippner, Stanley, and Alberto Villoldo. *The Realms of Healing*. Millbrae, CA: Celestial Arts, 1976.

Kuhn, Thomas S. *The Structure of Scientific Revolutions*. Chicago: University of Chicago Press, 1970.

Lakoff, George. *Don't Think of an Elephant: Know Your Values and Frame the Debate*. White River Junction, VT: Chelsea Green Publishing, 2004.

Landone, Brown. *Prophecies of Melchi-Zedek in the Great Pyramid and the Seven Temples*. New York: Book of Gold, 1940.

Lang, C. R. "The Reverse Side of the Seal of the United States and Its Symbolism." *Divine Life Magazine*. (15 May 1917): 1, 7, 18, 9. Chicago: Independent Theosophical Society of America.

Lannin, W. H. *The Great Seal of Our Nation*. Portland, ME: Smith & Sale, 1931.

Larsen, Stephen. "Our Inner Cast of Characters." *The Humanistic Psychologist* 18 (2) (1990): 176–87.

Lawrence, R. B. *George Washington Plays*. Washington, DC: Washington's Bicentennial Commission, 1931.

Lawton, Ian, and Chris Ogilvie-Herald. *Giza: The Truth*. Montpelier, VT: Invisible Cities Press, 2001.

Leach, Edmund Ronald. "Genesis as Myth." In *Myth and Cosmos,* edited by J. Middleton. New York: Natural History Press, 1967.

Leadbeater, Charles W. *The Hidden Life in Freemasonry*. Adyar, India: Theosophical Publishing House, 1963.

Lehner, Ernst. *Symbols, Signs and Signets*. New York: World Publishing Co., 1950.

Lester, Ralph P. *Lester's Look to the East*. Danbury, CT: Behreus Publishing, 1927.

Lewis, H. Spencer. "The Great Seal of the United States." *The Rosicrucian Forum*. (February 1956): 90–92. San Jose, CA: Rosicrucian Order.

———. *Rosicrucian Questions and Answers*. San Jose, CA: Rosicrucian Press, 1941.

———. *The Symbolic Prophecy of the Great Pyramid*. Kingsport, TN: Kingsport Press, 1964.

Locke, Alain, and Bernhard J. Stern, eds. *When Peoples Meet: A Study in Race and Culture Contacts*. New York: Hinds, Hayden, & Eldredge, 1946.

Lossing, Benson J. "The Great Seal of the United States." *Harper's New Monthly Magazine* (13 July 1856): 178–86.

Lunn, Martin. *Da Vinci Code Decoded*. New York: Disinformation Co., 2004.

MacGregor-Mathers, S. L. *The Book of the Sacred Magic of Abra-Melin, the Mage*. Chicago: De Laurence Co., 1939.

Mackey, Albert G. *Revised Encyclopedia of Freemasonry*. 3 vols. New York: Macoy Publishing and Masonic Supply, 1966.

Malone, Dumas. *Jefferson and His Time*. Vol. 1, *Jefferson the Virginian*. Boston: Little, Brown & Co., 1948.

———. *Jefferson and the Ordeal of Liberty*. Boston: Little, Brown & Co., 1962.

———. *Jefferson and the Rights of Man*. Boston: Little, Brown & Co., 1951.

Mann, Barbara A., and Jerry L. Fields. "A Sign in the Sky: Dating the League of the Haudenasaunee." *American Indian Culture and Research Journal* 21 (2) (1997): 105–63.

Marrs, Texe. *Dark Secrets for the New Age: Satan's Plan for a One World Religion*. Westchester, IL: Crossway Books, 1987.

———. *Power of Prophecy*. The Newsletter Ministry of Texe Marrs. www.texemarrs.com/061999/content.htm (June 1999, vol. 99–6).

Maslow, Abraham H. "Comments on Dr. Frankl's Paper." *Journal of Humanistic Psychology* 6 (2) (1966): 107–12.

———. *The Further Reaches of Human Nature*. New York: Penguin Books, 1978.

———. *Motivation and Personality*. 2nd ed. New York: Harper & Row, 1970.

———. *Religious Values and Peak Experiences*. New York: Penguin Books, 1977.

Maxwell, Jordan. *Matrix of Power*. Escondido, CA: Book Tree, 2000.

May, Rollo. *The Courage to Create*. New York: Bantam Books, 1976.

———. *The Cry for Myth*. New York: W. W. Norton & Co., 1991.

———. *The Meaning of Anxiety*. New York: Simon & Schuster, 1977.

May, Wayne N. "Tomb of the Embarras River or Burrows Cave?" *Ancient American Magazine* 9 (59) (October 2004): 2–9.

Mayo, P. E. Review of *Personal Mythology: The Psychology of Your Evolving Self*, by David Feinstein and Stanley Krippner. *The Humanistic Psychologist* 18 (2) (1990): 225–29.

McClain, Alva. *Freemasonry and Christianity*. Winoa Lake, IN: Brethren Missionary Herald Co., n.d.

McGavin, E. Cecil. *Mormonism and Freemasonry*. Salt Lake City, UT: Bookcraft, 1949.

McGrath, Ken. Interview by Dr. Bob Hieronimus. *21ˢᵗ Century Radio*, radio program, 10 July 2005, www.21stCenturyRadio.com.

———. *The Secret Geometry of the Dollar*. San Diego, CA: AuthorHouse, 2002.

McTaggart, Lynne. *The Field: The Quest for the Secret Force of the Universe*. New York: HarperCollins Publishers, 2002.

Mehler, Stephen. *The Land of Osiris*. Kempton, IL: Adventures Unlimited Press, 2001.

Millegan, Kris, ed. *Fleshing Out Skull and Bones*. Walterville, OR: Trine Day, 2003.

Mishlove, Jeffrey. *Psi Development Systems*. New York: Ballantine Books, 1983.

Morey, Grace Kincaid. *Mystic Americanism*. New York: Eastern Star Publishing, 1924.

———. *The Seal of the United States: Its Message*. Quakertown, PA: Philosophical Publishing, 1923.

Morgan, E. S. *The Mirror of the Indian: An Exhibition of Books and Other Source Materials*. Providence, RI: Associates of the John Carter Brown Library, 1958.

Morgan, Lewis Henry. *League of the Ho-de-no-sau-nee or Iroquois*. New York: Dodd, Mead & Co, 1902. First edition printed in 1851.

Morgan, William T. "The Five Nations and Queen Anne." *Mississippi Valley Historical Review* 13 (1927): 169–89.

Morse, Sidney. *Freemasonry in the American Revolution*. Washington, DC: Masonic Service Association of the United States, 1924.

Mosley, J. L. *The Great Seal of the United States of America*. Amherst, WI: Aquarian Age Research Society, 1974.

Mullins, Eustace. *The World Order: Our Secret Rulers*. Staunton, VA: Ezra Pound Institute of Civilization, 1992.

Murphy, Gardner. *Personality: A Biosocial Approach to Origins and Structure*. New York: Harper, 1947.

Musès, Charles, and Arthur M. Young, eds. *Consciousness and Reality*. New York: Outerbridge & Lazard, 1972.

Nelson, Dee Jay, and David H.Coville. *Life Force in the Great Pyramids*. Marina del Rey, CA: De Vorss, 1977.

Neumann, Erich. *Art and the Creative Unconscious*. Translated by R. Manheim. Bollingen Series 41. Princeton, NJ: Princeton University Press, 1974.

———. *The Great Mother*. Translated by R. Manheim. Bollingen Series 47. Princeton, NJ: Princeton University Press, 1970.

———. *The Origins and History of Consciousness*. Translated by R. F. C. Hull. Bollingen Series 42. Princeton, NJ: Princeton University Press, 1971.

Newhouse, Seth. *Constitution of the Five Nations' Indian Confederation*. Washington, DC: National Anthropological Archives, Smithsonian Institution, 1880.

Newman, Eric P. *The Early Paper Money of America*. Racine, WI: Whitman Publishing, 1967.

Noll, Gary, et al. "Self-Actualization, Self-Transcendence, and Personal Philosophy." *Journal of Humanistic Psychology* 14 (3) (1974): 53–73.

Odajnyk, Walter. *Jung and Politics*. New York: Harper & Row, 1976.

Orlandi, Enzo, ed. *The Life and Times of Washington*. New York: Curtis Publishing, 1967.

Ornstein, Robert E. *The Psychology of Consciousness*. New York: Viking Press, 1972.

Osten, Gar. *The Astrological Chart of the United States*. Briarcliff Manor, NY: Stein & Day, 1976.

Ovason, David. *The Secret Architecture of Our Nation's Capital*. New York: HarperCollins, 1999.

———. *The Secret Symbols of the Dollar Bill*. New York: HarperCollins, 2004.

Parker, Arthur Caswell. *The American Indian, the Government and the Country*. New York: New York Public Library, 1915.

———. *An Analytical History of the Seneca Indians*. Rochester, NY: Lewis H. Morgan Chapter, New York State Archaeological Association, 1926.

———. "The Constitution of the Five Nations." In *Parker on the Iroquois*, edited by W. N. Fenton. Syracuse, NY: Syracuse University Press, 1968.

———. *Parker Papers, 1860–1952*. University of Rochester River Campus Libraries. Reports and articles about Indians of North America, particularly New York State, n.d.

Patterson, Richard. *The Great Seal of the United States*. Washington, DC: Department of State Publication 8868, 1976.

———. *The Old Treaty Seal of the U.S.A.* Washington, DC: American Foreign Service Association, 1949.

———. "Seal of the United States." In *Encyclopedia Britannica*. Chicago: William Benton, 1971.

Patterson, Richard, and Richardson Dougall. *The Eagle and the Shield*. Washington, DC: Department of State, 1976.

Bibliography 231

Patton, John S. *Jefferson, Cabell, and the University of Virginia*. New York: Neal Publishing Co., 1906.
Pavitt, William Thomas, and Kate Pavitt. *The Book of Talismans, Amulets and Zodiacal Gems*. London: Aquarian Press, 1970.
Pearce, Joseph Chilton. *Spiritual Initiation and the Breakthrough of Consciousness*. Rochester, VT: Park Street Press, 2003.
Pearce, Roy Harvey. *The Savages of America: A Study of the Indian and the Idea of Civilization*. Baltimore, MD: Johns Hopkins University Press, 1965.
Pegler, Westbrook. "The Guru Letters: Wallace Meets the Roerich Cultists." *Newsweek*, 22 March 1948.
Pelletier, Kenneth R. *Towards a Science of Consciousness*. New York: Dell, 1978.
Penfield, Marc. *An Astrological Who's Who*. York Harbor, ME: Arcane Publications, 1972.
Perkins, Lynn F. *Masonry in the New Age*. Lakemont, GA: CSA Press, 1971.
Petrie, W. M. F. *Amulets*. London: Constable & Co., 1914.
Pieracci, Michael. "The Mythopoesis of Psychology." *The Humanistic Psychologist* 18 (2) (1990): 208–24.
———. Review of *Personal, Marital and Family Myths: Theoretical Formulations and Clinical Strategies*, by Dennis A. Bagarozzi and Stephen A. Anderson. *The Humanistic Psychologist* 18 (2) (1990): 240–49.
Pike, Albert. *Morals and Dogma of the Ancient and Accepted Scottish Rite of Freemasonry*. Charleston, SC: Southern Jurisdiction, F. M, 1906.
Pinkham, Mark Amaru. *Guardians of the Holy Grail: The Knights Templar, John the Baptist, and the Water of Life*. Kempton, IL: Adventures Unlimited Press, 2004.
Pitt, Valerie, ed. *Penguin Dictionary of Physics*. New York: Penguin, 1977.
Pound, Arthur. *Johnson of the Mohawks*. New York: Macmillan, 1930.
Preble, George Henry. *History of the Flag of the United States of America*. Boston: A. Williams & Co., 1880.
Preston, S. B. "From Radionics to Electronic Talismans." *Gnostica News* 5 (5) (1977).
Price, P. W. *The Great Seal: Key to Our Destiny*. New York: Exposition Press, 1952.
Progoff, Ira. *The Death and Rebirth of Psychology*. New York: Julian Press, 1969.
———. *Depth Psychology and Modern Man*. New York: McGraw-Hill, 1973.
———. *Jung, Synchronicity, and Human Destiny*. 2nd ed. New York: Dell, 1973.
Prophet, Elizabeth Clare, and Mark L. Prophet. *Saint Germain on Alchemy*. Vol. 1. Livingston, MT: Summit University Press, 1987.
Puharich, Andrija, ed. *The Iceland Papers*. Amherst, WI: Essential Research Associates, 1979.
Quaife, Milo Milton, et al. "The Seal of the United States." In *The History of the United States Flag*. New York: Harper & Row, 1961.
Quimby, George Irving. *Indian Culture and European Trade Goods: The Archaeology of the Historic Period in the Western Great Lakes Region*. Madison: University of Wisconsin Press, 1966.
Radin, Dean. *The Conscious Universe*. San Francisco: Harper Edge, 1997.

Ray, Paul H., and Sherry Ruth Anderson. *The Cultural Creatives: How 50 Million People Are Changing the World.* New York: Harmony Books, 2000.

———. Interview by Dr. Bob Hieronimus. *21ˢᵗ Century Radio,* radio program, 3 January 2001, www.21stCenturyRadio.com.

Raymond, E. *The Great Seal of America.* Thousand Oaks, CA: Artisan Sales, 1979.

Read, Herbert. *Icon and Idea.* Cambridge, MA: Harvard University Press, 1955.

Reaman, G. E. *Trait of the Iroquois Indians: How the Iroquois Saved Canada for the British Empire.* New York: Barnes & Noble, 1967.

Regardie, Israel. *How to Make and Use Talismans.* New York: Samuel Weiser, 1972.

———. *My Rosicrucian Adventure.* St. Paul, MN: Llewellyn Publications, 1971.

Renn, Bernice. Personal correspondence between Bernice Renn, keeper of the Seal, U. S. State Department, and J'Nevelyn Terrell, January 8, 1980.

Richards, A., and F. Richards. "The Whole Person." *Journal of Humanistic Psychology* 14 (3) (1974): 21–27.

Richards, M. C. *Centering.* Middletown, CT: Wesleyan University Press, 1974.

Richardson, Jabez. *Richardson's Monitor of Freemasonry.* Philadelphia: David McKay, n.d.

Robbins, Alexandra. Interview by Dr. Bob Hieronimus. *21ˢᵗ Century Radio,* radio program, 22 February 2004, www.21stCenturyRadio.com.

———. *Secrets of the Tomb: Skull and Bones, the Ivy League, and the Hidden Paths of Power.* New York: Little, Brown & Co., 2002.

Robbins, C. "Lincoln's Dream." *Parapsychology: An Insider's View of ESP.* Quoted in *Strange Stories, Amazing Facts.* Pleasantville, NY: Reader's Digest Association, 1976.

Robinson, John J. *Born in Blood: The Lost Secrets of Freemasonry.* New York: M. Evans & Co., 1989.

Robison, John. *Proofs of a Conspiracy against All the Religions and Governments of Europe Carried On in the Secret Meetings of Freemasons, Illuminati, and Reading Societies (1798).* Boston: Western Islands, 1967.

Roerich, Nicholas. "Cultural Unity." In *The Cochin Argus,* 1943.

———. *Realms of Light.* New York: Roerich Museum Press, 1931.

Rogers, Carl R. *Client-Centered Therapy.* New York: Houghton Mifflin, 1965.

Rogers, Earl M. Personal correspondence with the author, February 27 and March 19 and 25, 1974.

Root, Elihu. "The Iroquois and the Struggle for America." Address on the Tercentennial celebration of the discovery of Lake Champlain, Plattsburgh, NY, July 7, 1909. Washington, DC: Sudworth Printing Company.

Rosicrucian Order. Personal correspondence between A. C. Piepenbrink, Supreme Secretary, Rosicrucian Order, San Jose, CA, and the author, August 1, 1972.

Rubin, Allen. *Inner Wealth: Eight Ways to Discover Your Hidden Dimensions with the Symbols on the Dollar Bill.* N.p.: Harmony International, 2002.

Rubincam, M. "A Memoir of the Life of William Barton, A. M. (1754–1817)." *Pennsylvania History* 12 (3) (1945): 179–93.

Sachse, Julius F. *Benjamin Franklin as a Freemason*. Lancaster, PA: New Era Publishing, 1906.

———. *The German Pietists of Provincial Pennsylvania*. Philadelphia: Stockhausen, 1895.

———. *Old Masonic Lodges of Pennsylvania, Moderns and Ancients*. Philadelphia: Grand Lodge of Pennsylvania, 1912.

———. *Washington's Masonic Correspondence*. Lancaster, PA: New Era Printing Co., 1915.

Said, Boris. Interview by Dr. Bob Hieronimus. *21ˢᵗ Century Radio,* radio program, 8 March 1998, www.21stCenturyRadio.com.

Samohvalov, V., and V. S. Crilov. "Myth as a Bridge for the Languages of Mental Activity." *The Humanistic Psychologist* 18 (2) (1990): 143–50.

Schaaf, Gregory. *Wampum Belts, Peace Trees: George Morgan, Native Americans, and Revolutionary Diplomacy*. Golden, CO: Fulcrum Publishing, 1990.

Schlesinger, Arthur M. *The Age of Roosevelt: The Coming of the New Deal*. New York: Houghton & Mifflin, 1958.

———. "Liberty Tree: A Genealogy." *New England Quarterly* 25 (1952): 435–58.

Schoch, Robert M. "How Old Is the Sphinx?" A paper written to accompany a presentation at the 1992 American Association for the Advancement of Science, Annual Meeting, Chicago, February 7, 1992.

Schoch, Robert M., and Robert Aquinas McNally. *Pyramid Quest: Secrets of the Great Pyramid and the Dawn of Civilization*. New York: Jeremy P. Tarcher/Penguin, 2005.

Schoch, Robert M., with Robert Aquinas McNally. *Voices of the Rocks: A Scientist Looks at Catastrophes and Ancient Civilizations*. New York: Harmony Books, 1999.

———. *Voyages of the Pyramid Builders: The True Origins of the Pyramids from Lost Egypt to Ancient America*. New York: Jeremy P. Tarcher/Putnam, 2003.

Schwaller de Lubicz, R. A. *Sacred Science*. Translated by A. Vandenbroeck. Rochester, VT: Inner Traditions, 1982.

———. *Symbol and the Symbolic*. Translated by R. Lawlor and D. Lawlor. Brookline, MA: Autumn Press, 1978.

Seiss, Joseph A. *The Great Pyramid: A Miracle in Stone*. New York: Rudolph Steiner Publications, 1973.

Sepharial. *The Book of Charms and Talismans*. New York: Arc Books, 1969.

Serlin, I. Review of *The Chalice and the Blade: Our History, our Future*, by Riane Eisler. *The Humanistic Psychologist* 18 (2) (1990): 238–39.

Sheldrake, Rupert. "Memory and Morphic Resonance." *ReVision* 10 (1) (1987): 9.

———. *A New Science of Life: The Hypothesis of Formative Causation*. Rochester, VT: Park Street Press, 1995.

———. *The Presence of the Past: Morphic Resonance and the Habits of Nature*. Rochester, VT: Park Street Press, 1995.

———. *The Rebirth of Nature: The Greening of Science and God*. Rochester, VT: Park Street Press, 1994.

Singer, June. *Androgyny: Toward a New Theory of Sexuality*. Garden City, NY: Anchor Books, 1977.

———. *Boundaries of the Soul*. Garden City, NY: Anchor Books, 1973.

Sinnott, Edmond W. *Biology of the Spirit*. New York: Viking Press, 1957.

———. *Cell and Psyche*. Garden City, NY: Anchor Books, 1950.

Sitchin, Zecharia. *The Stairway to Heaven*. New York: Avon Books, 1980.

———. *The 12ᵗʰ Planet*. Santa Fe, NM: Bear & Co., 1991.

———. *The Wars of Gods and Men*. New York: Avon Books, 1985.

Smyth, Piazzi. *Our Inheritance in the Great Pyramid*. London: William Isbister, 1880.

Sora, Steven. *The Lost Colony of the Templars*. Rochester, VT: Destiny Books, 2004.

———. *The Lost Treasure of the Knights Templar*. Rochester, VT: Destiny Books, 1999.

———. *Secret Societies of America's Elite*. Rochester, VT: Destiny Books, 2003.

Sparks, Jared. *The Writings of Washington*. Vol. 11. New York: Harper & Bros., 1848.

Speck, Frank Gouldsmith. "The Iroquois: A Study in Cultural Evolution." Bloomfield Hills, MI: *Cranbrook Institute of Science Bulletin* 23 (1945).

Spence, Lewis. *Encyclopedia of Occultism*. New York: University Books, 1968.

Spenser, Robert Keith. *The Cult of the All-Seeing Eye*. Hawthorne, CA: Christian Book Club of America, 1968.

Stauffer, Vernon. *New England and the Bavarian Illuminati*. New York: Columbia University Press, 1918.

Steiner, Rudolf. *The Secret Stream: Christian Rosenkreutz and Rosicrucianism*. Great Barrington, MA: Anthroposophic Press, 2000.

Steinmetz, George H. *The Royal Arch: Its Hidden Meaning*. New York: Macoy Publishing, Masonic Supply Co., 1946.

Still, William T. *New World Order: The Ancient Plan of Secret Societies*. Lafayette, LA: Huntington House Publishers, 1990.

Strickland, Edward D. *Iroquois Past and Present*. Buffalo, NY: A.M.S. Press, 1901.

Sutton, Antony C. *America's Secret Establishment: An Introduction to the Order of Skull and Bones*. Walterville, OR: Trine Day, 2002.

Swann, Ingo. *Natural ESP*. New York: Bantam, 1987.

Taliaferro, A. A. "The Great Seal of the United States." *The Rosicrucian Digest* (June 1972): 9–11, 33, 36.

Tanner, Sandra. "Where Did Joseph Smith Get His Ideas for the Book of Mormon?" Salt Lake City: Utah Light Ministry Online Resources, n.d. Contains a partial list of books published prior to 1830 dealing with the Indians. (Condensed from Dan Vogel, *Indian Origins and the Book of Mormon*. Salt Lake City, UT: Signature Books, 1986, 105–32.)

Targ, Russell, and K. Harary. *The Mind Race: Understanding and Using Psychic Abilities*. New York: Villard Books, 1984.

Targ, Russell, and Harold E. Puthoff. *Mind-Reach: Scientists Look at Psychic Abilities*. Charlottesville, VA: Hampton Roads Publishing, 1977.

Tart, Charles T., ed. *Body, Mind, Spirit.* Charlottesville, VA: Hampton Roads Publishing, 1997.

Taylor, Greg. *Da Vinci in America.* Brisbane, Australia: Daily Grail Publishing, 2004.

Temple, Robert. *The Sirius Mystery.* Rochester, VT: Destiny Books, 1998.

Thomson, I. L. "The Great Seal of the United States." In *Encyclopedia Americana.* Vol. 13. New York: American, 1962.

Tiller, William A. Interview by Zohara Hieronimus. *Future Talk,* radio program, 16 March 2002, www.FutureTalkRadio.com.

———. *Science and Human Transformation.* Walnut Creek, CA: Pavior, 1997.

Tiller, William A., Walter E. Dibble Jr., and Michael J. Kohane. *Conscious Acts of Creation.* Walnut Creek, CA: Pavior, 2001.

Tillich, Paul. *Dynamics of Faith.* New York: Harper & Bros., 1958.

———. *Systematic Theology.* Vol. 3. Chicago: University of Chicago Press, 1963.

Tompkins, Peter. *Secrets of the Great Pyramid.* New York: Harper & Row, 1971.

Tooker, Elisabeth, ed. *Iroquois Culture, History, and Prehistory: Proceedings of a Conference in Iroquois Research, Glens Falls, NY, 1965.* Albany, NY: State Education Department, 1967.

Toth, Max. *Pyramid Prophecies.* Rochester, VT: Destiny Books, 1988.

Toth, Max, and Greg Nielsen. *Pyramid Power.* Rochester, VT: Destiny Books, 1974.

Totten, Charles. *The Great Seal of the United States, Its History and Heraldry.* Vols. 1 and 2. New Haven, CT: Our Race Publishing, 1897.

———. *An Important Question in Metrology.* New York: John Wiley & Sons, 1884.

Trenchard, James. "Description of the Arms of the United States." *Columbia Magazine* (September 1786): 33–34.

Ullman, Montague, and Stanley Krippner, with Alan Vaughn. *Dream Telepathy.* New York: Macmillan, 1973.

Underhill, Ruth M. *Red Man's Continent: A History of the Indians in the United States.* Chicago: University of Chicago Press, 1953.

U.S. Department of State. *The Seal of the United States.* Department of State publication 1314, Washington, DC: U.S. Government Printing Office, 1939.

———. *The Seal of the United States.* Department of State publication 2860, Washington, DC: U.S. Government Printing Office, 1947.

———. *The Seal of the United States.* Department of State publication 6455, Washington, DC: U.S. Government Printing Office, 1957.

———. *The Great Seal of the United States.* Washington, DC: U.S. Government Printing Office, 1970.

———. *The Great Seal of the United States.* Washington, DC: U.S. Government Printing Office, 2003.

Valentine, Tom. *The Great Pyramid: Man's Monument to Man.* New York: Pinnacle Books, 1975.

Van Doren, Carl. *Benjamin Franklin.* New York: Viking Press, 1938.

Vaughan, Alan. *Incredible Coincidence: The Baffling World of Synchronicity*. New York: Ballantine Books, 1979.

Vickers, Brian, ed. *Occult and Scientific Mentalities in the Renaissance*. New York: Cambridge University Press, 1984.

Von Franz, Marie-Louise. *On Divination and Synchronicity*. Toronto: Inner City Books, 1980.

Wadhams, A. *An Essay upon the Origin and Use of Seals, Also Introducing a Design for an Improved Seal of the United States*. Albany, NY: Weare C. Little, 1865.

Waite, Arthur E. *Brotherhood of the Rosy Cross*. New York: University Books, n.d.

Wallace, Henry A. *America Must Choose*. New York: Foreign Policy Association & World Peace Foundation, 1934.

———. Personal correspondence between Wallace and Hon. George M. Humphrey, February 10, 1955.

———. Personal correspondence between Wallace and Mr. Dal Lee, February 6, 1951.

———. *Statesmanship and Religion*. New York: Round Table Press, 1934.

Wallace, Paul A. W. "The Return of Hiawatha." *New York State History* 39 (1948): 385–403.

———. *The White Roots of Peace*. Saranac Lake, NY: Chauncy Press, 1986.

Watch Tower Bible and Tract Society. *The Divine Plan of the Ages, as Shown in the Great Pyramid*. Brooklyn, NY: Watch Tower Bible and Tract Society, 1886.

Waterman, E. "In God We Trust." *Rosicrucian Fellowship Magazine* 65 (7) (1973): 294–97, 303.

Webster, Nesta. *Secret Societies and Subversive Movements*. 9th edition. Originally published in 1924. N.p.: Christian Book Club of America, n.d.

Weiser, Conrad. *Narrative of a Journey from Tulpehocken in Pennsylvania to Onondago, the Headquarters of the Six Nations of Indians in 1737*. Philadelphia: J. Pennington, 1853.

West, John Anthony. *Serpent in the Sky*. New York: Harper & Row, 1979.

———. *The Traveler's Key to Ancient Egypt*. New York: Alfred A. Knopf, 1989.

Whalen, W. *The Rosicrucians*. Chicago: Claretian Publications, 1965.

Wiesenthal, Simon. *Sails of Hope: The Secret Mission of Christopher Columbus*. New York: Macmillan, 1973.

Williams, Robert C. *Russian Art and American Money*. Cambridge, MA: Harvard University Press, 1980.

Wilson, Edmund. *Apologies to the Iroquois*. New York: Farrar, Straus & Cudahy, 1960.

Wilson, L. *The Coat of Arms: Crest and the Great Seal of the United States of America*. San Diego, CA: N. Francis Maw, 1928.

Wilson, Robert Anton, and Robert Shea. *Illuminatus: Part 1, the Eye in the Pyramid*. New York: Dell, 1975.

Wingate, Richard. *Lost Outpost of Atlantis*. New York: Everest House, 1980.

Wise, Jennings C. *The Legacy of Jefferson: An Appeal to the Alumni of the University*. N.p.: published by the author, 194?.

Wittemans, Fr. *History of the Rosicrucians*. London: Rider & Co., 1938.

Wolf, Fred Alan. *The Dreaming Universe*. New York: Touchstone, 1994.

Wright, J. G. *The National Identity of the United States with Manesseh*. Vancouver: British Israel Association, n.d.

Wright, Robert C. *Indian Masonry*. Whitefish, MT: Kessinger Publishing, 1997.

Wyckoff, H. S. "The Great American Seal." *The Mystic Light, the Rosicrucian Magazine* (n.d.): 56–62.

Yates, Frances A. *The Art of Memory*. Chicago: University of Chicago Press, 1966.

———. *Giordano Bruno and the Hermetic Tradition*. Chicago: University of Chicago Press, 1979.

———. *Ideas and Ideals in the North European Renaissance*. Vol. 3, *Collected Essays*. Boston: Routledge & Kegan Paul, 1984.

———. *The Occult Philosophy in the Elizabethan Age*. London: Ark Paperbacks, 1983.

———. *The Rosicrucian Enlightenment*. London: Routledge & Kegan Paul, 1972.

———. *Theatre of the World*. Chicago: The University of Chicago Press, 1969.

Yates, J. and M. Yates. *History of the State of New York*. N.p., 1824.

Young, Arthur M. *The Bell Notes*. New York: Delacorte Press, 1979.

———. *The Reflexive Universe*. San Francisco: Robert Briggs Associates, 1976.

Zieber, J. J. "Charles Thomson, the Sam Adams of Philadelphia." *Mississippi Valley Historical Review* 45 (3) (1968): 464–80.

INDEX

Adams, John, 16, 18–19, 24, 82–83, 96, 98

Advancement of Learning, The, 38

affect image, 119, 140

Akhenaton (pharaoh), 35

Albany Congress, 13

Albany Plan, 11–14

alchemy, 23, 35, 36, 132

almanacs, 23–24. See also *Poor Richard's Almanac*

American Heraldic Institution, 90

American Philosophical Society, 56, 71, 86, 90

American Quarterly, 107

Ames, Nathaniel, 23

AMORC, 35, 47, 58, 60

Anderson, James, 26

androgyny, 143

Anglo-Iroquois alliance, 11–16

anima and animus, 127

Annuit Coeptis, 97, 109, 111, 138, 171, 173

antithesis, 122, 164

Apollonian Society, 56

aprons, Masonic, 43, 56

archetype

of collective unconscious, 127, 146, 158, 202

functions of, 203

magician, 134–35

mountain, 127–28, 130

psyche and, 118, 127, 164

seal's reverse as, 3, 126–27, 132, 134

squaring the circle and, 143–45

sun, 130–32

synchronicity and, 196

talismans and, 202–4

of unknown man and the seal, 97–98, 134–35

Argüelles, José and Miriam, 139

Arundel, Russell, 54, 67, 125

Assassins, 33

astrological charts, 52–55, 65–66, 77–78

Bacon, Roger, 76

Bacon, Sir Francis, 3, 5, 36, 37, 76

Barruel, Abbé Augustin de, 26, 72, 73

Barton, David, 51

Barton, Thomas, 79

Barton, William

esoteric fraternities and, 79

eye in the triangle and, 119–21, 122, 130

Great Seal and, 88, 90, 97

pyramid and, 122–26

Barton, William (Mason), 79

Bauval, Robert, 181–82, 183, 184

Bavarian Society of the Illuminati, 38–39

Beatles' yellow submarine, 245

Beissel, Conrad, 47, 60

Bigelow, Timothy, 44

Blavatsky, H. P., 171

Book of Constitutions, 26

Bork, Robert, 16

Boudinot, Elias, 88, 90

Bradshaw, Wesley, 48–49

Brant, Joseph, (Thayendanegea), 27–28

Brasington, Virginia, 98, 135

About the Author

Robert R. Hieronimus received his Ph.D. for the doctoral thesis "An Historic Analysis of the Reverse of the American Great Seal and Its Relationship to the Ideology of Humanistic Psychology" at Saybrook Institute in 1981 under Stanley Krippner. Hieronimus's research on the Great Seal has been used in the speeches, literature, and libraries of the White House, the State Department, and the Department of Interior. In June of 1976 President Gerald Ford used Hieronimus's research in his speech at the opening of the centennial safe during the nation's bicentennial. In 1976 and again in 1981 Hieronimus was invited to the White House to discuss the history and meaning of the two Great Seals of America. His Independence Hall speech on the Great Seal's bicentennial was published in the Congressional Record. In 1981 he had a personal meeting with Egyptian president Anwar el-Sadat who wanted to know why an Egyptian pyramid was on the back of the American dollar. Hieronimus and his wife, Zohara, lobbied the House and Senate on the Great Seal Act after decades of speaking about the symbolism of the reverse of the seal in hundreds of interviews for print media, radio, and TV (including *Voice of America*), and on the lecture circuit to colleges and universities and conferences around the country. He served on local and state bicentennial commissions and with Zohara was instrumental in establishing a sister-city relationship between both Baltimore and Luxor, Egypt, and Baltimore and Alexandria, Egypt.

Hieronimus is also an artist and has included elements of the seal's reverse in many of his dozens of murals including the 2,700-square-foot *Apocalypse* at Johns Hopkins University and the 800-square-foot

E Pluribus Unum at Lexington Market in Baltimore. (*E Pluribus Unum* also contains portraits of all the Founding Fathers who have eaten at the Lexington Market, including George Washington, Ben Franklin, Thomas Jefferson, John Eager Howard, and even Maryland's state comptroller and former governor and mayor of Baltimore, William Donald Schaefer— another Freemason.) During the summer of 1968 he shared his research with Elektra recording artists Jimi Hendrix, the Doors, and Earth Opera while he worked backstage in preparation for a job designing album covers that never came to fruition. In addition to his murals, he has painted the eye in the triangle and pyramid onto faces, bodies, cars, and busses. His VW bus "Light" (better known as "the Woodstock bus") was photographed by the Associated Press at the original 1969 Wood-stock and is still seen today regularly reprinted in *Rolling Stone* magazine, Woodstock compilations, and elsewhere.

Since 1988 Hieronimus has been the host of the radio talk show *21st Century Radio,* a forum he uses to continue his education and outreach about the symbolism on the Great Seal. The radio program explores the unknown with the world's leading-edge thinkers, researchers, and practitioners in such fields as parapsychology, holistic health, UFOs, and the environment. He and Zohara also use their media appearances to encourage the appreciation of modern mythologies to fill the void in our society that has been described by humanistic psychologists such as Rollo May, Abraham Maslow, and others. In the early nineties Hieronimus & Co. brought *21st Century News* to television on the local FOX-TV channel and a Baltimore community cable channel, and again took advantage of the opportunity to promote cultural heroes such as the Negro League's baseball players, Baltimore's legendary Babe Ruth, and the works of J. R. R. Tolkien. The common thread in these endeavors is an attempt to provide modern-day heroes that will inspire the viewers and listeners to find wholeness in their own lives. More can be learned at 21stCenturyRadio.com.

In 2002 Hieronimus published *Inside the Yellow Submarine: The Making of the Beatles' Animated Classic* (Krause) after many years of research, finding in this film another clear reflection of the Hero's Journey or monomyth. Look for a key scene in this film when the Yellow Submarine, flying through the air, lands atop an unfinished pyramid in the symbolic pose of the sun over the mountain. It is yet one more example of the resonating power of the archetypal symbol that is the subject of this book: the radiant eye in the triangle over the unfinished pyramid.